COMPUTER FUNDAMENTALS

CS-611

For
Bachelor of Computer Applications

S. Roy
Dinesh Verma

Useful For

IGNOU, Jamia Millia Islamia, Jammu & Kashmir University, Vinayaka Mission University, IP University, CCS University, Kota Open University (KOU), Yashwantrao Chavan Maharashtra Open University, *Nasik* (*Maharastra*), Amity University, Nalanda University, YCM Open University (Maharashtra), and all other Indian Universities.

GPH BOOK

GULLYBABA PUBLISHING HOUSE (P) Ltd.
AN ISO 9001:2008 CERTIFIED CO.

GullyBaba Publishing House (P) Ltd.

2525/193, Ist Floor, Onkar Nagar-A,
Tri Nagar, Delhi-110035
Ph: 9350849407, 9312235086, 011-27387998
E-mail: info@gullybaba.com / info@degreewala.com
Website: www.gullybaba.com / www.ignouonline.com

2011 Edition
ISBN: 978-81-89086-38-1

Price : 260/-

Preface

This book is mainly targeted for BCA exam of Introduction to Computer Fundamentals and PC Software. It has been introduced in market after seeing the huge demand of ready to grasp material for exams with high level of quality, and its un-availability in market. We the GullyBaba Publishing House took a step ahead to publish the quality material focusing on exams at the same time giving you indepth knowledge about the subject.

GPH Book is the pioneer effort that provides a unique methodology so as to perform better in exams. If your goal is to attain higher grade use this powerful study tool independently or along with your text.

On the Web : ***www.gullybaba.com*** *is the vital resource for your exams acting as catalyst to boost up your preparation. Gullybaba.com has been Listed* ***no.1*** *in www.google.com and www.yahoo.com when you search "IGNOU MCA BCA MBA". Now you can access us on the net through* ***www.doctorignou.com, www.doeacconline.com, www.gphindia.com, and www.gullybabapublishinghouse.com.***

Feedback about the book can be sent at **cs611writers@gullybaba.com.**

Acknowledgments :

We appreciate the staff and facility support provided by GullyBaba Publishing House. In particular, we appreciate the encouragement and professional advises received from Mr. Ajay Saini, Mr. Tarun Sharma, B. K. Krishna and many more.

Also we would like to thank typesetting and designing team Mrs. Bhawna Verma, Mr. Shravan Vats, Mr. Parveen Kumar, and Mr. Mukesh.

We gratefully acknowledges the significant contributions of Mr. Mahesh Chand, Mrs. Bimla Devi, Mrs. Bhawna Verma and our experts in bringing out this publication.

New Delhi ***Publisher***

CONTENTS

STUDY MATERIAL

SOLVED PAPERS

Chapter - 1

Computer System & Memory

INTRODUCTION

Q1. What is a Computer?

ANS : Computer is an electronic device, which operates on the principle of input, process and output. The whole process becomes possible when computer parts works with the instructions given in the form of programs. The computer parts are called hardware and all sort of programming is called software. So these two terms gave new definition of computer as follows : ***Computer is an electronic device or a system based on electricity, which works with the synchronistic working of hardware and software. All communications inside the computer is done with the combination of hardware and software.***

Computers are used in multi-faceted ways in various fields. If we see the applicability of computers, it's very wide. It is used in electricity bills, weather forecasts, airlines, and railway reservations, telephone, banking transactions, and so on. The list is endless. All these applications of computers have made the life easier for us.

Computer works on the basic principles of input, process, output, i.e., there is some data to which we need to modify according to our needs, then this data is processed and after processing what we get is the output. In other words we can say that computer accepts unprocessed data then processes it according to our definition and gives out processed data or output.

Now-a-days we call computers as electronic digital computers. We may, define digital computer as a machine which takes a stream of data, stores them, process them according to defined rules and produces a stream of data as its output. A digital computer may accept a single number as its input, process it and produce it after processing. The data for input may include numeric data (0-9), alphabetic data (A-Z) and special character data (+, -, ÷, x, %, >, <, = etc.)

Q2. What are the bottlenecks of Von Neumann architecture? How does multiprocessor architecture try to overcome this bottleneck? What are the advantages of multiprocessor systems? What are the problem of multiprocessor systems?

The von Neumann machine uses stored program concept, i.e., the program and data are stored in the same memory unit. The computers prior to this idea used to store programs and data on separate memories. Entering and modifying these programs were very difficult as they were entered manually by setting switches and plugging and unplugging.

◆ Each location of the memory of von Neumann machine can be addressed independently.

◆ Execution of instructions in von Neumann machine is carried out in a sequential fashion (unless explicitly altered by the program itself) from one instruction to the next.

Basic Structure of a conventional von Neumann machine.

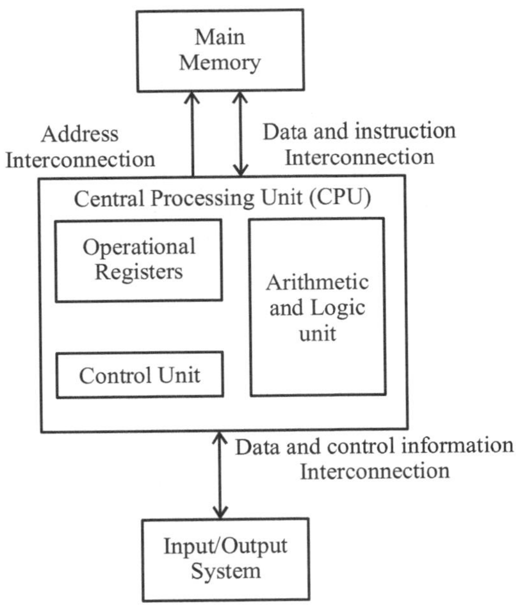

Structure of a computer

Von Neumann bottleneck

A von Neumann machine has only a single path between the main memory and control unit (CU). This feature/constraint is referred to as von *Neumann bottleneck*.

Advantages of Multiprocessor :-

(1) The performance of computer systems by allowing parallel processing of It improves segments programs.
(2) In addition to the CPUs, it also facilitates more efficient utilization of all the other devices of the computer system.
(3) It provides a built-in back up. If one of the CPUs break-down, the other CPU automatically takes over the complete work load until repairs are made.
(4) Significant speedup of an application may be possible by devoting multiple processors to it.
(5) Functionally specialized processors can be added to improve performance of particular applications.

Problems of Multiprocessor System :

(1) One of the central difficulties in the design of any multiprocessor system is the partitioning of software among the processor. In the general purpose case, this is a very difficult task. Consider, for example, a multiprocessor system, in which a number of processors are used to execute a standard program supplied by the user. For common assembly languages, as well as high-level languages such as BASIC, FORTRAN, COBOL, PASCAL, it is difficult to devise a general method for splitting up the program to be executed among the various processors. These languages do not make clear which subroutines or tasks may be executed in parallel and which must be executed in series, but PASCAL and ADA languages allows programs to be written as independent tasks that can be concurrently executed. However the number of processors that can be effectively utilized is limited by the number of concurrent tasks in the application program.
(2) In most multiple-microprocessor system, the various microprocessors are not cooperating to execute parts of one large program, but are each executing a program of their own. Each processor is assigned a function, when the system is designed and that function does not change regardless of the task the system performing.
(3) Software development is relatively straightforward in loosely coupled hardware architecture, since each processor has a particular task to perform and is isolated from the others. Communications protocols define instructions among the processors, and each process needs only to maintain its part of the protocol. It is complete isolated from the internal structure of the other processor systems. Each processor's software can be separately developed.

Solutions of these problems :

(1) Each processor's software can be separately developed and tested.

(2) Debugging can also be hampered by subtle interaction between the processor

(3) Proper protocol designs.

(4) Mutual suspicion helps avoid interaction problems.

(5) Messages set over communication links subject to noise should have a check sum or CRC appended to allow error detection.

Q3. Describe the following terms in brief :
Program, Bits/Binary digits, Byte, Word, Mega Byte, Giga Byte

Program : A program is a set of instructions, which operates on data to perform certain specified task.

Bits/Binary digits : Data in computer is represented in binary form by using two symbols 0 and 1 which are called Binary digits or bits.

Byte : Eight bits constitutes one byte.

Word : A word may be defined as a unit of information, which a computer can process at a time.

Mega Byte : 1 Mega byte stands for 2^{20} bytes which is equal to 1048576 bytes.

Giga Byte : 1 Giga byte stands for 2^{30} bytes.

Q4. Define Memory Hierarchy

✓ **Memory hierarchy** ⇒ The levels of memory in a computer. From fastest to slowest speed, they are:

1. CPU registers
2. L1 cache
3. L2 cache
4. Main memory
5. Virtual memory

The hierarchical arrangement of storage in current computer architectures is called the **memory hierarchy**. Each level of the hierarchy is of higher speed and lower latency, and is of smaller size, than lower levels. Most modern CPUs are so fast that for most program workloads the locality of reference of memory accesses, and the efficiency of the caching and memory transfer between different levels of the hierarchy, is the practical limitation on processing speed. As a result, the CPU spends much of its time idling, waiting for memory I/O to complete.

The memory hierarchy in most computers is as follows:

- **Processor registers** → fastest possible access, only hundreds of bytes

• **Level 1 (L1) cache** → often accessed in just a few cycles, usually tens of kilobytes

• **Level 2 (L2) cache** → higher latency than L1 by 2x to 10x, often 512KB or more

• **Level 3 (L3) cache** → (optional) higher latency than L2, often multiple MB's

Memory Hierarchy

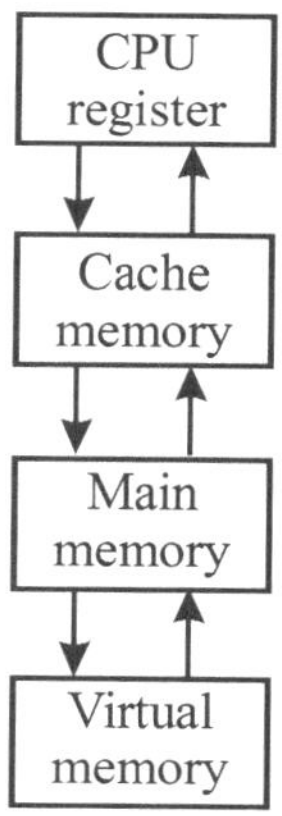

• **Main memory (DRAM)** → may take hundreds of cycles, but can be multiple gigabytes

• **Disk storage** → hundreds of thousands of cycles latency, but very large

Need of cache and Main memory : The above principles suggest that we should try to keep recently accessed items in the fastest memory. Because the smaller memories are more expensive and faster, we want to use smaller memories to try to hold the most recently accessed items close to the CPU and successively larger (and slower, and less expensive) memories as we move away from the CPU. This type of organization is called **a memory hierarchy** . Two important levels of the memory hierarchy are **the cache** and **virtual memory.** Primary storage is used to store data that is likely to be in active use, so it is usually faster than long-term secondary storage. Today, many computers have cache memory located in between the central processing unit and primary storage in order to further increase speed.

A particular location in storage is selected by its physical memory address. That address remains the same, no matter how the particular value stored there changes

Memory hierarchy is required for increased processing speed. This hierarchy permits fetching of instructions and operands at a rate that is high enough to prevent pipeline stalls. A typical hierarchy includes high-speed registers, cache, and/or buffers located on the CPU chip, and complex memory management schemes to support off-chip cache and memory devices.

Q5. Difference between

(i) Volatile and non-volatile memory → Memory technologies can be divided into two categories, volatile and nonvolatile. Volatile memories lose their contents when power is removed, nonvolatile memories do not. Traditional volatile technologies include SRAM and DRAM. The common factor is they are RAM-based technology, Random Access Memory. The main advantage of RAMs is they are easy to use, read and write operations are similar. The main disadvantage of traditional RAMs is that they can only be used for temporary storage. Traditional nonvolatile technologies are based on ROM-based technology, Read Only Memory. Various improvements to the underlying technology have created Flash and EEPROM memory, these variations of ROM can be written. The process or writing ROM-based memories is difficult and destructive. Traditional ROM based technologies are not suitable for applications requiring many write operations. FRAM is he first nonvolatile RAM. It offers the easy write access of SRAM or DRAM and the nonvolatility of Flash or EEPROM.

(ii) Static Vs Dynamic memories

Static Memory	Dynamic
(i) Losses its signal	(i) Does not loose the signal strength
(ii) Periodic refreshing of memory is needed	(ii) No refreshing
(iii) Expensive	(iii) Cheap
(iv) Used as cache	(iv) Used as main memory

Chapter - 2

Input/Output Organisation & New Technologies

Q1. Define input/output devices.

INPUT DEVICES

• **Keyboard** → This is another input device that is used to print letters of the alphabet on the screen. You cannot use your computer without a keyboard.

• **Light Pen** → A computer input device that acts somewhat like a mouse. A user points a wand or pen at the monitor and the computer responds to commands sensed from the emission of light from the device. Light pens are rare in modern computing due to the popularity of the mouse. Light pens are sometimes used in casinos to mark numbers in computerised Keno games.

• **Mouse** → This device is used to move a pointer on your screen, which is a form of navigation. A mouse can be a big help when the operating system you use is based on a GUI (graphical user interface). A mouse is a small handheld pointing device that is used mostly in graphics programs to manipulate what is on the screen. The mouse has two parts: what you can feel and touch (usually having a body and two "buttons"); and the software which is the program that controls the mouse and allows your applications to access it.

• **Scanner** → A device that digitises images so that they can be used in electronic document assembly. Scanners are available for a very wide range of prices, and their quality tends to vary accordingly. Thanks to scanner technology, a whole lot of really bad photos can be miraculously incorporated into a whole lot of really bad newsletters, brochures, and websites.

OUTPUT DEVICES

• **CRT** → Cathode Ray Tube, a sort of nickname for your monitor or screen. This CRT was used when the parts of the atom were discovered. Back around 100 years ago

• **LCD →** This means liquid crystal display - applies mostly to laptop computers. They are akin to the desktop computers VGA display.

• **Printer →** This is a device which attaches to the computer and prints information. This is necessary to give you a "hard copy" or printed output of the information on your files in the computer.

Q2. Define RISC and Characteristics of RISC.

RISC is an acronym for Reduced Instruction Set Computing, a description applied to microprocessors optimized for carrying out a relatively small number of instructions extremely quickly. In terms of the simple instructions most often carried out by computers, RISC chips are faster. For complex instructions that must be broken down into numerous simpler ones. A processor whose design is based on the rapid execution of a sequence of simple instructions rather than on the provision of a large variety of complex instructions Features which are generally found in RISC designs are uniform instruction encoding (e.g. the op-code is always in the same bit positions in each instruction which is always one word long), which allows faster decoding; a homogenous register set, allowing any register to be used in any context and simplifying compiler design; and simple addressing modes with more complex modes replaced by sequences of simple arithmetic instructions.

Certain design features have been characteristic of most RISC processors:

• *one cycle execution time*: RISC processors have a CPI (clock per instruction) of one cycle. This is due to the optimization of each instruction on the CPU and a technique called I.PIPELINING;

• *pipelining: a technique that allows for simultaneous execution of parts, or stages, of instructions to more efficiently process instructions;*

• *large number of registers: the RISC design philosophy generally incorporates a larger number of registers to prevent in large amounts of interactions with memory*

Q3(i) Difference between CRT display and LCD display
(ii) Laser and Dotmatrix Printer
(iii) Serial and Parallel Interface

(i)

CRT	LCD
(i) CRT is bulky (ii) High energy requirement (iii) Normally high resolution graphics	(i) LCD is Compact (ii) Low energy requirement (iii) Low resolution

(ii)

Laser	Dot Matrix Printer
(i) High cost	Low cost
(ii) Print Quality Superior	Print Quality much lower than Laser Printer
(iii) Non-inipact printer	Impact printer
(iv) High quality output	Output is of low quality
(v) Noiseless operation	Noisy

(iii) Serial and parallel interface → Serial interface - In serial interface only one line is used to transmit data, therefore, only one bit is transferred at a time. Serial interface is used for serial printers and terminals. In serial interface the i/o devices receives or send bytes one by one in serial fashion e.g. Keyboard is a serial interface. The most common serial interface is RS-232-C

Serail Interface

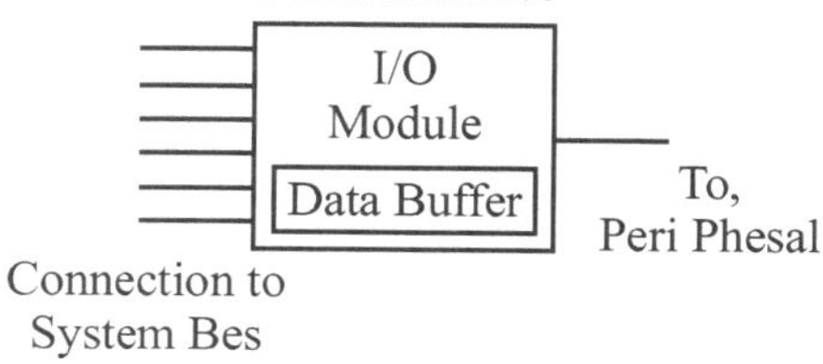

✓ **Parallel interface ⇒** In parllel interface multiple bits can be transferred simultaneously. The parllel interfaces are normally used for high-speed peripherals such as tapes and disks. In this the data is send or received block wise parallely such as printer. It is faster than serial interface. A common parllel interface is centronics.

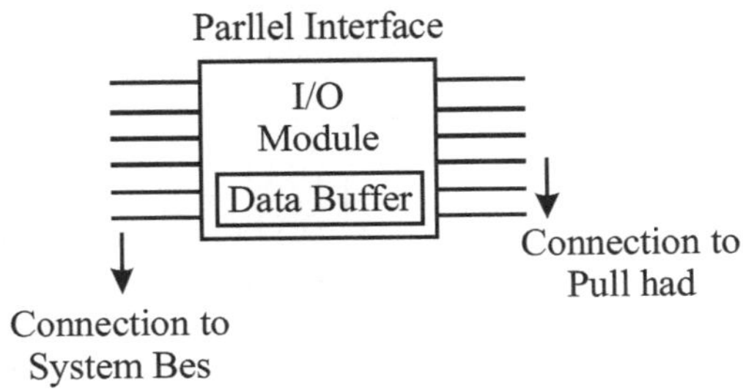
Parllel Interface
I/O
Module
Data Buffer
Connection to
Pull had
Connection to
System Bes

Chapter - 3

Software concepts And Terminology

Q1. Define Application Software.

✓ **Application software** ⇒ application software is written to enable the computer to solve a specific data processing task. A number of powerful software packages, which doesn't require significant programming knowledge, have been developed. These are easy to learn & use as compared to the programming languages. Although these packages can perform many general & special functions, there are applications where these packages are not found adequate. In such cases, application program is written to meet the exact requirements. A user application program is written using one of these packages or a programming language. The most important categories of software packages available are:

- Data Base Management Software (DBMS)
- Spreadsheet Software
- Word Processing desktop Publishing (DTP) & presentation Software, Graphics Software
- Data Communication Software.

Q2. Define Machine language.

This is a sequence of instructions written in the form of binary numbers consisting of 1s and 0s to which the computer responds directly. The machine language was initially referred to as code, although now term code is used more broadly to refer to any program text. It is faster in execution since the computer directly starts executing it. It is very difficult to understand.

Q3. Define Assembly language.

To facilitate programmer easily understandable language is developed. Assembly language is one of them. Programs can easily be written in alphanumeric symbols instead of 0s and 1s.

- Meaningful and easily rememberable symbols are selected for this purpose. For Example SUB for subtraction, ADD for addition, CMP for comparison etc.
- Writing of programs in assembly language is easier and faster as compared to written of programs in machine language.

• No assembly language is not still needed because now a days high level programming language are designed. Low level language like assembly language is hard to write, understand and debug. The syntax and instruction in high level is nearer to the instructions and high level is nearer to the English an these programs are easy to write and debug and understand.

Assembly Language	3rd Generation
(1) The computation like of and assembly language program is less	(1) Programming is difficult and time consuming
(2) This program runs faster to produce the desired result.	(2) This program takes time to produce the result
(3) This language contains more instructions.	(3) It contains less instruction compared to assembly language.
(4) The program written on one computer cannot be used on any other computer	(4) The program can run on the other computers making some changes.

Q4. Difference between
(i) Compiler & interpreter
(ii) 3rd generation language VS 4th generation language

(i) COMPILER → A compiler is used when the programmer wishes to write his code in a high-level language, such as C, Pascal, or sometimes Basic. In the 8052 community, C is the most popular compiled language. A compiler translates the source code written in the high-level language to machine language; thus the resulting output is the same as the output of an assembler which is pure executable machine code. Most modern compilers are relatively efficient and produce relatively tight code. However, an equivalent C program will almost require more code size than the same program in assembly language—unless the assembly language program was very poorly written.

✓ **INTERPRETER ⇒** An interpreted program is one in which the program must be analyzed each time the program is run to determine what actions the processor should execute. Since the program is essentially “compiled on the fly,” program execution is generally slow in comparison to other options. Code size is often larger, too, since not only is your program held in code memory but also the “kernel” which actually interprets and executes your program. Interpreted languages are usually only useful for learning purposes and are seldom used in commercial projects.

(ii) 4th generation language-these are used to get information from files and database and to display to print the information. It contains a query language which is used to answer queries or questions with the data from, database example SQL. All 4GLs are designed to reduce programming effort, the time it takes to develop software, and the cost of software development. They are not always successful in this task, sometimes resulting in inelegant and unmaintainable code. However, given the right problem, the use of an appropriate 4GL can be spectacularly successful. 4th GL don't have functions or subroutines as these are procedural and 4 GL is non procedural

4GL (4th Generation Language)	Third generation Language
(i) Mostly forth generation languages are non-procedural languages.	(i) Mostly third generation languages are procedural languages.
(ii) Fourth generation language are mostly machine independent.	(ii) Most third generation languages are machine dependent.
(iii) Fourth generation languages contain a query language which, is used to answer queries or question with data from a database.	(iii) Third generation language are procedure based, the computer has to follow in a program.
(iv) These are mostly used for office automation or business application	(iv) These are used for scientific programs
(v) Example : FORTRAN, COBOL	(v) Example : SQL

Q5. What are the elements of any programming language? Describe with the help of an example. Compare and contrast functions with subroutines.

Please Refer JUNE03 Q1(e)

Chapter - 4

Operating System Concepts

Q1 Define operating system.

✓ **OPERATING SYSTEM ⇒** An operating system is program that acts as an intermediary between a user of a computer and the computer hardware. The purpose of an operating system is to provide an environment in which a user can execute programs. The primary goal of an operating system is thus to make the computer system convenient to use. A secondary goal is to use the computer hardware in an efficient manner. An operating system is an important part of almost every computer system.

Q2 Define the following terms.

- **Multiprogramming →** A form of processing in which a computer holds more than one program in memory and works on them in round-robin fashion that is, by sharing out the processor's time so that each program receives some attention some of the time. This way of working is in contrast to using the processor to run one program at a time

- **Real time operating system →** A **Real Time Operating System (RTOS)** is an operating system that has been developed for real-time applications. It is typically used for embedded applications, such as mobile telephones, industrial robots, or scientific research equipment. A real-time operating system does not necessarily have high throughput — the specialized scheduling algorithm and a high clock-interrupt rate can both interfere with throughput. That is to say, RTOS are valued more for how quickly they can respond to input than for the total amount of work they can do. An early example of a large-scale real-time operating system was the so-called "control program" developed by American Airlines and IBM for the Sabre Airline Reservations System.

- **System call →** In computing, a **system call**, or **software interrupt** is the mechanism used by an application program to request service from the operating system. System calls often use a special machine code instruction which causes the processor to change mode (e.g. to "supervisor mode" or "protected mode"). This allows the OS to perform restricted actions such as accessing hardware devices or the memory management unit. When a system call is invoked by a program in the "running" state, the context of this program - values of the CPU registers - have to be stored into the program´s stack area in the main memory. After that, the Instruction Pointer register will point to a memory address that is the first executable instruction of the system call code. At the end of the execution, the system call will return the previous value of the Instruction Pointer from the stack area of the program to the CPU. If the system call performs any kind of I/O operation (e.g. disk/ network access) the program will switch from the "running" state to the "blocked" state and will wait until the hardware generates an interruption request to return the I/O operation data and change the program to the "ready" state.

- **Multitask** → This refers to a computer's ability to perform different operations simultaneously, such as saving a file while applying a Photoshop filter. In other words it refers to executing many processes on a single processor. Most operating systems support multitasking, but it can be costly if the need to switch large caches or execution pipelines makes context switching expensive in time. Multitasking can be either cooperative or preemptive. In the former, the operating system relies on the task to voluntarily cede control to another task; in the latter, the operating system decides which task receives priority.

Q3. Difference b/w system call & common line interface.

Please Refer DEC01 Q2(d)

Q4. Difference b/w Network operating system & Distribution operating system

Network OS	Distributed OS
(i) It allows a set of autonomous computers interconnected by a computer network to be used together in a convenient and cost-effective manner.	(i) It looks to its users like an ordinary centralized OS but runs on multiple independent CPUs.
(ii) In a network OS, the users are aware of existence of multiple computers and log in to remote machines and copy files from one machine to another machine.	(ii) In distributed OS, the use of multiple processors should be invisible to the user.
(iii) Each computer has its own private OS instead of running part of a global system wide OS.	(iii) All the machines are another area in which distributed OS are different.
(iv) Less efficient processing.	(iv) More efficient processing.
(v) Users are typically aware of where each of their files are kept.	(v) In a true distributed OS, users are not aware of where their programs are being run or where their files are residing, but can get when desired.
(vi) The system has little or no fault tolerance.	(vi) Fault tolerance is another area in which distributed OS are different.

Q5. What are the main advantages of multi programming ?

The main advantages of multiprogramming are

- Better CPU throughput
- Better resource utilization
- Can supports multiple users at a time

Q6. Define the essential difference between spooling and buffering

✓ **Spooling** ⇒ SPOOLING STANDS FOR SIMULTANEOUS PERIPHERAL OPERATIONS ONLINE. Buffering and Spooling are two methods to increase the system performance in case of batch processing.

Buffering	Spooling
(i) It is a method of overlapping input, output and processing of a Single job.	(i) To order items or jobs in a queue before sending them to an output device such as a printer.
(ii) If the CPU is much faster than an input device, buffering will be a little use.	(ii) Since it allows overlapping of more than one job, it is better approach than buffering.
(iii) A holding area for data shared by devices that operate at different speeds or have different priorities. A buffer allows a device to operate without the delays that other devices impose.	(iii) Spooling is more sophisticated form of buffering and allows overlapping of input, output of more than one job.

Chapter - 5

Fundamentals Of Data Communication

Q1. What do you understand by Simplex, Half-duplex, and Full-duplex modes? Explain with relevant examples.

Simplex	Half-duplex	Full-duplex
1. In simplex transmission, the communication is unidirectional.	**1.** In half-duplex transmission, each station can both transmit and receive, but not at the same time.	**1.** In full-duplex transmission, both stations can transmit and receive simultaneously.
2. It transmission is like a one-way street.	**2.** It transmission is like a one-lane road with two-directional traffic.	**2.** It transmission is like a two-way street with traffic flowing in both direction at the same time.
3. Example : Keyboards and Monitors, the key-board can only introduce input; the monitor can only accept output.	**3.** Example : Walkie-talkies & CB radio.	**3.** Example : Data transmission over Telephone lines.

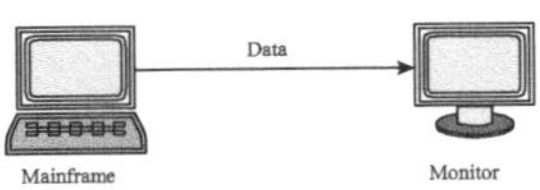

E.g keyboard, monitors are e.g. of simplex device

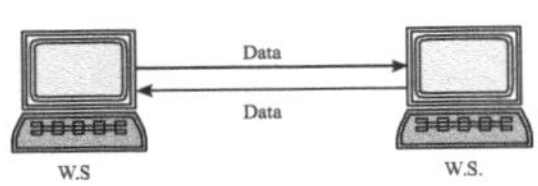

E.g Walkie takies is example of Half duplex

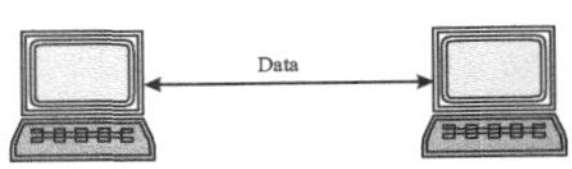

Telephone network is example of Full duplex.

Q2. Define :

(i) Multiplexer → Multiplexing is the form of data transfer in which communication channels are used for several transmissions. In other words multiplexing is a type of network mechanism, which allow a number of simple, low cost terminals to share each communication line,

(ii) Modem → A communications product that sends computer transmission over a standard telephone line at pre-set speeds. **MO**dulator/**DEM**odulator. A device that allows one computer to communicate with another by translating digital information from the computer into analogue data that can be transmitted by the phone lines.

Q3. Define various transmission media.

The popular communication media is:

✓ **Coax Cable** ⇒ Thin or thick coax cable used in Ethernet networking. This looks similar to cable TV coax but usually has BNC connectors on the ends. It is a round, flexible cable consisting of—from the center outwards—a copper wire, a layer of protective insulation, a braided metal mesh sleeve, and an outer shield, or jacket of PVC or fire-resistant material. Coaxial cable is widely used in networks.

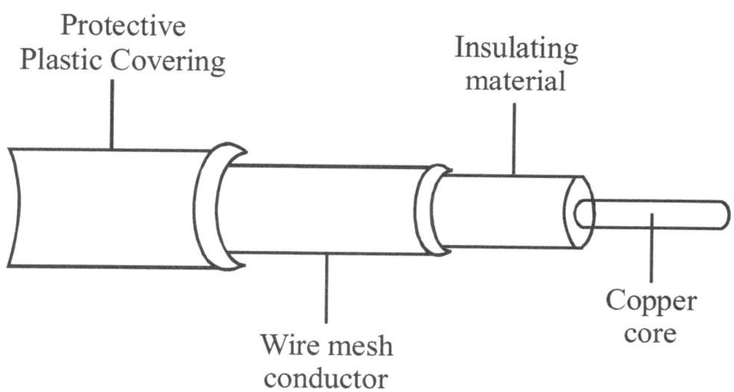

2. TWISTED PAIR CABLING (STP and UTP)

Coaxial and SHIELDED TWISTED PAIR (STP) have a copper braid of foil that offers good resistance to electrical noise, but the extra foil creates a larger, thicker cable, making it difficult to pull the cable through conduit and walls during installation. UNSHIELDED TWISTED PAIR (UTP) does not contain this aluminum shielding and is thinner and therefore easier to install. It offers less resistance to electrical noise.

STP is used in Token Ring, ARCnet and Appletalk networks. UTP is used in Star Topologies.

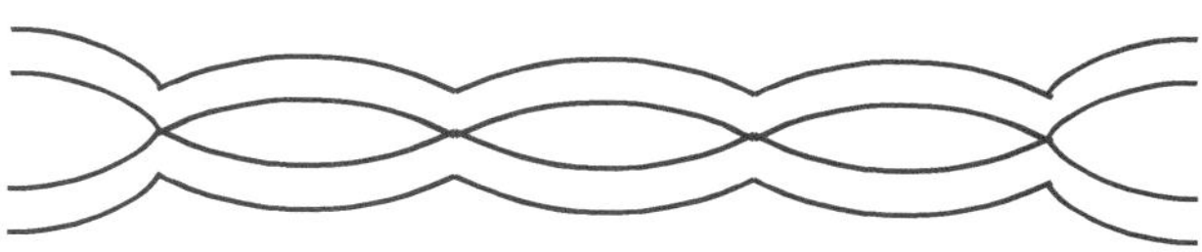

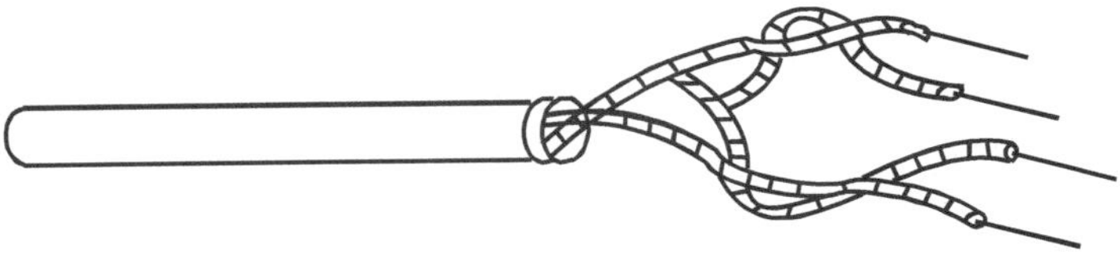

UTP (Unshieded Twisted Pair) is most commonly used in Category Three (CAT3) or Category Five (CAT5). The difference between the ratings is the number of twists per inch. Higher is better. CAT5 is probably the most commonly seen and used. It is inexpensive, reliable, easy to maintain and expand.

✓ **Fiber Optics** ⇒ The use of glass or plastic fibre's for the electronic transmission of data. The technology has several advantages over traditional wire cables in that transmission speed is greatly increased; fiber optics allow for greater bandwidth with no electromagnetic noise; fiber optic cables can carry more data; they transmit the data digitally; and they are lighter and thinner than wire cables.

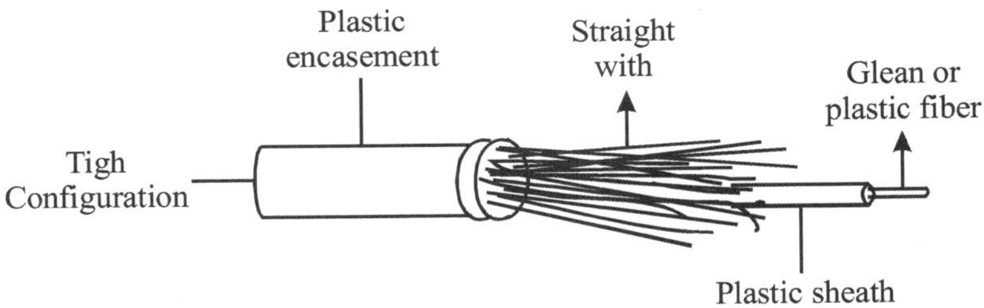

Chapter - 6

Introduction To Computer Networks And Emerging Trends

Q1. Define the following terms.

1. EDI → EDI is an acronym of Electronic Data Interchange. It is the computer-to-computer exchange of structured information, by agreed message standards, from one computer application to another by electronic means and with a minimum of human intervention. EDI documents contain the same data that would normally be found in a paper document used for the same organisational function. However, EDI is not confined to just business data related to trade but encompasses all fields such as medicine (patient records, laboratory results..), transport (container and modal information...), engineering and construction, etc.

2. e-mail → "Electronic Mail" An application of network connectivity and a communication standard to allow users on different computers to send messages (usually text only) back and forth. E-mail works in an analogous fashion to traditional paper mail. To compose an e-mail document, the user drafts a message and puts it in an electronic "envelope." This message is then delivered to the electronic "post office" (actually a computer acting as a mail server) that is responsible for that user. Upon receipt of the message, the "post office" decodes the electronic envelope and gleans from it which "post office" or mail server is responsible for the person defined as the recipient. The "post offices" then exchange the contents of the message, which is then handed off to the recipient by that person's local mail server. The only real problem with this model is that the mail servers will occasionally become "disgruntled" and fail to deliver the messages as instructed.

3. WAN → Wide Area Network" A WAN is a connection of two or more computers that are not at the same physical location. Using a modem or a T1 line to connect multiple computers is a common application of a WAN. Without the presence of WAN technology, there could be no such thing as the Internet, which would indeed be quite sad.

4. LAN → "Local Area Network" A LAN is a group of computers within the same physical location that are capable of communicating data to one another. A network allows users to share resources such as file storage and print services. A group of computers linked together in close proximity such as a building, a suite of offices, or even a single room. Due to the limited size of the network, data is usually transferred rapidly. This arrangement is useful in business for the sharing of information.

Q2. Define Protocol and explain a protocol used in LAN. Is protocol is topology dependent? Justify your answer.

✓ **Protocol ⇒** When data is being transmitted between two or more devices something needs to govern the controls that keep this data intact. A formal description of message formats and the rules two computers must follow to exchange those messages. Protocols can describe low-level details of machine-to-machine interfaces (e.g., the order in which hits and bytes are sent across wire) or high-level exchanges between application programs (e.g., the way in which two programs transfer a file across the Internet). It is A set of rules that specify how two network devices talk to each other. A protocol controls the way information is sent or received over the network.

One protocol used for lan :

✓ **Token passing ⇒** A means of controlling network access through the use of a small packet, the token, which is circulated through the network from node to node. A node can transmit only when it holds the token.

No, protocols are not topology oriented. Topology is just the way of interconnection between machines. Protocols are the rules which facilitates communication among all computers over a network. Protocol works on particular layer and independent to the topology used.

Q3. Describe different communication switching techniques.

(i) Circuit Switching → If two processes want to communicate, a permanent physical link is established between them. This link is allocated for the duration of the communication, and no other processes can use that link during this period (even if the two processes are not actively communicating for a while). This scheme is similar to that used in the telephone system. Once a communication line has been opened between A and B, no one else can use this circuit, until the communication is terminated explicitly.

(ii) Message Switching → If two processes want to communicate, a temporary link is established for the duration of one message transfer. Physical links are allocated dynamically among correspondents as needed, and are allocated for only short periods. Each message is a block of data, with system information (such as the source, the destination and the error correction codes) that allows the communication network to deliver the message to the destination correctly. This scheme is similar to the post office mailing system. Each letter is considered a message that contains both the destination address and source(return) address. Note that many messages (from different users) can be shipped over the same link.

(iii) Packet Switching → Messages are generally of variable length. To simplify the system design, we commonly implement communication with fixed length messages called packets, frames or datagrams. One logical message may have to be divided into a number of packets. Each packet may be sent to its destination separately, and therefore must include a source and destination address with its data. Each packet may take a different path through the network. The packets must be reassembled into messages as they arrive.

Q4. Describe the hardware devices used in WAN

Various types of hardware devises are

✓ **Routers ⇒** A router is like super-intelligent bridge. They can link multiple LANs and look deeper into the data packet to determine its destination. Routers not only know the addresses of the computers on the network but are aware of all the other bridges and routers on the network and can decide the most efficient path in which to send data. The router uses a routing table of network addresses to determine where to forward the packet. When a router receives data, it discards the outer packet or frame or MAC address, repackages the data with network address, and retransmits the signal. By stripping off the outer layers of data before sending a packet, the total number of bits moving across the network is reduced. The router at the receiving end then repackages the data into a packet of frame that is appropriate for its network. There are ROUTABLE and NON-ROUTABLE protocols.

✓ **Gateways ⇒** A gateway is like a super-intelligent router. Gateways are designed to connect radically different networks. Although slower than a bridge or router, a gateway has its own processor and memory to perform complex functions such as interpreting between computers that speak different languages through both protocol and bandwidth conversion. A gateway can convert a TCP/IP packet to a NetWare IPX packet and vice versa. An example of a gateway is a messaging gateway, which converts messages between different protocols.

✓ **Bridge ⇒** A bridge is like a smart repeater. Bridges, like repeaters, can connect two network segments, but bridges are a little smarter about the data they transport. Most bridges have the capacity to listen to the network and figure out the address of each computer on both sides of the bridge. The bridge can then inspect each message that comes from one side and broadcast it to the other side of the bridge, if the message is intended for a computer that is on the other side. If the packet's destination is on the same side of the bridge, it is discarded. This creates a more efficient scheme for data transport

Q5. Describe WAN and LAN. Which topology can be used in LAN and WAN? Also explain communication channel in context of LAN.

A **wide area network** or **WAN** is a computer network covering a wide geographical area, involving a vast array of computers. This is different from local area networks (LANs) that are usually limited to a room, building or campus. The best example of a WAN is the Internet. WANs are used to connect local area networks (LANs) together, so that users and computers in one location can communicate with users and computers in other locations. Many WANs are built for one particular organization and are private. Others, built by Internet service providers, provide connections from an organization's LAN to the Internet. WANs are most often built using leased lines. At each end of the leased line, a router connects to the LAN on one side and a hub within the WAN on the other. Network protocols including TCP/IP deliver transport and addressing functions.

In making LAN we have more options of choosing topologies than in WAN. As LAN can support BUS, RING, and STAR topologies whereas WAN can support MESH topology. As it a wide area network spreaded across the countries with thousands or even more computers and LANs are connected. All make MESH when combined in WAN so MESH topology is well suited for WAN. It does not mean that we cannot use MESH topology in LAN. If we want to have each computer connected with every computer over a network then its a preferred choice.

Star Topology is well suited for a LAN which is to be built in building : It uses a central hub through which all components are connected. In a computer network, the central hub is the host computer, and at the end of each connection is a terminal. An advantage of the star topology is failure in one of the terminals does not affect any other terminal, however, failure of the central hub affects all terminals.

Communication Channel :

✓ **Coax Cable ⇒** Thin or thick coax cable used in Ethernet networking. This looks similar to cable TV coax but usually has BNC connectors on the ends. It is a round, flexible cable consisting of—from the center outwards—a copper wire, a layer of protective insulation, a braided metal mesh sleeve, and an outer shield, or jacket of PVC or fire-resistant material. Coaxial cable is widely used in networks.

✓ **Twisted-pair wiring** ⇒ Wiring consisting of two insulated strands of copper twisted around one another to form a cable. Twisted-pair wiring comes in two forms, unshielded twisted pair (UTP) and shielded twisted pair (STP), the latter named for an extra protective sheath wrapped around each insulated pair of wires. Twisted-pair wiring can consist of a single pair of wires or, in thicker cables, two, four, or more pairs of wires. Twisted-pair wiring is typical of telephone cabling.

Depending on the budget these two can be selected we can not prefer to choose optical fibre as these are very expensive. And coax cable lies in middle when quality and cost are compared. So, coax cable will be well suited for LAN in a building.

Chapter - 7

Computer Virus

Q1. Define the following terms.

1. Data Encryption Standard (DES) → A standard method of encryption and decrypting data, developed by the U.S. National Bureau of Standards. DES is a block of cipher that works by a combination of transposition and substitution, and was developed after years of work at IBM, rigorously tested by the National Security Agency, and finally accepted as being free of any mathematical or statistical weaknesses. This mean, that it is impossible to break the system using statistical frequency tables or to work the algorithm backwards using standard mathematical methods. DES has remained unbroken despite years of use; it completely randomizes the information so that it is impossible to determine the encryption key even if some of the original text is known. DES is used by the federal government and most banks and money-transfer systems to protect all sensitive computer information

2. RSA ALGORITHM → RSA is an Internet encryption and authentication system that uses an algorithm developed in 1977 by Ron Rivest, Adi Shamir, and Leonard Adleman. The RSA algorithm is the most commonly used encryption and authentication algorithm and is included as part of the Web browsers from Microsoft and Netscape. It's also part of Lotus Notes, Intuit's Quicken, and many other products. The encryption system is owned by RSA Security. The company licenses the algorithm technologies and also sells development kits. The technologies are part of existing or proposed Web, Internet, and computing standards.

3. Virus → A computer virus is a computer program that infects other computer programs and reproduces itself without the knowledge of the PC user. A virus may be destructive, and should never be ignored. Contrary to popular belief, not all viruses are dedicated to performing overt harm on computers that they inhabit. The vast majority of viruses would never perform such fabled destructive behaviour as reformatting the hard drive or spiking the water cooler. There are some nasty ones, though. A virus is a clear example of an area in which it is better to give than to receive. A proper measure must be taken to cope with the virus when encountered.

4. Cryptography → Cryptography is the study and practice of scrambling information in a manner that is difficult to unscramble, and making scrambled information intelligible. It is used as the basis of much computer security, in that it can be used to keep information confidential, and also preserve the integrity of data, particularly when being stored or being transmitted. It is the science and technology of keeping information secret from unauthorised parties by using a code or a cipher. Cryptography can be used for many applications that do not involve confidentiality. Cryptography is commonly used for securing communications.

5. Worm → In a computer, a worm is a self-replicating virus that does not alter files but resides in active memory and duplicates itself. Worms use parts of an operating system that are automatic, and are usually invisible to the user. Like a virus, worms can be transmitted to a computer through e-mail attachments, downloads, or infected floppy disks or CD's. It is important to have updated antivirus software so that the newest viruses and worms will be detected and halted. A program that enters a computer and replicates itself, often causing damage to the system.

6. Trojan Horse → A program downloaded from the Internet that contains destructive elements to a computer. Unlike a true virus, the Trojan horse does not replicate itself, it simply erases the users hard drive. A Trojan horse can come disguised as a useful application such as a game or even a virus protection program.

7. Authentication → Authentication is the recognition of a user as having a valid account on the system with legitimate access to its resources, usually determined during login by username and password. It is a security service that provides a user with a means of verifying the identity of the sender of a message, a file, a computer system, a software process, or even a database or individual software component. In other words it is the act of verifying the identity of a user

Q2. Give four ways of protecting your computer against virus

Following are basic ways to protect computer against virus attack.

- Many virus detection programs are available in market. Regularly run these type of software in computer and also keep upgrading antivirus software.
- Avoid to copy data from one computer to other computer.
- Whenever any files are downloaded from internet or any other place, first scan those data from antivirus. If data is without virus then only download it.

- Do not download or install any illegal or unauthorized software. Also avoid purchasing pirated software.

Q2. How can virus can be categorised ?

Viruses are classified on the basis of their mode of existence and there are three categories of viruses

1. Boot infectors → Boot infectors display information originally residing on the location, which they occupy while writing onto the boot sector, the virus ensures that the boot record is not deleted. Once the virus is loaded, it automatically transfers control to the area where the boot record is available. Boot infectors typically create "BAD SECTORS". Boot infectors are the types which once loaded would stay in the memory until the system is shut off, and until the disk reforms.

2. System Infectors → This second categories of viruses deals with the components of the system itself. All machines without exception require an operating system in order to create an environment in which the operator works. The system infectors attach themselves to a file such as COMMAND.COM.

3. GENERAL.COM Infectors →These viruses are most dangerous they attach themselves to program files and can spread to almost any executable program in any system. This virus change the original program instructions into a jumpto its own code and follows that code with a return to the original; program and the exclusive use of the cable tends to be prohibitive.

Solved Papers
CS-611

CS-611 : COMPUTER FUNDAMENTALS AND PC SOFTWARE
JAN 2001

Note: *There are five questions in this paper. Question 1 is* ***compulsory*** *and carries 30 marks. Attempt any* ***three*** *from the rest.*

1(a) Describe the components of von Neumann architecture. What is the purpose of defining any architecture of a computer system? Can a computer system be made by just a single chip? Justify your answer. **[5]**

Most of today's computer designs are based on concepts developed by john von newmann referred to as the "von newmann architecture". There are basically three components for the von newmann architecture :

✓ **Central Processing Unit** ⇒ The central processing unit or CPU is responsible for all the computations, control of the address and data busses, generating the required timing and control signals for the memory and the I/O (input/output) devices, and any other system-level tasks. In principle, the CPU consists of the arithmetic logic unit or ALU, the datapath, the instruction decoder and control subsystem, and a set of registers.

✓ **Memory** ⇒ Any stored-program computer must have some form of storage or memory. In embedded systems, this normally consists of a combination of random access memory, or RAM, and read-only memory, or ROM In a RAM memory, the system can change the contents of each and every memory location under the command of the CPU. In a ROM memory, the contents are "written" at the time the ROM is produced and cannot be changed. Hence, a ROM is "read-only". Memory temporarily holds data and instructions for the CPU. Defined as the internal storage areas of the computer. This is where the computer stores information as it is working on it.

✓ **Input/Output Devices** ⇒ This means Input/Output. This is the way the computer actually works. They take in information, process it then, give it back out! It Refers to the hardware and software mechanisms connecting a computer with its environment. This includes connections between the computer and its disk and bulk storage system, connections to user terminals, graphics systems, and networks to other computer systems or devices.

Structure of Basic Computer

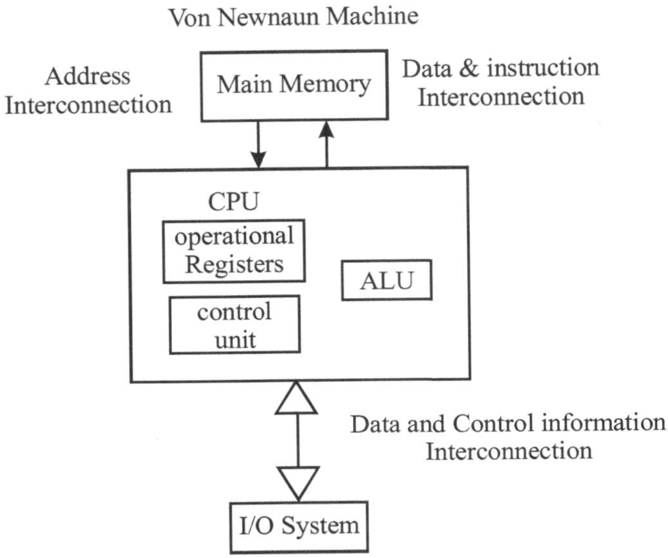

✓ **Purpose of defining any architecture** ⇒ In terms of networks, architecture covers the infrastructure, functionality, protocols, and standards implemented in a particular network design. Architecture - Design; the way components fit together. May be conceived of any complex system such as "software architecture" or "network architecture. In information technology, architecture is a term applied to the process and the outcome of planning and specifying the overall structure, logical components, and logical interrelationships of a computer, its operating system, a network, or other conception. An architecture can be a reference model, such as the Open Systems Interconnection (OSI) reference model, intended as a model for specific product architectures, or it can be a specific product architecture, such as that for an Intel Pentium microprocessor or for IBM's OS/390 operating system. Computer architecture can be divided into five fundamental components: input/output, storage, communication, control, and processing. In practice, each of these components (also called subsystems) is sometimes said to have an architecture.

Yes, a computer system can be made by just a single chip by fabricating all the units in a single chip there can be a cpu in on a single chip and that can be performed by designing all the units using transistors/resistors kind of discrete elements which can be fabricated in the integrated chip.

(b) Compare and contrast the following: **[5]**
(i) Static versus Dynamic random access memories
(ii) Serial versus Parallel interfaces
(iii) Mainframe computers versus Super computers

(i) DRAM → (Dynamic Random Access Memory) The most common form of RAM. DRAM can hold data for only a short time. To retain data, DRAM must be refreshed periodically. If the cell is not refreshed, the data disappear.

SRAM → (Static Random-access Memory) Pronounced S-ram,. It is used in caches and video memory, where speed is of the essence. The term *static* is derived from the fact that it doesn't need to be refreshed like dynamic RAM. Consequently, it is faster, more reliable and more expensive
Point of Difference

- Unlike dynamic RAM, which requires refreshing with electrical current thousands of time per second to function, Static RAM does not need to be refreshed

- While DRAM supports access times of about 60 nanoseconds, SRAM can give access times as low as 10 nanoseconds. In addition, its cycle time is much shorter than that of DRAM

- It is also much more expensive to produce than DRAM. Due to its high cost, SRAM is often used only as a memory cache.

- Data stored in SRAM is lost when the system is powered down or reset. Compare to DRAM.

- Static RAM is fast and expensive, and dynamic RAM is less expensive and slower. Therefore static RAM is used to create the CPU's speed-sensitive cache, while dynamic RAM forms the larger system RAM space.

(ii) Serial and parllel interface → Serial interface - In serial interface only one line is used to transmit data, therefore, only one bit is transferred at a time. Serial interface is used for serial printers and terminals. In serial interface the i/o devices receives or send bytes one by one in serial fashion e.g. Keyboard is a serial interface. The most common serial interface is RS-232-C

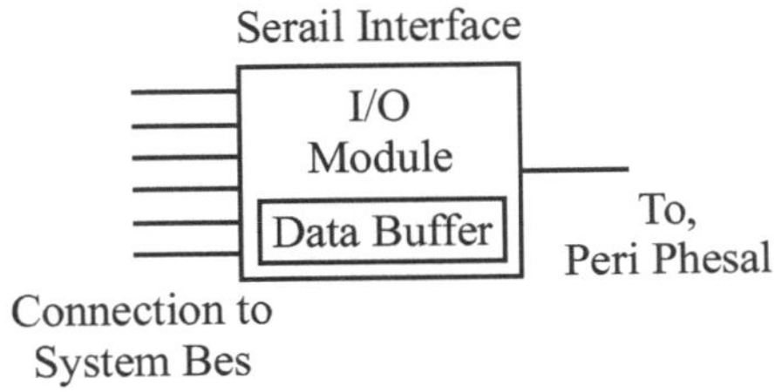

✓ **Parllel interface** ⇒ In parllel interface multiple bits can be transferred simultaneously. The parllel interfaces are normally used for high-speed peripherals such as tapes and disks. In this the data is send or received block vise parallely such as printer. It is faster than serial interface. A common parllel interface is centronics.

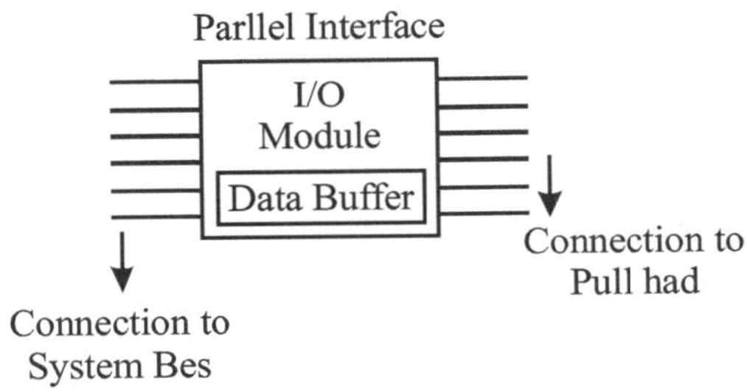

(iii) Mainframe computer → A very large and expensive computer capable of supporting hundreds, or even thousands, of users simultaneously and run a wide variety of applications all at one time .mainframes are just below supercomputers. They are generally 32 bit machines they are used as central host computers in distributed systems. They were used by governments worldwide and large corporations. IBM and Unisys are the leading manufacturers of mainframe computers. A large, stationary computer that requires space in an air conditioned room. Such machines are able to store massive amounts of data, support many users simultaneously corporations. IBM and Unisys are the leading manufacturers of mainframe computers.

✓ **Super computer** ⇒ A very large mainframe computer whose primary activity is carrying out sophisticated and complex calculations. The fastest type of computer in terms of processing speed and use multiprocessing techniques. Supercomputers are very expensive and are employed for specialized applications that require immense amounts of mathematical calculations. For example, weather forecasting requires a supercomputer. Other uses of supercomputers include animated graphics, fluid dynamic calculations, nuclear energy research, and petroleum exploration. In other words, A time dependent term which refers to the class of most powerful computer systems world-wide at the time of reference. Example are CRAY XMP-14. The chief difference between a supercomputer and a mainframe is that a supercomputer channels all its power into executing a few programs as fast as possible, whereas a mainframe uses its power to execute many programs concurrently.

In some ways, mainframes are more powerful than supercomputers because they support more simultaneous programs. But supercomputers can execute a single program faster than a mainframe.

(c) What are the basic components of a Graphical user Interface? Why is Windows a popular graphical user interface? [5]

Please Refer JUNE01, Q1(f)

(d) Why do you use arrays in a programming language? Describe with the help of an example. What is the need of subroutines and functions? Give one example for each. [5]

Arrays are simple and efficient way of referring and performing computation on data of similar types in programming we deal with large amount of related data. To represent each data element we have to consider them as separate variables for example if we have to analyse for the sale performance of a particular company for the last ten years, we can take ten different variables(names) each one representing sales of a particular year. If we analyse sales information for more than ten years, then accordingly number of variables will further increase. It is very difficult to manage with large numbers of variables in a program to deal with such situation an array is used.

Example :

List of 5 years sales information of a company can be referred to by same array name A.

A(0)	A(1)	A(2)	A(3)	A(4)
50000	100,000	5,00,000	8,00,000	9,00,000

A(0) specifies sale information of a firstyear

A(1)specifies sale information of a second year

A(4) specifies sale information of a fifth year

Subroutines and functions are needed almost everywhere while dealing with programming. It provides us better understanding and manageability of code.

As all code related to particular activity can be combined to form a function or subroutine and later called as many as times in coding whereever needed. Thus making the code easily understandable. Functions are made where we need to return some value upon calling. While subroutine do not return any value so used where no need to return value.

(e) What is authentication? Is it related to cryptography? Describe the logic of the RSA algorithm for encryption. [5]

Authentication is the recognition of a user as having a valid account on the system with legitimate access to its resources, usually determined during login by username and password. It is a security service that provides a user with a means of verifying the identity of the sender of a message, a file, a computer system, a software process, or even a database or individual software component. In other words it is the act of verifying the identity of a user.
NO, it is not related to cryptography because cryptography is related to hiding information from an unauthorized attempts. It is the technology of keeping information secret from unauthorised parties by using a code or a cipher. Cryptography can be used for many applications that do not involve confidentiality.

✓ **RSA ALGORITHM ⇒** The Rivest-Shamir-Adelman public-key encryption algorithm.

Please Refer DEC03, Q1(c).

(f) What are the features needed for communication channels of a Local Area Network? How will these features be different for a wide area network? Describe a popular communication media for WAN. [5]

A LAN, or local area network, is a group of computers, printers or other hardware that are all connected in a reasonably small geographic location like a office or home. A LAN makes it possible for the connected users to share files and applications that usually reside on a server or some type of shared computer it is a group of computers within the same physical location that are capable of communicating data to one another. A network allows users to share resources such as file storage and print services.. Due to the limited size of the network, data is usually transferred rapidly. This arrangement is useful in business for the sharing of information. LANs were invented to let people and computers share information. A server can have an application or database that is accessed by all the other computers on the LAN. This allows users to share information quickly and easily different features required for lan communication are:

1. Capacity to transfer signal from one place to other
2. Capacity to keep the signal ineffective from external interference
3. Bandwidth to allow multiple signal through channels

Basic features are same for WAN but the difference is :

1. Bandwidth
2. Distance (Strength of channel) are the main issues

A wide area network or WAN is a computer network covering a wide geographical area, involving a vast array of computers. This is different from local area networks (LANs) that are usually limited to a room, building or campus. The best example of a WAN is the Internet. Along the long way, optical fiber is well suited. A fiber optical carries a signals in the form of fluctuating light in a glass or plastic fiber cable. A form of network cabling that transmits signals optically, rather than electrically as do coaxial and twisted-pair cable. The light-conducting heat of a fiber optic cable is a fine glass or plastic fiber called the core. Fiber optic cable can transmit clean signals at speeds as high as 2 Gbps. Because it transmits light, not electricity, it is also immune to eavesdropping.

Q2. Compare and contrast the features of the following in the context of computer hardware and software: [10]

(a) Dot matrix printer versus Inkjet printer.

• **Dot-matrix** → Creates characters by striking pins against an ink ribbon. Each pin makes a dot, and combinations of dots form characters and illustrations. This is a type of printer which uses a series of pins to create an image on paper. Dot matrix printers are the most economical way to print information. Because the printing involves mechanical pressure, these printers can create carbon copies and carbonless copies. These machines can be highly durable, but eventually wear out. In the 1970s and 1980s, dot matrix impact printers were generally considered the best combination of expense and versatility, and until the 1990s they were by far the most common form of printer used with personal computers.

✓ **Inkjet Printer** ⇒ A printer that creates characters and images by spraying fine streams of ink onto paper at high speeds. Inkjet printers are relatively inexpensive and produce high quality text and graphics in both black and white and colour. Ink jet printers are the most common type of computer printer; and industry and commerce also use them extensively for special-purpose applications. For example, many ATMs, stock control systems, and cash registers use an inkjet printer. Inkjets are usually inexpensive, quiet, reasonably fast, and many models can produce high quality output Compared to earlier consumer-oriented printers, ink jets have a number of advantages. They can print finer, smoother details through higher printhead resolution, and many ink jets with photorealistic-quality color printing are widely available.

Difference between inkjet or Dotmatrix printer :

• **Quality of type →** The output produced by printers is said to be either *letter quality* (as good as a typewriter), *near letter quality*, or *draft quality.* , ink-jet printers produce letter-quality type. Some dot-matrix printers claim letter-quality print, but if you look closely, you can see the difference.

• **Impact or non-impact →** Impact printers include all printers that work by striking an ink ribbon. dot-matrix, printers are impact printers. Non-impact printers include ink-jet printers. The important difference between impact and non-impact printers is that impact printers are much noisier.

• **fonts →** Some printers, notably dot-matrix printers, are limited to one or a few fonts. In contrast, and ink-jet printers are capable of printing an almost unlimited variety of fonts.

• **Price →** dot matrix printers are relatively cheaper than inkjet printers

(b) High-level languages versus Fourth generation languages.

High level Language	4th Generation Language
(i) High level languages are designed because the low level programs were hard to write, understand and debug.	(i) 4th generation language is used to get information from files and data base and to display, to print the information.
(ii) The syntax and instruction in high level is nearer to the English and hence programs are easy to write, debug and understand in the case of High level language	(ii) The 4th generation language contains a query language which is used to answer queries of questions with the data from database. Example SQL(Structured Query Language).

(c) Access mechanism magnetic tapes versus Access mechanism on Winchester disks.

✓ **Access mechanism on magnetic tape** ⇒ Magnetic tape is a sequential access device and hence data recorded on tape can not be addressed directly they can only be retrieved serially

✓ **Access mechanism on Winchester disk** ⇒ Access mechanism on Winchester disk is based on direct access mechanism. In this the information is neither accessed randomly nor in sequence but somewhere in between. In these kind of access, a separate read/write head exists for a track .

(d) Direct Memory Access Module versus Input/Output Module.

✓ **Direct memory access (DMA)** ⇒ A method of transferring information directly from a mass-storage device such as a hard disk or from an adapter card in memory (or vice versa), without the information passing through the processor. Because the processor is not involved in the transfer, direct memory access is usually very fast. It allows certain hardware subsystems within a computer to access system memory for reading and/or writing independently of the CPU. Many hardware systems use DMA including disk drive controllers, graphics cards, network cards, and sound cards. DMA is an essential feature of all modern computers, as it allows devices of different speeds to communicate without subjecting the CPU to a massive interrupt load. Otherwise, the CPU would have to copy each piece of data from the source to one of its registers, and then write it back again to the new location. During this time the CPU would be unavailable for other tasks.

✓ **I/O Module** ⇒ This means Input/Output. This is the way the computer actually works. They take in information, process it then, give it back out! It Refers to the hardware and software mechanisms connecting a computer with its environment. This includes connections between the computer and its disk and bulk storage system, connections to user terminals, graphics systems, and networks to other computer systems or devices.

(e) Reduced Instruction Set Computers versus von Neumann machine.

✓ **Von newmann machine** ⇒ An early computer created by Hungarian mathematician John von Neumann (1903-1957). It included three components used by most computers today: a CPU; a slow-to-access storage area, like a hard drive ; and secondary fast-access memory (RAM). The machines stored instructions as binary values (creating the stored program concept) and executed instructions sequentially - the processor fetched instructions one at a time and processed them. Today "von Neumann architecture" often refers to the sequential nature of computers based on this model.

✓ **RISC** ⇒ An acronym for Reduced Instruction Set Computing, a description applied to microprocessors optimized for carrying out a relatively small number of instructions extremely quickly. In terms of the simple instructions most often carried out by computers, RISC chips are faster. For complex instructions that must be broken down into numerous simpler ones, A processor whose design is based on the rapid execution of a sequence of simple instructions rather than on the provision of a large variety of complex instructions Features which are generally found in RISC designs are uniform instruction encoding (e.g. the op-code is always in the same bit positions in each instruction which is always one word long), which allows faster decoding; a homogenous register set, allowing any register to be used in any context and simplifying compiler design; and simple addressing modes with more complex modes replaced by sequences of simple arithmetic instructions.

3(a) What is a network operating system. Suggest an application where you will prefer network operating system instead of distributed operating system. Give the name of an operating system which is a network operating system. [5]

✓ **Network Operating System** ⇒ A special application that allows computers and other devices on the network the ability to communicate and accept and receive information. It is a : Software that (a) controls a network and its message (e.g. packet) traffic and queues, (b) controls access by multiple users to network resources such as files, and (c) provides for certain administrative functions, including security. A NOS is not the same as the networking tools provided by some existing OS's, windows XP for instance. A NOS is an OS that has been specifically written to keep networks running at optimal performance. It is An operating system specifically designed to support networking. A server-based network operating system, or NOS, provides networking support for multiple simultaneous users as well as administrative, security, and management functions. On the desktop, a network-aware operating system provides users with the ability to access network resources. Some popular NOS's include:

- Windows NT
- Windows 2000 Server
- Windows 2003 Server
- Novell NetWare
- Linux Red Hat

A network operating system is most frequently used with local area networks and wide area networks, but could also have application to larger network systems. Applications using NOS is in lab, where each person works on the computer separately and uses the resources such as software, hardware etc.

(b) What is multiprogramming? How is it different from multi-tasking? What is real-time operating system? Suggest one application for a real-time system. **[5]**

Please Refer JUNE03, Q4(a).

✓ Application for real time operating system ⇒ Flight control.

4(a) What are the components that will be needed to create a local area network at your lab? Which topology and protocol will you suggest for the above LAN? Give reasons for your selection. **[5]**

In LAN several functions are to be performed. These are some specialized in nature that they require hardware specially build for such purpose. For implementing LAN in a lab we require.

1. Transmission channels are required (medial) : For the connectivity and transmission of data and message were require some connecting media such as wires. These can be of the following type :

(a) Twisted pair cable

(b) 2 wire opens line

(c) Co-axial cable

(d) Optical fibre.

2. Servers are needed to provide services : These gives the benefits of sharing expensive resources like printers, storage devices, etc. Server is a dedicated computer which control one or more resources. This contains both hardware and software interface of LAN. The server can be classified as file server, printer server and mail server.

3. Network Interfaces : These connects the transmission channel with the computer and other network resources. It is also used to implement LAN protocol and for device attachments & depends on topologies, it is also called the Ethernet card used in micro computers. Topologies for LAN are bus topology, ring topology, star topology. In bus topology all stations are corrected via a single communication line.

Protocol in-LAN :- Protocol is an agreement between the communicating

parties and how communication is to proceed.
LAN can be accessed in either or the following ways.

1. CSMA/CD (Carries Sense Multiple Access with Collision Detection)
2. Token passing.

CSMA/CD access method is used with bus network. The bus operates in a multiple Access mode. It is the medium is free the node is allowed to transmit. In token passing a logical ring of all modes connected to the physical medium is first established & a single token is generated, the control token passes from one hole to other. After receipt of the token writing station transmits the waiting frames on the physical medium after which it posses the control token to the next node on the logical ring.

(b) Describe the following terms in the context of Computer networks: [5]

(i) Optical Fiber
Please Refer JUNE3, Q3(b)(iv).

(ii) Transport Layer
Please Refer JUNE03, Q3(b)(i).

(iii) EDI
Please Refer JUNE01, Q4(b)(ii).

(iv) BUS
✓ **Bus Topology** ⇒ A networking set-up in which a single cable, such as thin Ethernet, is used to connect one computer to another like a daisy chain to carry data over a network. A network configuration based on a single main communication line (trunk) to which nodes are attached; also known as linear bus. In this, a bus is a central cable that connects all devices on a local-area network (LAN). It is also called the backbone.

Advantage :
- Ease of installation
- Uses less cabling

Disadvantage :
- Difficult reconfiguration and fault isolation.

(v) Switching
Please Refer JUNE02, Q3(c).

5(a) Describe five most important features that exist in a word processor. Explain why do you think that they are most important. [5]

Most Word Processor available today allows more than just creating and editing documents. They have wide range of other tools and functions, which are used in formatting the documents. The following are the main features of a Word Processor.

i. Text is typing into the computer, which allows alterations to be made easily.
ii. Words and sentences can be inserted, amended or deleted.
iii. Paragraphs or text can be copied /moved throughout the document.
iv. Margins and page length can be adjusted as desired.
v. Spelling can be checked and modified through the spell check facility.

(b) What are the security threats to a computer if it is connected to Internet? What are worms? How are they different from computer viruses? [5]

Please Refer DEC02, Q1(f).

CS-611 : COMPUTER FUNDAMENTALS AND PC SOFTWARE
JUNE 2001

Note: *There are five questions in this paper. Question 1 is* ***compulsory*** *and carries 30 marks. Attempt any* ***three*** *from the rest.*

1(a) What are the functional components of a Computer System? What configuration will you suggest for these components? Suggest hardware devices which you would like to procure with a computer. Justify the suggested configuration and devices. [5]

Components of a computer system - Please Refer JAN01, 1(a).

Configuration to be suggested for these components :

• **Microprocessor/CPU →** A piece of silicon containing a general-purpose CPU. P-IV of any GHz speed is preferred configuration for CPU.

• **Bus Speed [Input/Output]→** This is a speed measured in MegaHertz that determines how fast the memory and CPU run. High-quality memory is required for the higher bus speeds. Now a days 133 MHz speed buses are in market which are faster than earlier 100 MHz buses.

• **Main Memory→** At least 256 MB of main memory is preferred most of the present day softwares occupies more memory. E.g. even Windows XP needs at least 256 MB of main memory to work smoothly.

Hardware devices we would like to procure with a computer :

• **Uninterrupted power supply (UPS) →** A unit that switches to battery power whenever the power cuts out. It is must for todays computers. If we taking one computer then UPS of minimum 500 VA is sufficient which normally comes for Rs. 1500 and provides 15 to 20 minutes backup.

• **CD-ROM Drive →** Reads compact disks in the form of audio or CD-ROM. A CD-ROM holds data (perhaps audio as well). Newer CD-ROM drives will read CD-R (Writable CDs) and CD-RW (ReWritable CDs). The speed of a CD-ROM drive is not usually very important except when installing programs, running games that require use of the CD-ROM drive. 52 x CD-ROM are the latest available in market.

• **Hard Drive** → The hard drive stores all the computer's information and retains the information when the computer is turned off. A fast hard drive is needed to supply the CPU with data as fast as it needs it. Hard drive sizes are typically measured in GigaBytes. The larger the number, the more applications and games you can have installed. 80 GB is preferred capacity for Hard Drive as there is very less price difference between 40 GB and 80 GB.

• **Modem** → It stands for Modulator Demodulator, but it's use is much simpler. It enables a computer to "dial-up" to another computer for a variety of purposes including Fax, Gaming, or Internet connections. There is a large variety of modems available now including the original 14.4, 28.8, 33.6, and 56k modems as well as newer ISDN (128k) and ADSL (256k) modems. To use any modem, your Internet Service Provider must support the format (modem, ISDN, or ADSL).

• **Monitor** → A device connected to the computer that visually displays accessed information. A monitor may be either monochrome (black and white) or color (RGB), and can come in sizes ranging from 14" to 21". You can also control the brightness, contrast, and size of the display through buttons located on the monitor.

• **Printer** → A printer outputs data that is seen on the computer screen. Most printers are used through a parallel port, but some newer ones use USB connections. USB is somewhat faster, but there's not much of a difference for printers. Networked computers usually print to a printer through the network card. The most crucial printer measurement is its dots per inch rating. Although this can be misleading, a higher number is generally better. Printers are best chosen by actually seeing the quality of the printer output. Inkjet printers are highly used as these can provide color and black prints.

• **Video Card** → This component is used to transfer data to your monitor so that it can be displayed. Today's video cards have a variety of "3D" capabilities. 3D video cards are only needed for playing games though. When playing 3D games, the video card is the most important component.

• **Floppy Drive** → (Or "floppy disk drive") A peripheral device that reads and writes floppy disks. The drive contains a motor to rotate the disk at a constant rate and two read/write heads which are positioned over the desired track to access the data contained there. Floppy disks must be formatted in order to be used to save information on.

• **Keyboard** → This is another input device that is used to print letters of the alphabet on the screen. You cannot use your computer without a keyboard.

(b) Why do you need an operating system in a computer? Which operating system will you suggest for your lab computers? Give reasons of your selection. [5]

"Operating System" The OS is the base layer of a computing environment, upon which the application level software (or programs) can be run. Examples of popular operating systems are Macintosh, Windows, and UNIX. Without an operating system, a computer would be unable to work at all, and without application programs, a computer would work but be unable to perform any useful tasks. This is the piece of software on your computer which takes instructions from you, and does the task you desire. They also aid in organisation, and can play a big role in the speed of your computer.

For lab computer I suggest network operating system based on client/server technology. It is an operating system specifically designed to support networking. A server-based network operating system, or NOS, provides networking support for multiple simultaneous users as well as administrative, security, and management functions. On the desktop, a network-aware operating system provides users with the ability to access network resources. I suggest this OS in the lab as there is a need of sharing the data and resources in a lab.

(c) What are the basic looping constructs in a programming language? Write an algorithm for reading one dimensional array and then printing it. [5]

Generally there are 4 mainly looping structure available in the programming language :

(i) For loop

(ii) Until loop

(iii) While loop

(iv) Loop using if and goto

(i) For loop → For loop is a for the situation when number of iterations are known to the programmer in advance.

(ii) While loop → It is the loop which is used in the situation where number of iterations are not known before entering in the loop. But some condition decides whether to continue in the loop or stop execution.

(iii) Until loop (or Do......while loop) → It is bottom tasted loop. Here it works like while loop but only difference is that it execute once because the condition is checked after entering into the loop.

(iv) If ....and Goto → It construct any kind of loop.

Algorithm :

To read the array and then print the same array, in the case of array in advance you know the size of an array so you can use the for loop.

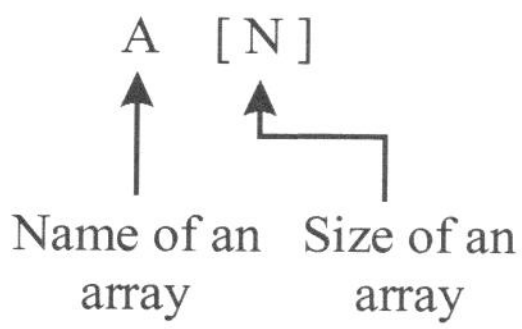

Construct

For I = 1, 2,... To N
    Read A(I)
For J = 1, ... To N
    Print A(J)

Algorithms

Step – 1 : For I = 1 to N repeat step – 2
Step – 2 : Read A(I)
Step – 3 : For J = 1 to N repeat step – 4
Step – 4 : Print A(J)

(d) What is a protocol? Describe one protocol used for Local Area Network. Can a specific protocol be linked to only a single topology? Give reasons in support of your answer. [5]

✓ **Protocol** ⇒ When data is being transmitted between two or more devices something needs to govern the controls that keep this data intact. A formal description of message formats and the rules two computers must follow to exchange those messages. Protocols can describe low-level details of machine-to-machine interfaces (e.g., the order in which hits and bytes are sent across wire) or high-level exchanges between application programs (e.g., the way in which two programs transfer a file across the Internet). It is A set of rules that specify how two network devices talk to each other. A protocol controls the way information is sent or received over the network.

One protocol used for lan :

✓ **Token passing** ⇒ A means of controlling network access through the use of a small packet, the token, which is circulated through the network from node to node. A node can transmit only when it holds the token.

No, protocols are not topology oriented. Topology is just the way of interconnection between machines. Protocols are the rules which facilitates communication among all computers over a network. Protocol works on particular layer and independent to the topology used.

(e) Can a file infector virus, infect your system on receiving e-mail?

Justify your answer. How is a typical virus different from a Trojan Horse? How can you control virus infection to your system?

[JUN02, Q5(b)][JUN99, Q1(e)][5]

Yes, file infecting virus, infect the system on receiving the email. As some of the emails brings virus with them as attachments and due to curiosity the receiver opens the attachments and the virus is triggered, infecting the various files in the systems.

A *Trojan Horse* is full of as much trickery as the mythological Trojan Horse it was named after. The Trojan Horse, at first glance will appear to be useful software but will actually do damage once installed or run on your computer. Those on the receiving end of a Trojan Horse are usually tricked into opening them because they appear to be receiving legitimate software or files from a legitimate source. When a Trojan is activated on your computer, the results can vary. Some Trojans are designed to be more annoying than malicious (like changing your desktop, adding silly active desktop icons) or they can cause serious damage by deleting files and destroying information on your system. Trojans are also known to create a backdoor on your computer that gives malicious users access to your system, possibly allowing confidential or personal information to be compromised. Unlike viruses and worms, Trojans do not reproduce by infecting other files nor do they self-replicate.

✓ **Controlling Virus infection ⇒** The first steps to protecting your computer are to ensure your operating system (OS) is up-to-date. This is essential if you are running a Microsoft Windows OS. Secondly, you should have anti-virus software installed on your system and ensure you download updates frequently to ensure your software has the latest fixes for new viruses, worms, and Trojan Horses. Additionally you want to make sure your anti-virus program has the ability to scan e-mail and files as they are downloaded from the Internet. This will help prevent malicious programs from even reaching your computer. If this isn't enough protection, then you may want to consider installing a firewall as well.

A firewall is a system which prevents unauthorized use and access to your computer. A firewall can be either hardware or software. Hardware firewalls provide a strong degree of protection from most forms of attack coming from the outside world and can be purchased as a stand-alone product or in broadband routers. Unfortunately, when battling viruses, worms and Trojans, a hardware firewall may be less effective than a software firewall, as it could possibly ignore embedded worms in out going e-mails and see this as regular network traffic. For individual home users, the most popular firewall choice is a software firewall. A good software firewall will protect your computer from outside attempts to control or gain access your computer, and usually provides additional protection against the most common Trojan programs or e-mail worms. The downside to software firewalls is that they will only protect the computer they are installed on, not a network.

It is important to remember that on its own a firewall is not going to rid you of your computer virus problems, but when used in conjunction with regular operating system updates and a good anti-virus scanning software, it will add some extra security and protection for your computer or network

(f) What are the basic components of a Graphical User Interface? Describe each of the components and give example for that component in the context of Windows. [JUN02, Q1(c)][DEC98, Q5(a)][5]

Please Refer JUNE03, Q1(c).

Q2. Compare and contrast the following : [10]

(a) SPOOLING versus BUFFERING

✓ **Spooling** ⇒ SPOOLING STANDS FOR SIMULTANEOUS PERIPHERAL OPERATIONS ON LINE. To order items or jobs in a queue before sending them to an output device such as a printer. Spooling furnishes a waiting area for documents to pause while waiting for the printer to accommodate each item in the queue.

✓ **Buffering** ⇒ A holding area for data shared by devices that operate at different speeds or have different priorities. A buffer allows a device to operate without the delays that other devices impose.

An area of RAM reserved for temporary storage of data that is waiting to be sent to a device. The data is usually on its way to or from the hard disk drive or some other peripheral device.

(b) Compiler versus Interpreter

Please Refer DEC01, Q2(c).

(c) EEPROM versus ROM

✓ **EEPROM** ⇒ (Electrically Erasable Programmable Read-Only Memory) A memory chip that retains data content after power has been removed. EEPROM can be erased and reprogrammed within the computer or externally. **A** type of ROM that can be erased electronically and reprogrammed in-circuit (or with a device programmer). EEPROMS ARE MAINLY USED BY R&D PERSONNEL BECAUSE THEY FREQUENTLY CHANGES THE MICROPROGRAM TO test the efficiency of the computer system with new programs

✓ **ROM** ⇒ Acronym for read only memory. Integrated circuit chip containing programs and data that can be accessed and read but cannot be modified. These are special chips in the computer that contain instructions that are permanently stored. It is not possible to write the information on it.. These are read-only files and the information cannot be changed. In this mode data or programs are written to it once, at the time of manufacture, and always retained thereafter, even when the computer's power is turned off. In other words it is a ; memory that can be read but not updated or changed. Memory that is nonvolatile and does not disappear when power is shut off. Commonly used in computers and CD formats such as CD-ROMs.

(d) Registers versus Cache memory in memory hierarchy.

✓ **Register** ⇒ A high speed storage space within a CPU. The size and number of registers in the central processing unit are critical in determining the speed and power of a computer. As the instructions are interpreted and executed by the cpu, there is a movement of information between the various units of the computer system. In order to handle this process satisfactorily and to speed up the rate of information transfer ,the computer uses a number of special memory units called register.

✓ **Cache Memory** ⇒ A small amount (normally less than 1 MB) of high-speed memory residing on or close to the CPU. Cache memory supplies the processor with the most frequently requested data and instructions. **cache memory** is a mechanism interposed in the memory hierarchy between main memory and the CPU to improve effective memory transfer rates and raise processor speeds. The name refers to the fact that the mechanism is essentially hidden and appears transparent to the user. Cache memory is the fastest type of RAM available and is used in CPUs, hard drives

(e) CD-ROM versus Hard Disk (HD)

✓ **CD-ROM** ⇒ Compact Disc Read-Only Memory. A form of write-once, disc-based, random-access data storage, usually mass-produced and distributed as a publication. At present, capable of holding approximately 640 megabytes of data. It allows the information to be stored and retrieved. Once a CD-ROM is pressed, new data cannot be stored and the disc cannot be erased for reuse. Although CD-ROMs look like music discs, they can only be used with a computer equipped with a CD-ROM drive .it is a secondary memory device

✓ **HARD DISK** ⇒ Hard disks contains One or more rigid magnetic disks rotating about a central axle with associated read/write heads and electronics, used to store data. Most hard disks are permanently connected to the drive (fixed disks) though there are also removable disks. Each surface of each disk is divided into a number of evenly spaced concentric circular tracks. The set of all tracks at a given radius on all surfaces (the tracks which can be accessed without moving the heads) are known as a cylinder. Each track is divided into sectors. Because hard disks spin more rapidly than floppy disks, and the flies closer to the other on disk, hard disks can transfer data faster and store more in the same volume. A hard drive is the mass storage device in your computer. Whenever you make a document, you save it to your hard disk. The hard disk stores pretty much everything you see on the screen.

Q3. Write short note on the following giving one example each (wherever applicable): [10]

(a) Network Operating System

Please Refer JAN01, Q3(a).

(b) Distributed Operating System

✓ **DOS** ⇒ The DOS operating system contains commands such as COPY and RENAME for copying files and changing the names of files, respectively. The commands are accepted and executed by a part of the operating system called the command processor or command line interpreter. Graphical user interfaces allow you to enter commands by pointing and clicking at objects that appear on the screen. A DOS is one that looks to its users like an ordinarily centralized OS but runs on multiple independent CPUs. The key concept here is transparency. In other words ,the use of multiple processors should be invisible to the users.

(c) Time-sharing Operating System

✓ **Time Sharing OS** ⇒

A Real Time Operating System (RTOS) is an operating system that has been developed for real-time applications. It is typically used for embedded applications, such as mobile telephones, industrial robots, or scientific research equipment.

An RTOS facilitates the creation of real-time systems, but does not guarantee that they are real-time; this requires correct development of the system level software. Nor does an RTOS necessarily have high throughput — rather they allow though specialized scheduling algorithms and deterministic behavior the

guarantee that system deadlines can be met. That is, an RTOS is valued more for how quickly it can respond to an event than for the total amount of work it can do. Key factors in evaluating an RTOS are therefore maximal interrupt and thread latency.
An early example of a large-scale real-time operating system was the so-called "control program" developed by American Airlines and IBM for the Sabre Airline Reservations System.

(d) System Calls and Command Line Interfaces
Please Refer DEC01, Q2(d).

(e) Batch Systems
✓ **Batch system ⇒** Executing a series of noninteractive jobs all at one time. The term originated in the days when users entered programs on punch cards. They would give a batch of these programmed cards to the system operator, who would feed them into the computer. Batch jobs can be stored up during working hours and then executed during the evening or whenever the computer is idle. Batch processing is particularly useful for operations that require the computer or a peripheral device for an extended period of time. Once a batch job begins, it continues until it is done or until an error occurs. Note that batch processing implies that there is no interaction with the user while the program is being executed. An example of batch processing is the way that credit card companies process billing. The customer does not receive a bill for each separate credit card purchase but one monthly bill for all of that month's purchases. The bill is created through batch processing, where all of the data are collected and held until the bill is processed as a batch at the end of the billing cycle.

4(a) Describe briefly the various wired transmission media used in LANs. Compare and contrast their features. [5]
Please Refer DEC01, Q4(a).

(b) Describe the following terms in the context of computer networks (any *two*): [5]
(i) TCP/IP
(ii) EDI
(iii) MODEM
(i) Transmission Control Protocol/Internet Protocol (TCP/IP) → A set of protocols, resulting from ARPA efforts, used by the Internet to support services such as remote login (TELNET), file transfer (FTP) and mail (SMTP). The primary protocols that allow the Internet to transfer data among the various

networks that make up the Internet. IP protocol deals only with packets of data. TCP enables two hosts to establish a connection and exchange streams of data. TCP guarantees delivery of data and also guarantees that packets will be delivered in the same order in which they were sent. TCP defines how a message is broken up and communicated using these packets. TCP/IP can handle errors, multiple paths through the Internet for packets and message reconstruction even when packets arrive out of order

(ii) EDI → Electronic Data Interchange. Contact between companies exchanging orders via intra- or internet. **EDI** is the computer-to-computer exchange of structured information, by agreed message standards, from one computer application to another by electronic means and with a minimum of human intervention. EDI documents contain the same data that would normally be found in a paper document used for the same organisational function. However, EDI is not confined to just business data related to trade but encompasses all fields such as medicine (patient records, laboratory results..), transport (container and modal information...), engineering and construction, etc.

(iii) Modem → MOdulator/DEModulator. A device that allows one computer to communicate with another by translating digital information from the computer into analogue data that can be transmitted by the phone lines. A device which converts digital data to and from a form that it can be transmitted over a phone line. Modems suitable for graphics transmission on the Internet are 14.4 kbps or higher. Now a days minimum 56 Kbps speed modems are in market. A hardware device that connects your computer and to a phone line, allowing a computer to talk to other computers, usually servers, through the public telephone system

5(a) Describe the following features of Word processor giving one example each: [6]
(i) Mailmerge
(ii) Macro [JUN00, Q5(b)]
(iii) Autotext and find.

(i) Mail merge → A feature supported by many word processors that enables you to generate form letters. To use a mail-merge system, you first store a set of information, like a list of names and addresses, in one file. In another file, you write a letter, substituting special symbols in place of names and addresses (or whatever other information will come from the first file). The power and flexibility of mail merge systems varies considerably from one word processor to another. Some word processors support a full set of logical operators that enable you to specify certain conditions under which information should be merged. Also, some merge systems allow you to merge data from several files at once. Mail merge is sometimes called *print merge.*

(ii) Macro → This is a program within a program which can carry out a preset complex function with the stroke of one or two keys. You can preset your name and address, for example, and then every time you need to use it, in a particular program, just hit the macro key that you already preset as your name and address, and it will be all printed out for you. Saves time!

(iii) Auto text and find → MS-WORD provides some excellent features as Find and Replace, which may be used for a number of tasks with flexibility. Using these features it is possible to find a specific text in a document, search for a particular pattern of text etc. To find a particular text in a document, choose the EDIT → Find Option. A dialog box appears which is used to specify the text to be found. The text found by this option can be changed, by clicking the mouse at the position required in the document. The dialog box can be reused to fetch the next instance of the text.

Following steps are to followed to execute Find and Replace command.

1. Type the text to be searched in the find dialog box.
2. Click on Find Next (only to Find)
3. Click at replace on the top left hand corner (for Find & Replace). You will find another box where you can type text which has to be replaced by the found text.
4. Type the text which will replace the text.
5. Click on Replace or Replace All as per requirement.
6. Click on Close to resume editing.

(b) Describe the various security threats to a compute system. [4]

Please Refer DEC02, 1(f).

CS-611 : COMPUTER FUNDAMENTALS AND PC SOFTWARE
DEC 2001

Note: *There are five questions in this paper. Question 1 is* ***compulsory*** *and carries 30 marks. Attempt any* ***three*** *from the rest.*

1(a) What should be the configuration of a computer that is to be used at your home? Justify your answer. Categorise the various terms used for configuration description under the broad categories: CPU, Memory, Input/Output devices and Bus or Interconnection structures. [5]

Please Refer JUNE01, 1(a).

(b) How does a user interact with an operating system of computer? What is the need of an operating system in a computer? Can two operating systems be loaded in a computer at a time? Justify your answer. [5]

As a user, you normally interact with the operating system through a set of commands. For example, the DOS operating system contains commands such as COPY and RENAME for copying files and changing the names of files, respectively. The commands are accepted and executed by a part of the operating system called the command processor or command line interpreter. Graphical user interfaces allow you to enter commands by pointing and clicking at objects that appear on the screen

The most important program that runs on a computer. Every general-purpose computer must have an operating system to run other programs. Operating systems perform basic tasks, such as recognizing input from the keyboard, sending output to the display screen, keeping track of files and directories on the disk, and controlling peripheral devices such as disk drives and printers.

For large systems, the operating system has even greater responsibilities and powers. It is like a traffic cop — it makes sure that different programs and users running at the same time do not interfere with each other. The operating system is also responsible for *security*, ensuring that unauthorized users do not access the system.
Operating systems provide a software platform on top of which other programs, called *application programs,* can run. The application programs must be written to run on top of a particular operating system. Your choice of

operating system, therefore, determines to a great extent the applications you can run. For PCs, the most popular operating systems are DOS, OS/2, and Windows, but others are available, such as Linux.

Yes, there is a mechanism to store two OSs in a computer system in such a way that at a time one of them is active. Means booting can only be done through one operating system.

(c) What is meant by the term "Iteration"? Describe the use of a two dimensional array with the help of Iteration. How is iteration different or similar to Recursion. [5]

It is the repetition of a process, typically within a computer program. It can be used both as a general term, synonymous with repetition, and to describe a specific form of repetition with a mutable state. When used in the first sense, recursion is an example of *iteration*, but typically using a *recursive notation*, which is typically not the case for *iteration*. However, when used in the second (more restricted) sense, iteration describes the style of programming used in imperative programming languages. This contrasts with recursion, which has a more declarative approach.

Here an example of iteration using two dimensional array :

```
For m=1 to 3
        For n=1 to 4
            Read  A[m][n]     // two diamensional array
            i=A[m][n]
            Print i
        End for
End for
```

This algorithm prints values in the two diamensional array depending on the values of m, n it fetches the actual value at that location in array and store in variable i then prints.

(d) The protocol used on Internet is "TCP/IP"? What does the above statement mean in the context of data communication? Suppose that a LAN protocol which has been implemented on STAR topology LAN, can it be implemented on RING topology network? Justify your answer.[5]

TCP/IP capability is built into virtually every computer and device capable of connecting to the Internet. It is a transmission and packet protocol used on the Internet. IP defines packets, chunks of about 500 characters with attached header information such as to/from addresses of machines on the Internet. TCP defines how a message is broken up and communicated using these packets. TCP/IP can handle errors, multiple paths through the Internet for packets and message reconstruction even when packets arrive out of order. TCP/IP is the common data communication mode that makes the Internet work. TCP/IP is not a program or a language, but a protocol that defines how data packets are to be transferred from one computer or network to another computer or network lan can be implemented on both star and ring topology, sharing data and communication to all connected nodes.

Yes, a LAN protocol which has been implemented on STAR topology LAN, can be implemented on RING topology network because protocols are not topology dependent. It works on a particular layer with a objective to make communication happen.

(e) Describe the basic components of the graphical user interface giving an example each from MS-Windows.

[JUN02, Q1(c)][JUN01, QI(c)][DEC98, Q5(a)][5]

Please Refer JUNE03, Q1(c)

(f) What is a WORM in the context of computers? How is it different than computer virus? Can a worm be spread through e-mail messages? Can a virus spread through e-mail messages? Justify your answer.

[JUN02, Q5(b)][JUN99, Q1(e)][5]

Refer to JUNE 2003, Q5(b)

Yes, a virus and worm can spread through E-mail. A virus is often designed so that it is automatically spread to other computer users. Viruses can be transmitted as attachments to an e-mail note, as downloads, or be present on a diskette or CD. While a worm can spread unknowingly to all mails.

Q2. Compare and contrast the following : [10]

(a) Batch Processing versus Multiprogramming.

(b) Registers versus Main memory versus Cache memory

(c) Assembler versus Compiler versus Interpreter

(d) System calls versus Command line interfaces.

(a)

Batch processing	Multiprogramming
(i) Executing a series of noninteractive jobs all at one time. The term originated in the days when users entered programs on punch cards. They would give a batch of these programmed cards to the system operator, who would feed them into the computer.	(i) Multiprogramming Operating system provides sophisticated form of memory protection and enforces concurrency control when processes access shared I/O devices and files i.e. it usually supports multiple users.
(ii) It has less resources utilization compared to multiprogramming operating system	(ii) it has a significant potential for improving system throughout and resource utilization.
(iii) At most one program is in execution at any time	(iii) Not necessary that at most one program is in execution
(vi) Scheduling in batch system is very simple	(iv) A multiprogramming operating system monitors the state of all active programs and system resources. When important changes of state occur, or when explicit called the operating system is activated to allocate resources and to provide certain form of services.

(b)

Register	Main Memory	Cache
(i) A high speed storage space within a CPU.	(i) Main memory is placed between the cache memory secondary memory	(i) Cache memory is placed between CPU and main memory
(ii) It is set of flip-flop fabricated within CPU and hence provide fast access	(ii) Not very fast as compared to cache and register	(ii) Cache memory is designed and implemented to provide fast access
(iii) Register is a set of Flip-flops fabricated with in the CPU	(iii) It is mainly based on integrated Circuits (ICs)	(iii) Cache memory is associative type of semiconductor memory.
(iv) Register are essential part of memory	(iv) Main memory is a heart of computer system and is accessed directly by the processor	(iv) Cache memory is used to improve performance of improve performance of computer. Faster than Main memory.

(c) Interpreter →

(i) An interpreted program is one in which the program must be analyzed each time the program is run to determine what actions the processor should execute.

(ii) Since the program is essentially "compiled on the fly," program execution is generally slow in comparison to other options. Code size is often larger, too, since not only is your program held in code memory but also the "kernel" which actually interprets and executes your program.

(iii) Interpreted languages are usually only useful for learning purposes and are seldom used in commercial projects.

✓ **Assembler →**

(i) An assembler allows you to write your program in assembly language which is one step away from pure machine language. The assembler actually translates your assembly program into machine language.

(ii) A well-written assembly language program will provide the most speed and smallest code size, but writing a program in assembly language is generally considered to be more advanced and more difficult than writing a similar program in an interpreted or compiled language.

(iii) Using assembly language also gives you complete control over what the processor is doing.

✓ **Compiler →**

(i) A compiler is used when the programmer wishes to write his code in a high-level language, such as C, Pascal, or sometimes Basic.

(ii) A compiler translates the source code written in the high-level language to machine language; thus the resulting output is the same as the output of an assembler—pure executable machine code. Most modern compilers are relatively efficient and produce relatively tight code.

(iii) However, an equivalent C program will almost require more code size than the same program in assembly language—unless the assembly language program was very poorly written.

(d)

System Call	Command Line Interface
(i) In computing, a system call, or software interrupt is the mechanism used by an application program to request service from the operating system. System calls often use a special machine code instruction which causes the processor to change mode (e.g. to "supervisor mode" or "protected mode").	(i) Command line interface is a terminal type means for sending commands to the shell and entering data into the computer. The command line is indicated by a symbol, or prompt (e.g., >, %, $), showing the user where to enter commands.
(ii) These system calls can be used by user interface layer to execute user requirements	(ii) Command line interface a way of interface between user and system
(iii) System calls can be called with different arguments/different order to get required task done.	(iii) Example : MS-DOS, UNIX, LINUX } Commands in textual form

3(a) Describe the characteristics of distributed operating system. How is it different to that of Network Operating System? Is it essential that a distributed operating system must be a network operating system also. Justify your answer. [6]

Please Refer JUNE03, Q4(b).

(b) Differentiate the basic requirements of multitasking, multi process and time sharing operating systems. What are the basic requirements for a real-time operating system. [4]

✓ **Multitasking** ⇒ This refers to a computer's ability to perform different operations simultaneously, such as saving a file while applying a Photoshop filter. In other words it refers to executing many processes on a single processor.. Most operating systems support multitasking, but it can be costly if the need to switch large caches or execution pipelines makes context switching expensive in time.. Multitasking can be either cooperative or preemptive. In the former, the operating system relies on the task to voluntarily cede control to another task; in the latter, the operating system decides which task receives priority.

✓ **Time sharing OS** ⇒ A Real Time Operating System (RTOS) is an operating system that has been developed for real-time applications. It is typically used for embedded applications, such as mobile telephones, industrial robots, or scientific research equipment.

An RTOS facilitates the creation of real-time systems, but does not guarantee that they are real-time; this requires correct development of the system level software. Nor does an RTOS necessarily have high throughput — rather they allow though specialized scheduling algorithms and deterministic behavior the guarantee that system deadlines can be met. That is, an RTOS is valued more for how quickly it can respond to an event than for the total amount of work it can do. Key factors in evaluating an RTOS are therefore maximal interrupt and thread latency.

An early example of a large-scale real-time operating system was the so-called "control program" developed by American Airlines and IBM for the Sabre Airline Reservations System.

✓ **Multiprogramming** ⇒ A form of processing in which a computer holds more than one program in memory and works on them in round-robin fashion that is, by sharing out the processor's time so that each program receives some attention some of the time. This way of working is in contrast to using the processor to run one program at a time.

Requirements for Real time operating system :

- Real time operating system are used in environments where a large number of events, mostly external to the computer system, must be accepted and processed in a short time or within certain deadlines.
- This system provides quick event-response and meets the scheduling deadlines.

• Real time operating system usually rely on some specific policies & techniques for doing this job.
• File management is usually found only in larger installation of real–time systems.
• Time–critical device management is one of the main characteristics of real – time systems.

4(a)Compare and contrast the feature of various wired transmission media used in local area networks? What are the limitations of these wired medias for Wide Area Network. [JAN01, Q1(f)][6]

Transmission media used in LAN are:

✓ **Coax Cable** ⇒ Thin or thick coax cable used in Ethernet networking. This looks similar to cable TV coax but usually has BNC connectors on the ends. It is a round, flexible cable consisting of—from the center outwards—a copper wire, a layer of protective insulation, a braided metal mesh sleeve, and an outer shield, or jacket of PVC or fire-resistant material. Coaxial cable is widely used in networks.

✓ **Fiber optic cable** ⇒ A form of network cabling that transmits signals optically, rather than electrically as do coaxial and twisted-pair cable. The light-conducting heart of a fiber optic cable is a fine glass or plastic fiber called the core. This core is surrounded by a refractive layer called the cladding that effectively traps the light and keeps it bouncing along the central fiber. Outside both the core and the cladding is a final layer of plastic or plastic-like material called the coat, or jacket. Fiber optic cable can transmit clean signals at speeds as high as 2 Gbps. Because it transmits light, not electricity, it is also immune to eavesdropping.

✓ **Twisted-pair wiring** ⇒ Wiring consisting of two insulated strands of copper twisted around one another to form a cable. Twisted-pair wiring comes in two forms, unshielded twisted pair (UTP) and shielded twisted pair (STP), the latter named for an extra protective sheath wrapped around each insulated pair of wires. Twisted-pair wiring can consist of a single pair of wires or, in thicker cables, two, four, or more pairs of wires. Twisted-pair wiring is typical of telephone cabling.

Comparison and untrusting of
various transmission made

Factor Cost	TP Low	C C Moderate	F O High
Instillation	Easy	Easy	Difficult
Attenuator	High	Lower	Lowest
Hectricity effect	Most	Less	Not effected

✓ **LIMITATION OF WIRED TRANSMISSION** ⇒ A Wan spans a large geographical area often a country while lan uses a single cable to which all machines are connected such use of single cable lengths is not possible in wan.

(b) What is Electronic Data Interchange (EDI)? How is it different to E-mail? What are the hardware needed for connecting your computer to make use the features of EDI?. **[4]**

✓ **EDI** ⇒ Electronic Data Interchange, Contact between companies exchanging orders via intra- or internet.(**EDI**) is the computer-to-computer exchange of structured information, by agreed message standards, from one computer application to another by electronic means and with a minimum of human intervention. In common usage, EDI is understood to mean specific interchange methods agreed upon by national or international standards bodies for the transfer of business transaction data, with one typical application being the automated purchase of goods and services.

EDI documents contain the same data that would normally be found in a paper document used for the same organisational function. However, EDI is not confined to just business data related to trade but encompasses all fields such as medicine (patient records, laboratory results..), transport (container and modal information...), engineering and construction, etc.- (Electronic Data Interchange) The exchange of information between two or more companies with mutual interests over a network.

E-mail	EDI
(i) E-mail is an acronym of electronic mail	(i) EDI is an acronym of Electronic Data interchange
(ii) E-mail system is basically used for sending message electronically to individuals or group of individuals in an inter and intra office environment. It requires network to connect them.	(ii) EDI is the inter-organisatonal exchange of business documentation in structured, machine processable form.
(iii) No such need.	(iii) EDI provides communication between trading partners that agree to exchange EDI transactions.
(iv) One of the advantages of E-mail is that if gives users ability to review, respond message quickly.	(iv) EDI eliminates the paper documents associated with common business transactions.
(v) No processing of the message received.	(v) EDI message can be immediately processed by receiving computer without any human intervention or interpretation or re-keying
(vi) No such facility	(vi) One other advantage of EDI is that it generates the functional acknowledgment whenever an EDI message is received, and is electronically transmitted to the sender.

Hardware required for EDI are :
Modem, NIC, Telephone connection, cable.
Modem : Modem is called modulator/demodulator. It converts digital signal into analog for transmission and Vice versa.

NIC (Network Interface Card) : It is the means by which the workstations are connected functionally and physically to the network. It is microprocessor bases device. Comes with software/driver which is to be installed. Software supplies the intelligence to control access to and communications across the network and to perform all communication processing.

5(a)In what situation/application would you like to use 'Mailmerge' feature of a Word Processor? Describe with the help of suitable example. [3]

Word's Mail Merge feature is a quick and easy way for mass producing of form letters, envelopes, mailing labels, phone lists etc.

➢ Mail Merge feature can also be used to prepare other kind of merged documents such as catalogues, parts lists, directory list, forms or invoices, print addresses and envelopes and mailing labels.

➢ By using Mail Merge, the same letter can be sent to a number of people, without typing the original letter more than once.

➢ Word's Mail Merge feature lets you quickly create personalized correspondence and other documents by combining information from two different files. For example – a list of names and addresses from one file (your data document) could be merged with another file (you main document) to produce a number of personalized form letters.

(b) What are the basic utilities available in Windows to deal with some very basic problems such as bad sectors, bad response time etc? [3]

Please Refer JUNE04, Q2(b).

(c) What are the basic threats to computer security? How can you counter a threat like "occurrence of a disaster" in the area computer is placed? [4]

Please Refer DEC02, Q1(f).

CS-611 : COMPUTER FUNDAMENTALS AND PC SOFTWARE
JUNE 2002

Note: *There are five questions in this paper. Question 1 is* ***compulsory*** *and carries 30 marks. Attempt any* ***three*** *from the rest.*

1(a) What is the structure of a Basic computer? What is the need of various components of a Basic computer as defined by Von Neumann? Are they a must for a computer system? Justify your answer. [5]

Please Refer JAN01, Q1(a)

Yes, all of the above components are must for the computer system because it a system where all the units are connected together and working together to achieve a goal. No single unit can be removed from the system, if it is done then the system will be incomplete and will not work at all.

(b) Why is the main memory of a computer also called RAM? What is static RAM and how is it similar/different to dynamic RAM? Can RAM be totally replaced by Cache memory? Justify your answer. [5]

The main memory consist of semiconductor memory chips and is used to store the data and programs currently in use. All modern computers use semiconductor memory as its main memory. Semiconductor memory is known as Random Access Memory(RAM) since any part of the memory can be accessed for reading and writing. Hence the main memory in a computer is also called as RAM. A memory which can be accessed randomly.

✓ **DRAM ⇒** (Dynamic Random Access Memory) The most common form of RAM. DRAM can hold data for only a short time. To retain data, DRAM must be refreshed periodically. If the cell is not refreshed, the data disappear.

✓ **SRAM ⇒** (Static Random-access Memory) Pronounced S-ram,. It is used in caches and video memory, where speed is of the essence. The term *static* is derived from the fact that it doesn't need to be refreshed like dynamic RAM. Consequently, it is faster, more reliable and more expensive

Difference :

- Unlike dynamic RAM, which requires refreshing with electrical current thousands of time per second to function, Static RAM does not need to be refreshed.

• While DRAM supports access times of about 60 nanoseconds, SRAM can give access times as low as 10 nanoseconds. In addition, its cycle time is much shorter than that of DRAM

• It is also much more expensive to produce than DRAM. Due to its high cost, SRAM is often used only as a memory cache.

• Data stored in SRAM is lost when the system is powered down or reset. Compare to DRAM.

static RAM is fast and expensive, and dynamic RAM is less expensive and slower. Therefore static RAM is used to create the CPU's speed-sensitive cache, while dynamic RAM forms the larger system RAM space.

RAM cannot be totally replaced by cache memory because

• Limited size i.e less than the main memory

• It stores frequently visited contents

(c) What are the advantages of Graphical User Interface? What is the need of having various components of Graphical User Interface? [5]

✓ **GUI** ⇒ "Graphical User Interface" Though the use of a GUI, one may operate a computer by interacting with pictures and menus on the screen, as opposed to entering commands directly through the keyboard. The use of a GUI requires an input device in addition to the keyboard (such as a mouse, trackball, touchscreen, or stylus pad). The term GUI is usually pronounced "gooey", which makes it particularly fun to slip into conversation

Advantages of GUI :

A major advantage of GUIs is that they make computer operation more intuitive, and thus easier to learn and use. For example, it is much easier for a new user to move a file from one directory to another by dragging its icon with the mouse than by having to remember and type seemingly arcane commands to accomplish the same task.

In addition, GUIs allow users to take full advantage of the powerful *multitasking* (the ability for multiple programs and/or multiple instances of single programs to run simultaneously) capabilities of modern operating systems by allowing such multiple programs and/or instances to be displayed simultaneously. The result is a large increase in the flexibility of computer use and a consequent rise in user productivity.

But the GUI has became much more than a mere convenience. It has also become the standard in human-computer interaction, and it has influenced the work of a generation of computer users. Moreover, it has led to the development of new types of applications and entire new industries. An example is desktop publishing, which has revolutionized (and partly wiped out) the traditional printing and typesetting industry.

Despite the great convenience of the GUI however, system administrators and other advanced users tend to prefer the CLI for many operations because it is frequently more convenient and generally more powerful.

Need of various components :

feature the following basic components:

- **pointer :** A symbol that appears on the
- display screen and that you move to
- select
- objects and
- commands. Usually, the
- pointer appears as a small angled arrow.
- Text -processing
- applications, however, use an
- *I-beam pointer* that is shaped like a capital *I*.

- **pointing device :** A
- device, such as a
- mouse or
- trackball, that enables you to select objects on the display screen.
-

- **icons :** Small pictures that represent commands,
- files, or
- windows. By moving the pointer to the icon and pressing a
- mouse button, you can
- execute a command or
- convert the icon into a window. You can also move the icons around the display screen as if they were real objects on your desk.

- **desktop :** The area on the display screen where icons are grouped is often referred to as the desktop because the icons are intended to represent real objects on a real desktop.

- **windows:** You can divide the screen into different areas. In each window, you can
- run a different program or display a different file. You can move windows around the display screen, and change their shape and size at will.

• **menus :** Most graphical user interfaces let you execute commands by selecting a choice from a menu.

(d) What is the usefulness of Wide Area Network (WAN)? How is the topology of WAN different from that of Local Area Networks (LAN)? Which topology and communication channel will you suggest for LAN located in a building? Justify your answer. [5]

A **wide area network** or **WAN** is a computer network covering a wide geographical area, involving a vast array of computers. This is different from local area networks (LANs) that are usually limited to a room, building or campus. The best example of a WAN is the Internet. WANs are used to connect local area networks (LANs) together, so that users and computers in one location can communicate with users and computers in other locations. Many WANs are built for one particular organization and are private. Others, built by Internet service providers, provide connections from an organization's LAN to the Internet. WANs are most often built using leased lines. At each end of the leased line, a router connects to the LAN on one side and a hub within the WAN on the other. Network protocols including TCP/IP deliver transport and addressing functions.

In making LAN we have more options of choosing topologies than in WAN. As LAN can support BUS, RING, and STAR topologies whereas WAN can support MESH topology. As it a wide area network spreaded across the countries with thousands or even more computers and LANs are connected. All make MESH when combined in WAN so MESH topology is well suited for WAN. It does not mean that we cannot use MESH topology in LAN. If we want to have each computer connected with every computer over a network then its a preferred choice.

Star Topology is well suited for a LAN which is to be built in building : It uses a central hub through which all components are connected. In a computer network, the central hub is the host computer, and at the end of each connection is a terminal. An advantage of the star topology is failure in one of the terminals does not affect any other terminal, however, failure of the central hub affects all terminals.

Communication Channel :

✓ **Coax Cable** ⇒ Thin or thick coax cable used in Ethernet networking. This looks similar to cable TV coax but usually has BNC connectors on the ends. It is a round, flexible cable consisting of—from the center outwards—a copper wire, a layer of protective insulation, a braided metal mesh sleeve, and an outer shield, or jacket of PVC or fire-resistant material. Coaxial cable is widely used in networks.

✓ **Twisted-pair wiring ⇒** Wiring consisting of two insulated strands of copper twisted around one another to form a cable. Twisted-pair wiring comes in two forms, unshielded twisted pair (UTP) and shielded twisted pair (STP), the latter named for an extra protective sheath wrapped around each insulated pair of wires. Twisted-pair wiring can consist of a single pair of wires or, in thicker cables, two, four, or more pairs of wires. Twisted-pair wiring is typical of telephone cabling.

Depending on the budget these two can be selected we can not prefer to choose optical fibre as these are very expensive. And coax cable lies in middle when quality and cost are compared. So, coax cable will be well suited for LAN in a building.

(e) How will you represent a table in a computer using a programming languages? Give definition of the element used by you and give reason of your selection. To multiply two matrices would you like to define a function or a subroutine? Justify your answer. [5]

To represent a table in a computer using a programming language. We use an array of two dimensions, one for the row and the other dimension for the column. The two dimensional array can be called a matrix of any data type it depends as the type of data it is storing in it.

To multiply any two matrix we would like to define a function or a subroutine sending two pointers containing the base addresses of both the matrices and the return type of the function will also be a pointer type which will return base address of the resultant matrix.

By creating a function we get the modularity of code, which is universal for various number of rows & columns.

(f) What is the need of cryptography? Describe the data Encryption Standard (DES) with the help an example. [5]

Cryptography is the study and practice of scrambling information in a manner that is difficult to unscramble, and making scrambled information intelligible. It is used as the basis of much computer security, in that it can be used to keep information confidential, and also preserve the integrity if data, particularly when being stored or being transmitted. It is the science and technology of keeping information secret from unauthorised parties by using a code or a cipher. Cryptography can be used for many applications that do not involve confidentiality. Cryptography is commonly used for securing communications. Desirable properties due to which it is needed are:

1. Confidentiality, also known as secrecy: only an authorised recipient should be able to extract the contents of the message from its encrypted form.

Otherwise, it should not be possible to obtain any significant information about the message contents.

2. Integrity: the recipient should be able to determine if the message has been altered during transmission.

3. Authentication: the recipient should be able to identify the sender, and verify that the purported sender actually did send the message.

4. Non-repudiation: the sender should not be able to deny sending the message.

✓ **Data Encryption Standard (DES)** ⇒ A standard method of encryption and decrypting data, developed by the U.S. National Bureau of Standards. DES is a block of cipher that works by a combination of transposition and substitution, and was developed after years of work at IBM, rigorously tested by the National Security Agency, and finally accepted as being free of any mathematical or statistical weaknesses. DES works on bits, or binary numbers—the 0s and 1s common to digital computers. Each group of four bits makes up a hexadecimal, or base 16, number. Binary "0001" is equal to the hexadecimal number "1", binary "1000" is equal to the hexadecimal number "8", "1001" is equal to the hexadecimal number "9", "1010" is equal to the hexadecimal number "A", and "1111" is equal to the hexadecimal number "F". DES works by encrypting groups of 64 message bits, which is the same as 16 hexadecimal numbers. To do the encryption, DES uses "keys" where are also *apparently* 16 hexadecimal numbers long, or *apparently* 64 bits long. However, every 8th key bit is ignored in the DES algorithm, so that the effective key size is 56 bits. But, in any case, 64 bits (16 hexadecimal digits) is the round number upon which DES is organized.

For example, if we take the plaintext message "8787878787878787", and encrypt it with the DES key "0E329232EA6D0D73", we end up with the ciphertext "0000000000000000". If the ciphertext is decrypted with the same secret DES key "0E329232EA6D0D73", the result is the original plaintext "8787878787878787".

This example is neat and orderly because our plaintext was exactly 64 bits long. The same would be true if the plaintext happened to be a multiple of 64 bits. But most messages will not fall into this category. They will not be an exact multiple of 64 bits (that is, an exact multiple of 16 hexadecimal numbers).

2(a) What is meant by Serial and Parallel Interfaces? Where are they used? [2½]

Please Refer JAN01, Q1(b)(ii).

(b) What is an assembly language? Is it still needed? Give reason. Compare and contrast assembly language to third generation languages. [2½]

To facilitate programmer easily understandable language is developed. Assembly language is one of them. Programs can easily be written in alphanumeric symbols instead of 0s and 1s.

• Meaningful and easily rememberable symbols are selected for this purpose. For Example SUB for subtraction, ADD for addition, CMP for comparison etc.

• Writing of programs in assembly language is easier and faster as compared to written of programs in machine language.

• No assembly language is not still needed because now a days high level programming language are designed. Low level language like assembly language is hard to write, understand and debug. The syntax and instruction in high level is nearer to the instructions and high level is nearer to the English an these programs are easy to write and debug and understand.

Assembly Language	3rd Generation
(1) The computation in assembly language program is less	(1) Programming is difficult and time consuming
(2) This program runs faster to produce the desired result.	(2) This program takes time to produce the result
(3) This language contains more instructions.	(3) It contains less instruction compared to assembly language.
(4) The program written on one computer cannot be used on any other computer	(4) The program can run on the other computers making some changes.

(c) What is Direct Memory Access? Where is it used in a computer? How is it different from having the CPU doing Input/Output? [2½]

Please Refer JAN01, Q2(d).

(d) What is meant by the term Reduced Instruction Set Computers (RISC)? What are their characteristics? [2½]

RISC is an acronym for Reduced Instruction Set Computing, a description applied to microprocessors optimized for carrying out a relatively small number of instructions extremely quickly. In terms of the simple instructions most often carried out by computers, RISC chips are faster. For complex instructions that must be broken down into numerous simpler ones. A processor whose design is based on the rapid execution of a sequence of simple instructions rather than on the provision of a large variety of complex instructions Features which are generally found in RISC designs are uniform instruction encoding (e.g. the op-code is always in the same bit positions in each instruction which is always one word long), which allows faster decoding; a homogenous register set, allowing any register to be used in any context and simplifying compiler design; and simple addressing modes with more complex modes replaced by sequences of simple arithmetic instructions.

Certain design features have been characteristic of most RISC processors:

• *one cycle execution time*: RISC processors have a CPI (clock per instruction) of one cycle. This is due to the optimization of each instruction on the CPU and a technique called I.PIPELINING;

• *pipelining: a technique that allows for simultaneous execution of parts, or stages, of instructions to more efficiently process instructions;*

• *large number of registers: the RISC design philosophy generally incorporates a larger number of registers to prevent in large amounts of interactions with memory*

3(a) What is protocol in the context of Local Area Network? Define a protocol used in LANs. **[2½]**

✓ **Protocol ⇒** When data is being transmitted between two or more devices something needs to govern the controls that keep this data intact. A formal description of message formats and the rules two computers must follow to exchange those messages. Protocols can describe low-level details of machine-to-machine interfaces (e.g., the order in which hits and bytes are sent across wire) or high-level exchanges between application programs (e.g., the way in which two programs transfer a file across the Internet).

Protocols used in LAN : Token passing, CSMA/CD

CSMA/CD stands for *Carrier-Sense Multiple Access with Collision Detection*. It is a media access method which means it defines how the network places data on the cable and how it takes it off. CSMA/CD specifies how bus topologies such as Ethernet handle transmission collisions. A *collision* occurs when two or more computers transmit signals at the same time.

"*Carrier Sense*" means that each station on the LAN continually listens to (tests) the cable for the presence of a signal prior to transmitting. *"Multiple Access"* means that there are many computers attempting to transmit and compete for the opportunity to send data (i.e., they are in contention). *"Collision Detection"* means that when a collision is detected, the stations will stop transmitting and wait a random length of time before retransmitting. CSMA/CD works best in an environment where relatively fewer, longer data frames are transmitted. This is in contrast to token passing which works best with a relatively large amount of short data frames. Because CSMA/CD works to *control* or manage collisions rather than *prevent* them, network performance can be degraded with heavy traffic. The greater the traffic, the greater the number of collisions and retransmissions. CSMA/CD is used on Ethernet networks.

(b) What is multiplexing in the context of computer network? Where will it be needed? [2½]

✓ **Multiplex ⇒** No, this does not refer to a movie theatre with many screens. It is simply a fancy word for the process of taking a single communication channel and dividing it among several different signals. Multiplexing is a technique used in some global navigation satellite receivers to sequence the signals of two or more satellites through a single hardware channel. Multiplexing allows a receiver to track more satellites than the number of hardware channels at the cost of lower effective signal strength. It is the process of weaving multiple signals onto a single channel or communications line. In multiplexing, segments of information from each signal are interleaved and generally separated by time, frequency, or space. Used in radio transmission, video channel transmission etc.

(c) What are the various types of switching methods in LANs? Describe any one of those. [2½]

There are three types of switching methods :

✓ **Packet Switching ⇒** The method used to send information over a network. Each packet has the address of the sender as well as the destination address. This allows information to intermingle with other packets of data, without being lost or misdirected, while making it's journey over the network. In other words it is the method used to move data on the Internet. In a packet switching network, all the data coming from a machine is broken up into chunks. Each chunk includes the addresses of both the origin and the destination. This enables chunks of data from many different sources to intermingle on the same lines and be sorted and directed along different routes. In this way, many people can use the same lines at the same time. A second advantage of packet-switching networks is that since packets can take alternative routes through the network, data transmission can easily be maintained if parts of the network are damaged.

✓ **Message Switching ⇒** If two processes want to communicate, a temporary link is established for the duration of one message transfer. Physical links are allocated dynamically among correspondents as needed, and are allocated for only short periods. Each message is a block of data, with system information (such as the source, the destination and the error correction codes) that allows the communication network to deliver the message to the destination correctly.

This scheme is similar to the post office mailing system. Each letter is considered a message that contains both the destination address and source(return) address. Note that many messages (from different users) can be shipped over the same link.

✓ **Circuit Switching** ⇒ A means of connecting two communicating parties that relies on the creation of a physical link between the two. Circuit switching is characteristic of telephone connections. Unlike other methods of transmission, such as packet switching, it requires the link to be established before any communication can take place.

(d) What is the purpose of having layered architecture for computer networks? What is the purpose of Data-Link and Network layers?[2½]

✓ **Layered architecture** ⇒ The division of a network model into multiple discrete layers, or levels, through which messages pass as they are prepared for transmission. In a layered architecture, protocols at each layer provide specific services or functions and rely on protocols in the layers above and below them for other needed services.

Network Layer (Rx highway exit numbering scheme)	Establishes THE UNIQUE NETWORK ADDRESS AND MANAGES THE TRANSPORT OF INFORMATION PACKETS BETWEEN DIFFERENT NETWORKS. Routes the packets and determines the best rout for sending them. Manages network traffic problems, packet switching, routing, and resembling data.

✓ **Data-link layer** ⇒ The second of seven layers of the International Standards Organization's Open Systems Interconnection (ISO/OSI) model for computer-to-computer communications. The data-link layer validates the integrity of the flow of data from one node to another by synchronizing blocks of data, and by controlling the flow of data.

4(a) What is distributed operating system? How is it different to multiprogramming operating system? What are the applications where you would like to use distributed operating system? [5]

Multiprogramming Operating System	Distributed Operating system
In this operating system, there is a capability to store more than one program in the same memory.	It is an Operating System with its different components are stored on different machine, all components collectively performs a single job.

The distributed operating system as the name suggests is the OS to manage something which is distributed. This implies it is well suited for distributed applications. Where database is to be stored on different locations around the world and has to be managed.

(b) What is batch operating system? What were the disadvantages of this system that led to multiprogramming system? What is multitasking? What are its applications? [5]

✓ **Batch Processing Operating System ⇒** It means Executing a series of noninteractive jobs all at one time. The term originated in the days when users entered programs on punch cards. They would give a batch of these programmed cards to the system operator, who would feed them into the computer. Batch jobs can be stored up during working hours and then executed during the evening or whenever the computer is idle. Batch processing is particularly useful for operations that require the computer or a peripheral device for an extended period of time. Once a batch job begins, it continues until it is done or until an error occurs. Note that batch processing implies that there is no interaction with the user while the program is being executed. An example of batch processing is the way that credit card companies process billing. The customer does not receive a bill for each separate credit card purchase but one monthly bill for all of that month's purchases. The bill is created through batch processing, where all of the data are collected and held until the bill is processed as a batch at the end of the billing cycle.

Disadvantage :

(i) Non-interactive environment → Batch operating system allows little or no interaction between user and executing program. The time taken between job submission & job completion in batch operating system is very high.

(ii) Off-line debugging → Program must be differed which means a programmer cannot correct bugs the moment it occurs.

✓ **Multitasking ⇒** This refers to a computer's ability to perform different operations simultaneously, such as saving a file while applying a Photoshop filter. In other words it refers to executing many processes on a single processor. Most operating systems support multitasking, but it can be costly if the need to switch large caches or execution pipelines makes context switching expensive in time.. Multitasking can be either cooperative or preemptive. In the former, the operating system relies on the task to voluntarily cede control to another task; in the latter, the operating system decides which task receives priority.

Applications of Multitasking :

Multitasking is particularly useful when a software project has to be divided up among multiple programmers, because each programmer can concentrate on his particular section of code and not really worried too much about how his code will interact with the other sections. So, multitasking is useful in any embedded system. Multitasking concept is widely used in operating system also, and many more real time application like image processing, AI application, System application uses multitasking concept.

5(a) What is the need of a presentation software like Powerpoint? Describe five most important features needed in a presentation package. Give reason for your selection. [5]

A Presentation is a single way of communication of idea from one person to another. We use various types of presentation to convey our thoughts, ideas & subjects in our school or at home. And to convey our thoughts effectively we should give a good presentation so that it is well accepted by all. Thus a presentation can be said a type of communication where we put your thoughts ideas & feelings across to an individual or to thoughts before someone with the intention or convincing that person is important. That is why presentation is necessary.

Presentation software like Powerpoint is needed nowadays as this is an era of competition & the presentation must be very impressive so that every one is convinced. Power Point provides a wonderful combination of text, special effects, sound & graphics. The text has several fonts and sizes, special effects make your presentation more powerful and memorable, sound and picture make the presentation one convincing and easy to explain & present.

Most important features in a presentation package, which must be present, are :

1. Multiple fonts and sizes
2. Sound effects
3. Special effects
4. Graphics and pictures
5. Presentation Planner

Multiple font and sizes are required for the deep impact and attractive looks of the text material presented.

Sound Graphics and pictures are used for the easy understanding and explaining presentation.

Special effects to add overall effect of the presentation.

The presentation package should hold the above qualities for a successful presentation, which can be designed and displayed with intention of convincing people.

(b) What are the threats to computer security? What is computer virus? Does a password authentication mechanism prevent computer virus? Justify your answer. What are the areas a computer virus can destroy? [JUN99, Q1(e)][5]

Please Refer DEC02, Q1(f).

Yes, a password authentication mechanism can prevent computer virus.

Please Refer to JAN01, Q1(e)

Areas, a computer virus can destroy :

- Destruction of file allocation table
- User losses everything on his hard disk
- Erasing of specific programs or data on discs
- Distroy parts of programs
- Reduction of free spaces in disc
- Overwriting of entire disc directories
- Makes the system speed slow and sometimes very slow

CS-611 : COMPUTER FUNDAMENTALS AND PC SOFTWARE
DEC 2002

Note: *There are five questions in this paper. Question 1 is* ***compulsory*** *and carries 30 marks. Attempt any* ***three*** *from the rest.*

1(a)What is the purpose of having a hierarchy of memory (such as main memory, secondary etc.) in a computer system? What is the popular secondary storage technology presently available? What is the access mechanism used for those devices? Describe the characteristics of CD-ROM technology. [5]

Refer to JUNE, 2004, 1(a).

Popular secondary storage technology :

✓ **Flash memory devices,** being faster (no moving parts), with longer lifetimes, and being more portable are rapidly becoming the most popular secondary storage technology for computers as well as digital cameras.

✓ **Magnetic tape** ⇒ A sequential storage medium used for data collection, backup and historical purposes. Like videotape, computer tape is made of flexible plastic with one side coated with a ferromagnetic material. Tapes come in reels and cartridges of many sizes and shapes. Tape is more economical than disks for archival data. However, if tapes are stored for the duration, they must be periodically recopied or the tightly coiled magnetic surfaces may contaminate each other.

✓ **Optical Disk** ⇒ A data storage medium that utilises laser technology to read information. CD-ROMs and WORM (Write Once Read Many) are examples of optical disks.

✓ **CD-ROM** ⇒ Compact Disc Read-Only Memory. A form of write-once, disc-based, random-access data storage, usually mass-produced and distributed as a publication. At present, capable of holding approximately 640 megabytes of data. Version of the CD that allows the information to be stored and retrieved. Once a CD-ROM is pressed, new data cannot be stored and the disc cannot be erased for reuse. Although CD-ROMs look like music discs, they can only be used with a computer equipped with a CD-ROM drive. Each CD-ROM can hold up to 650 megabytes of data in any of several volume formats. Once a CD has been written to and finalised, no more data can be stored on that disc. Like any other common disk storage medium, a CD-ROM can be formatted as a Macintosh volume or a Windows volume.

Characteristics of CD-ROM technology : durability (the program is very robust and reliable in a technical sense), portability, accuracy, and rapid, easy access to the recorded information.

(b) What is a Supercomputer? What are its applications? Compare and contrast a supercomputer with mainframe and mini-computers. Are the present day micro-computers powerful enough to emulate a supercomputer? Justify your answer. [JUN00, Q1b(iii)][5]

A supercomputer is a computer that leads the world in terms of processing capacity, particularly speed of calculation, at the time of its introduction

✓ **Uses/Applications ⇒** Supercomputers are used for highly calculation-intensive tasks such as weather forecasting, climate research (including research into global warming), molecular modeling (computing the structures and properties of chemical compounds, biological macromolecules, polymers, and crystals), physical simulations (such as simulation of airplanes in wind tunnels, simulation of the detonation of nuclear weapons, and research into nuclear fusion), cryptanalysis, and the like. Military and scientific agencies are heavy users.

✓ **Design ⇒** Supercomputers traditionally gained their speed over conventional computers through the use of innovative designs that allow them to perform many tasks in parallel, as well as complex detail engineering. They tend to be specialized for certain types of computation, usually numerical calculations, and perform poorly at more general computing tasks. Their memory hierarchy is very carefully designed to ensure the processor is kept fed with data and instructions at all times—in fact, much of the performance difference between slower computers and supercomputers is due to the memory hierarchy design and componentry. Their I/O systems tend to be designed to support high bandwidth, with latency less of an issue, because supercomputers are not used for transaction processing.

As, the micro-computers can not be used in applications where supercomputer is used as stated above, also there design differs much as compared to supercomputers. Thus, we can conclude that micro-computers are not powerful enough to emulate a supercomputer.

(c) "UNIX operating system was not popular in the commercial business world because of Graphical User Interface." Comment on the above

statement. Describe the various components of a Graphical User Interface (GUI) and their usefulness with respect to GUIs.

[JUN02, Q1(c)][JUN01, QI(c)][DEC98, Q5(a)][5]

"Unix operating system was not popular in the commercial business world because of Graphical User Interface" because

- The Unix does not provide the expanded basis functionalities to support graphics but also not provides dimension, color, height, video and highly dynamic interaction.
- So it was not popular in the non-programmer like end-user.
- It is mostly used by engineers and programmers to develop high-end applications / softwares.

Now Refer JUNE03, Q1(c).

(d) Can a Wide Area Network (WAN) use optical fibre as transmission medium and bus topology? Justify your answer. Describe the term protocol, giving one example each for WAN and LAN protocols. What is EDI? Can it be supported on LANs? Justify your answer.

[JUN02, Q1(d)][JAN01,Q1(f)][5]

YES, A WAN can use the optical fiber as a transmission medium and can not use bus topology.

Because of the inherent distance problems in Wide Area Networks, fiber has found wide spread deployment. Carriers are migrating large portions of their networks to fiber to take advantage of its superior bandwidth and compact size. As more WAN services are provisioned to the customer premises via fiber, the need to convert from single mode (used almost exclusively in the WAN venue) to multi mode will grow. Some of the services that are being provided directly on fiber are ATM, SONET/SDH. Bus topology can not be used because it is a linear architecture, usually by one or more pieces of cable is used to form a single line, or bus. The signals sent by one station extend the length of this cable to be heard by other stations. Mesh topology is well suited for WAN as all are connected to all and can communicate easily. While in bus topology one signal sent by any node will be heard by all which will create huge traffic problem in case of WAN where millions of signals flows within a second.

✓ **Protocol** ⇒ When data is being transmitted between two or more devices something needs to govern the controls that keep this data intact. A formal description of message formats and the rules two computers must follow to exchange those messages. Protocols can describe low-level details of machine-to-machine interfaces (e.g., the order in which hits and bytes are sent across wire) or high-level exchanges between application programs (e.g., the way in which two programs transfer a file across the Internet. **CSMA/CD** is used in LAN. X.25 is used in WAN.

✓ **EDI** ⇒ Electronic Data Interchange, Contact between companies exchanging orders via intra- or internet. **EDI** is the computer-to-computer exchange of structured information, by agreed message standards, from one computer application to another by electronic means and with a minimum of human intervention. In common usage, EDI is understood to mean specific interchange methods agreed upon by national or international standards bodies for the transfer of business transaction data, with one typical application being the automated purchase of goods and services. The EDI standards were designed from the beginning to be independent of lower-level technologies and can be transmitted using Internet protocols as well as private networks. Yes, it can be supported on LAN. As in LAN exchange of data is possible among all computers present on the LAN easily through wires.

(e) What is meant by the term 4GLs (Fourth Generation Languages)? Explain with the help of an example. Does 4GLs contain functions and subroutines? Give reasons. Compare and contrast the features of 4GLs to third generation languages. [5]

4th generation language-these are used to get information from files and database and to display to print the information. It contains a query language which is used to answer queries or questions with the data from, database example SQL. All 4GLs are designed to reduce programming effort, the time it takes to develop software, and the cost of software development. They are not always successful in this task, sometimes resulting in inelegant and unmaintainable code. However, given the right problem, the use of an appropriate 4GL can be spectacularly successful. 4th GL don't have functions or subroutines as these are procedural and 4 GL is non procedural

4GL (4th Generation Language)	Third generation Language
(i) Mostly forth generation languages are non-procedural languages.	(i) Mostly third generation languages are procedural languages.
(ii) Fourth generation language are mostly machine independent.	(ii) Most third generation languages are machine dependent.
(iii) Fourth generation languages contain a query language which, is used to answer queries or question with data from a database.	(iii) Third generation language are procedure based, the computer has to follow in a program.
(iv) These are mostly used for office automation or business application	(iv) These are used for scientific programs
(v) Example : FORTRAN, COBOL	(v) Example : SQL

(f) What are the security threats to a computer which is a node on a Local Area Network? How can you minimise the possibility of information access from this computer by unauthorised users? Describe one method in detail. **[5]**

THREATS

✓ **Worm**. In a computer, a worm is a self-replicating virus that does not alter files but resides in active memory and duplicates itself. Worms use parts of an operating system that are automatic, and are usually invisible to the user. Like a virus, worms can be transmitted to a computer through e-mail attachments, downloads, or infected floppy disks or CD's. It is important to have updated antivirus software so that the newest viruses and worms will be detected and halted. A program that enters a computer and replicates itself, often causing damage to the system.

✓ **Virus** ⇒ A virus is a piece of programming code usually disguised as something else that causes some unexpected and usually undesirable event. It is important to have updated antivirus software so that the newest viruses and worms will be detected and halted. A computer program designed to copy itself into other software and spread through multiple computer systems, causing minor damage to completely destroying software systems

✓ **Trojan Horse** ⇒ A program downloaded from the Internet that contains destructive elements to a computer. Unlike a true virus, the Trojan horse does not replicate itself, it simply erases the users hard drive. A Trojan horse can come disguised as a useful application such as a game or even a virus protection program.

We can minimize the possibility of information access by the unauthorised user by following the methods below :

1. Identification
2. Authentication
3. Authorisation

Now Refer JAN01, Q1(e).

2(a) What is a multi-programming operating system? How is it different to a multi-tasking and real-time operating system? Is a network operating system also a multiprogramming operating system? Justify your answer. What are the advantages of a network operating system? [5]

Refer to JUNE 2003, 4(a).

No, network operating system is not a multiprogramming operating system. As NOS is a collection of software and associated protocols that allows a set of autonomous computers which are interconnected by a computer network to be used together in a convenient and cost effective manner.

The Advantages of network operating system are :-

(1) It allow users to access the various resources of the network hosts.

(2) Controlling access so that only users with proper authorization are allowed to access particular resources.

(3) Make use of remote resources appear to be identical to the use of local resources.

(4) Provides up to the minute network documentation online.

(b) What is a distributed operating system? What are its advantages/ disadvantages? For a company whose office is located in a building, which of the two - network OS or distributed OS - will you suggest to use? Justify your answer. [5]

A distributed operating system provides users with access to the various resources that the system provides. By resources, we mean both hardware (such as printers and tape drives) and software (such as files and programs). Access to these resources is controlled by the operating system. Distributed operating systems: The users do not need to be aware of the multiplicity of machines. They access remote resources in the same manner as they do local resources. Data and process migration from one site to another is under control of the distributed operating system. Access to a shared resource can be provided by data migration, computation migration or job migration. A distributed operating system must address two major issue; transparency (i.e. does all the users access all files in the same manner regardless of where they are in the network ?) and locality (where do the files reside in the system ?).

Advantages :

Resource Sharing. If a number of different sites (with different capabilities) are connected to one another, then a user at one site may be able to use the resources available at another. For example, a user at site A may be using a laser printer available at only site B. Meanwhile, a user B may access a file that resides at A. In general, resource sharing in a distributed system provides mechanisms for sharing files at remote sites, processing information in a distributed database, printing files at remote sites, using remote specialized hardware devices (such as a high-speed array processor), and performing other operations.

Computation Speedup. If a particular computation can be partitioned into a number of sub computations that can run concurrently, then the availability of a distributed system may allow us to distribute the computation among the various, to run the computation concurrently. In addition, if particular site is currently over loaded with jobs, some of them may be moved to other, lightly loaded, sites. This movement of jobs is called load sharing. Automated load sharing, in which the distributed operating system automatically moves jobs, is still uncommon in commercial systems. It remains an active research area, however.

Reliability. If one site fails in a distributed system, the remaining sites can potentially continue operating. If the system is composed of a number of large autonomous installations (that is, general-purpose computers), the failure of one of them should not affect the rest. If, on the other hand, the system is composed of a number of small machines, each of which is responsible for some crucial system function (such as terminal character I/O or the file system), then a single failure may halt the operation of the whole system. In general, if enough redundancy exists in the system (in both hardware and data), the system can continue with its operation, even if some of its sites have failed.

Communication. When several sites are connected to one another by a communication network the users at different sites have the opportunity to exchange information. The advantage of a distributed system is that the functions can be carried out over great distances. A project can be performed by two people at geographically separate sites. By transferring the files of the project, logging in to each other's remote systems to run programs, and exchanging mail to coordinate the work, the users are able to minimize the limitations inherent in long-distance work.

Disadvantages :

➢ Here the data is distributed and some critical data are duplicated, and the updation of data at one site should reflect to all the replicas. And in distributed operating system this updation is very difficult.

➢ Maintaining the consistency is very difficult.

For a company whose offices are located in a building, the network operating system is very much suitable because.................

• It is well suited where network is spread in a very large area.

• To establish the network within a building is not very difficult.

• And if the network fault occurs then it is very easy to find out the fault within the building.

• And to maintain the consistency is very easy in case of Network Operating system.

So, it is suggested that network operating system is much suitable for the company located within the building.

3(a) What are the hardware and software components one may need for a computer network? Describe two hardware components giving their characteristics. [5]

A NETWORK consists of two or more computers that are linked in order to share resources (such as printers and CD-ROMs), exchange files, or allow electronic communications. The computers on a network may be linked through cables, telephone lines, radio waves, satellites, or infrared light beams.

• When any one of these computers are connected to a LAN they are referred to as a WORKSTATION. All computing devices on a network; workstations, printers, etc., are referred to as NODES.

• When connecting a workstation, the interface hardware is referred to as an ADAPTER. Networking adapters are also commonly referred to as NETWORK INTERFACE CARDS or NICS.

A basic network is made up of primary components.

1. A hub (which acts as the traffic cop on your small information highway. The hub acts as a switch to route information from one terminal to another through the use of cables.
2. An interface card (hardware in each computer that connects to the hub)
3. A server (the central storage computer for information).
4. Special cabling
5. Computers, printers, scanners, etc.

✓ **Network Hardware** ⇒ More than any feature, network hardware may determine the speed, quality and performance of a network.

✓ **Hubs** ⇒ A hub is a central connecting device that joins computers in a star configuration. Hubs may be passive or active. A passive hub merely connects computers to the network and does not process data in any way. Active hubs, sometimes called repeaters, regenerate the data in order to maintain signal strength. Some hubs have intelligence and can perform additional duties such as bridging, routing and switching.

✓ **Switches** ⇒ Fast Ethernet switches allow dedicated, high-speed connections at either 10 BASE-T or 100BASE-TX. They are ideal for connecting servers or multiple hubs in small businesses that want the highest network performance possible to exchange large data files and images, and access real-time information. A switch does this by providing dedicated bandwidth to every device—server, PC, or hub—connected to one of its ports. They are intelligent in that they give priority to large bandwidth data

(b) XYZ Company has all its data available on a Local Area Network. The company decided to become international, and positioned its offices all over the world. What changes will you propose for the LAN of the company? You may suggest changes in hardware, software, protocol, topology, security, etc. [5]

XYZ Company has all its data available on a Local Area Network. The company decided to become international, and positioned its offices all over the world. This statement implies that company is shifting to WAN from LAN. As the LAN is under the compete control of the owner, whereas the WAN needs the involvement of another authority like telephone company and spread across the countries. So, the hardware changes suggested for implementing this new requirement of the company is :

✓ **Hardware** ⇒ Routers, LAN cables, Gateways

✓ **Software** ⇒ Novell netware, Windows NT (or any other network operating system)

✓ **Protocol** ⇒ TCP/IP protocol

✓ **Topology** ⇒ Point to point, mesh, tree or mixed topology as per the requirements

✓ **Security** ⇒ Antivirus softwares and firewalls.

4(a) What will you do if your computer has slowed down? What are the possible reasons? How will you try to resolve the problem? Assume that you are working with a computer having Windows 95 with all its utilities. [5]

Any computer having window95 with all its utilities, if slows down can be facing either any hardware problem like malfunction of RAM slots. (when there is more than one RAM slot) etc. There can also be software problems, like the common and major problem is of computer virus. A computer virus is a program which has the capabilities of terminate and stay resident, replicate itself and attach itself to any other executable programs. Virus can be detected by any antivirus software and finally cleaned it. Other problems due to which the system could be slow is the loading of extra applications while startup. These applications generally gets loaded while start up and could be found in the systray resulting slow booting and startup. The unwanted applications should be detected from the startup and also from the start up of Msconfig. These applications should be unchecked. This gives minimum load to the boot up sequence of the system.

The system should be scanned by scandisk application to check for the integrity of the file system on the disk drives. It also detects the physical damage of the disk drives. It removes cross liked files, lost file clusters and this give better performance to the system.

The temporary and swap files should be deleted periodically as it also helps in speeding up of the system.

The unwanted softwares should be detected and uninstalled as it occupies both system resources and hard disk space.

A periodic check for system's I/O conflicts should be done as it is also responsible for the malfunction of the system and the deterioration of speed in the system.

The less frequently desktop item's should be removed from the desktop, as it also slows the speed to some extent.

The System File Checker (SFC) should be executed for the checking of damaged or corrupted system files which can be extracted and fixed from the installation disk.

All the above factors are responsible for the slow speed of the system a periodical check up either manually or in the scheduler (for automatic check up) can be done for the smooth running of the CPU.

(b) What is the Mailmerge feature of a word processor? Why is it needed? Describe with the help of an example.

[JUN02, Q5(a)][JUN99, Q2(a)][5]

Please Refer DEC01, Q5(a)

5(a) Compare and contrast the following in the context of hardware and software of a computer : [5]
(i) Inkjet printer versus Dot matrix printer versus Laser printer
(ii) Sequential access versus Direct access versus Random access

(i) • Dot-matrix → Creates characters by striking pins against an ink ribbon. Each pin makes a dot, and combinations of dots form characters and illustrations This is a type of printer which uses a series of pins to create an image on paper. Dot matrix printers are the most economical way to print information.

• **Ink-jet →** Sprays ink at a sheet of paper. Ink-jet printers produce high-quality text and graphics. A printer that creates characters and images by spraying fine streams of ink onto paper at high speeds. Inkjet printers are relatively inexpensive and produce high quality text and graphics in both black and white and colour.

• **Laser →** Uses the same technology as copy machines. Laser printers produce very high quality text and graphics A special kind of printer that uses a laser beam create the image on paper. They produce really good graphics. And of course, they are more expensive than the traditional dot matrix printer.

Point of difference between inkjet, Dot matrix and laser are :

• **Quality of type →** The output produced by printers is said to be either *letter quality* (as good as a typewriter), *near letter quality*, or *draft quality*. Only , ink-jet, and laser printers produce letter-quality type. Some dot-matrix printers claim letter-quality print, but if you look closely, you can see the difference.

• **Speed →** Measured in characters per second (cps) or pages per minute (ppm), the speed of printers varies widely. Dot-matrix printers can print up to 500 cps, and laser printers range from about 4 to 20 text pages per minute.

• **Impact or non-impact →** Impact printers include all printers that work by striking an ink ribbon. Daisy-wheel, dot-matrix, and line printers are impact printers. Non-impact printers include laser printers and ink-jet printers. The important difference between impact and non-impact printers is that impact printers are much noisier.

• **Graphics →** Some printers (daisy-wheel and line printers) can print only text. Other printers can print both text and graphics.

• **Fonts →** Some printers, notably dot-matrix printers, are limited to one or a few fonts. In contrast, laser and ink-jet printers are capable of printing an almost unlimited variety of fonts.

(ii) Sequential Access vs. Random Access VS Direct Access →

Sequential	Direct (Semi random)	Random
1. Memories where storage locations can be accessed only in certain predetermined sequence are called sequential access.	1. Memory device which contains a large number of independent rotating tracks. If each track has its own read-write head, the tracks may be accessed randomly although accessed within each track is serial.	1. If location may be accessed in any order and access time is independent of the location being accessed.
2. Example : Magnetic tape, Magnetic bubble memories.	**2. Example :** Magnetic disks	**2. Example :** Ferrite - Core and semiconductor memories are usually of this type.
3. Here the access mechanism need to be shared among different location. Thus, either the location or the read/write head or both should be moved to access the desired location.	3. In direct access, a separate read/write head exists for a track and on a track the information can be accessed serially	3. The storage location can be accessed independently.

(b) What is pipelining? Can it be done in Reduced Instruction Set Computers? Justify your answer. [3]

An **instruction pipeline** is a technology used on microprocessors to enhance their performance. Pipelining greatly improves throughput. Instructions consist of a number of steps. Practically every CPU ever manufactured is driven by a central clock. Each step requires at least one clock cycle. Each step of an instruction is performed by a different piece of hardware on the CPU. Early, non-pipelined, processors did only one step at a time. For example, they might perform these steps sequentially in order:

1. Read the next instruction
2. Read the operands, if any
3. Execute the instruction
4. Write the results back out

This approach, while simple, is wasteful. While the processor is adding numbers, for instance, the hardware dedicated to loading data from computer memory is idle, waiting for the addition to complete. Pipelining improves performance by reducing the idle time of each piece of hardware. Pipelined CPUs include circuitry that examines the instructions and breaks them down into their sub-instructions. Some sub-instructions of different instructions can be executed simultaneously by different pieces of hardware, exploiting more parallelism in the hardware. A control unit called the *pipeline controller* ensures that this is done in a safe way that does not change the end result.

Yes, pipelining can be done in Reduced Instruction Set Computers. Simple decoding and pipeline execution are more important than program size. At the peak rate a new instruction is started at every cycle. Pipelined execution gives a peak performance of one instruction at every step, so the longest piece determines the performance rate of the pipelined machine. So dealing each piece should take the same amount of time.

(c) To transfer data from a Winchester disk which method of data transfer with memory should be used? Give reasons. [2]

To transfer data from Winchester disk with memory module the most suitable method will be DMA i.e., Direct Memory Access. As DMA acts as it has taken over control from the CPU. It operates in the following ways :

1. When I/O requested the CPU instructs the DMA module about the operation by providing the information.

(a) Which operation (Read/write) to be performed.

(b) The address of I/O which is to be used.

(c) Starting location of memory from where information will be read be written to.

(d) Then number of words to be written or to be read.

2. The DMA module transfers the requested block byte by byte directly to the memory without intervening the CPU.

3. One completion of request DMA module send an interrupt signal to CPU. Thus in DMA the CPU involvement is restricted at the beginning and end of the transfer, so a DMA is a method suggested for the disk-memory transfer.

CS-611 : COMPUTER FUNDAMENTALS AND PC SOFTWARE
JUNE 2003

Note: *There are five questions in this paper. Question 1 is* ***compulsory*** *and carries 30 marks. Attempt any* ***three*** *from the rest.*

1(a) "A computer is basically an instruction execution machine." Is the above statement correct? Give reasons in support of your answer. How is an instruction executed by a computer? Explain in a stepwise fashion. [5]

The basic function performed by computer is the execution of a program. A program is a sequence of instructions, which operates on data to perform certain tasks.

❖ So, the above statement true.

❖ For the execution of the instruction different units performs different tasks.

- The data applied by the external environment comes into input devices (module)
- The input module puts the data in the form of signals that can be recognized by the system. The unique code is provided to each set of control signals.
- The unit that interpret a code to generate respective control signal is termed as Control Unit (CU) now the program consist of codes.
- The operation related to the arithmetic and logical function are performed by the another unit known as ALU. ALU performs arithmetic operation such as addition, subtraction, multiplication, division and the logical operation such as "IS A = B ?" (Where the A and B are the numeric values).
- The arithmetic and logical operation performed in the CPU in special storage area called registers.
- Whatever is the final results, it will report in the proper format to the module called as output device.

(b)What is the need of memory hierarchy in a computer system? Describe the memory hierarchy and the function of each level in memory hierarchy. Can we instead of having memory hierarchy just have a huge (GB) RAM? Justify your answer. [5]

Please Refer DEC02, Q1(a).

(c) What are the various components of Graphical User Interfaces? What is the purpose of each one of them?

[DEC01, Q1(e)][JUN01, Q1(f)][JUN99, Q1(f)][DEC99,Q1(b)][5]

✓ **GUI** ⇒ "Graphical User Interface" Though the use of a GUI, one may operate a computer by interacting with pictures and menus on the screen, as opposed to entering commands directly through the keyboard. The use of a GUI requires an input device in addition to the keyboard (such as a mouse, trackball, touchscreen, or stylus pad). The term GUI is usually pronounced "gooey", which makes it particularly fun to slip into conversation.

i. Windowing System → It allows programs to display multiple applications at the same time. Windowing system include programming tools for building movable and resizable windows, menus, dialog boxes and other items on the display.
Some GUI contain properly windowing system such as Macintosh. Other uses the common windowing system such as X windows or simple X.

ii. An imaging model → The imaging model defines how fonts and graphics are created on the screen. Imaging model handle for example, typeface and size in a word processor or curve and lines in a drawing program.
This component of the system environment has taken on increasing sophistication as application incorporate complex curves, colors, shading and dimensions.

iii. An Application program interface → API is a set of programming language functions that allow the programmer to specify how the actual application will control the menus scrollbars and icons that appear on the screen

- Linking windowing models.
- APIs align with particular GUIs.
- Its feature varies from package to package.

iv. A set of tools and frame works for creating interface and developing integrated application :
GUI development environment can include looking and frame works Most of these tools kits are based on object oriented programming.

(d) A university has a Headquarters having about 200 computers in an office complex, and 30 Regional offices at the state capitals having 20 computers each. What kind of network will you suggest for this university? Suggest suitable topology, protocol and communication media in your answer. Justify your answer. **[5]**
For this university, both LAN and WAN networks are needed to enable communication between Headquarter and Regional Offices.

A LAN should be implemented at Headquarter and 30 Regional Offices with following specification at each office.

Topology : Star Topology using switches and hubs.

Protocol : Ethernet (CSMS/CD)

Communication Media : UTP Cable with RJ-45 cabling, 10-100mbps link. Since headquarter will be having many servers, they should be connected to switch. All other client PCs should be connected to hubs and these hubs should be connected to central switch. This will provide cost effective and faster network environment.

All regional Offices must be connected to Headquarter with a WAN link. This WAN link may be established through Modem (Cost effective, Low speed, useful when communication is not frequent) or any other WAN communication media such as Leased line, Frame Relay or ATM. The choice solely depends on the usage of line and cost to offices. If Video conferencing is required, ATM or Leased line may be considered. Budget and requirements are two things which directly effects the way in which it has to be connected.

(e) What are the elements of any programming language? Describe with the help of an example. Compare and contrast functions with subroutines. [JUN00, Q1(f)][5]

There are various elements of the programming language.

1. Variables, constants, data types, array and expressions are the elements of the programming language.

(i) Variables : Variable is a character or group of characters by the programmer to a single memory location and used in the program as the name of the memory location in order to access, the value stored in it on an memory location.

A = 9 i.e. 'A' is assigned the value 9 and 9 is stored on that memory location.

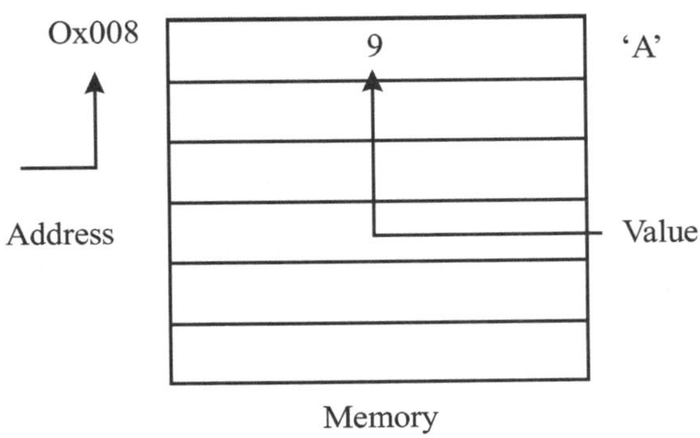

(ii) Constants : It is fixed value in the sense that 4 cannot be equal to 9.

➢ String constant is simply a sequence of character such as 'Computers'

➢ The numeric constant can be integer representing whole quantities or a number with a decimal point to represent numbers with fractional part.

➢ As string constants are a sequence of characters, a related string constant may be obtained from a given string expression. E.g. : "It is gone when water flows in this direction"

➢ From this you can obtain "one water", "It is one direction" etc.

(iii) Data types : In the terms of the computer programming the data refers to the anything and everything that can be processed by the computers.

➢ There are different types of data processed by the computers. E.g. : numbers, words etc. are the types of the data.

➢ The operations are performed on data different from one type of data to another type. E.g. : Multiplication applies to only numbers & not words.

➢ In 'C' int A = 9 that means A is a numeric data type and initially assign a value 9 and char ch = 'c' i.e. the ch is a data type with one or 2 letter.

(iv) Array : When there is large amount of related data is used then array comes into picture. It is also called as collection of elements of same data type.

Example :

A(0)	A(1)	A(2)	A(3)	A(4)
10000	20000	90000	80000	70000

Say the list of 5 years profit information of a company can be referred by some array name A.

A(0) Specify the information of 1st Year
A(1) Specify the information of 2nd Year
A(2) Specify the information of 3rd Year
A(3) Specify the information of 4th Year
A(4) Specify the information of 5th Year

Array usually starts with 0 where A[0] represents the first element of the array.

(v) Expression : We can express intended arithmetic operation using expression such as X+Y+Z and so on. Several simple expression can even be nested together using parentheses to form complex expression. Every computer language specifies an order in which various arithmetic operations are evaluated in a given expression. Every expression contains operators such as '+', '-',

’*’,’/’,’(‘,’)’,’^’ etc.

Example 4 + 6 * (11 – 17 / 7)

It is useful to remember the order of priority of various operators. But it is safe to simplify expression and enclose them parenthesis to avoid unpleasant surprise. For comparing the numbers or strings we are using the relational operators like :

= Equal to

<> Not Equal to

<, >, <=, >= etc.

Example :

If 5 > 7 returns false (or 0) and

If 11 > 7 returns true (or 1)

Apart from this we also have logical operations like

NOT, AND, OR, XOR

(a) NOT :

Simply negates a value.

Example : NOT (2 > 5) is true

(b) AND :

Returns true if both disjoint expression are true otherwise returns false

Example : (6 > 7) AND (9 < 12) returns, false.

(c) OR :

Returns false if both disjoint expression is true and otherwise it returns true.

Example : (6 > 4) OR (9 > 4) returns true.

(d) XOR :

True only if one of the disjoint expression is true and other is false.

Example : (6 < 9) XOR (9 < 12) returns false.

2. Input & Output Statements :

Input statements are normally used for supplying values to a list of variables through an Input devices such as Keyboard.

Example : In BASIC, INPUT A,B,C is an Input statement with list of 3 variables A,B & C.

3. In programming, a compiler directive that places a value into a variable. For example, counter=0 creates a variable named counter and fills it with zeros.

The VARIABLE=VALUE syntax is common among programming languages. There are four kinds of assignment statements:

1. Arithmetic
2. Logical
3. Statement label (ASSIGN)
4. Character

1 Arithmetic Assignment Statement

The form of an arithmetic assignment statement is:

v = *e*

where: *v* is the name of a variable or array element of type integer, real, double precision, or complex

• *e* is an arithmetic expression

2 Logical Assignment Statement

The form of a logical assignment statement is:

v = *e*

• where: *v* is the name of a logical variable or logical array element

• *e* is a logical expression

3 Statement Label Assignment (ASSIGN) Statement

The form of a statement label assignment statement is:

ASSIGN *s* TO *i*

• where: *s* is a statement label

• *i* is an integer variable name

Execution of a statement label assignment statement is the only way that a variable may be defined with a statement label value.

4 Character Assignment Statement

The form of a character assignment statement is:

v = *e*

• where: *v* is the name of a character variable, character array element, or character substring

• *e* is a character expression

4. In case of print statement the print option is used to either print a string or constant or the variable i.e. value of the variable. Different language has different statement for printing like in case of BASIC we have

Print "Computer" or Print B.

A conditional statement, or simply a conditional for short, is an "if-then" statement, written in the form: 'if P, then Q'. Here, 'P' is the *antecedent* (the

"if" part of the statement) and 'Q' is the *consequent* (the "then" part). For example, in "If you give me ten dollars, then I will be your best friend," the claim "you give me ten dollars" is the antecedent of the conditional, and "I will be your best friend" is the consequent.
In traditional logic, a statement *if A then B* is true if and only if either *A* is false or *B* is true, or both are false or both A and B are both true. There have been attempts in areas such as modal logic to find a formal definition that is closer to the 'intuitive' meaning: in the traditional logic interpretation *"If it is raining now, then I am a unicorn."* is true provided it is not raining now.
Conditional Statement: Is an "if… then…" statement; for example: *If all girls turn into women, then all boys turn into men.*
A looping statement that contains the word do followed by a statement (the action), the word while, and an expression in parentheses (the condition). It is used when the same task is to be performed number of times.
Subroutines &functions are used to avoid repeated programming of the same calculations, the programmer generally writes these same lines of codes in a function or subroutine and calls them when required these are used to get information from files and database and to display to print the information. It contains a query language which is used to answer queries or questions with the data from, database example SQL. All 4GLs are designed to reduce programming effort, the time it takes to develop software, and the cost of software development. They are not always successful in this task, sometimes resulting in inelegant and unmaintainable code. However, given the right problem, the use of an appropriate 4GL can be spectacularly successful.

5. Library Functions : These are the functions supplied with language compiler, interpreter. The code for a library function does not appear in the program.

➢ The computer inserts it when the program is translated into machine language. Some built in functions in C language are Printf, Scanf etc.

(f) What are the various threats faced by electronic data? Can cryptography solve all such problems? Justify your answer. [5]

There are various threats faced by electronic data :-
(i) Theft of PC and Media
(ii) Damage due to Breakage
(iii) Environment Damage
(iv) Inadvertent corruption/Loss
(v) Environmental losses
(vi) Malicious damage/Leakage
(vii) Unauthorized Access

(viii) Modifications / Erasures and
(ix) Computer viruses

No, cryptography can not solve all such problems.

➢ Cryptography is the process of transforming plain text or original information into an unintelligible form (Cipher text) so that it may be sent over unsafe channels of communication.

➢ Anyone getting hold of the cipher text while it is on the unsafe channel would need to have the appropriate key, to be, able to get it to the original form of information. The authorized receiver is assumed to have that key.

➢ So to prevent the unsafe text from the unauthorized uses, there is a need of cryptography.

➢ Thus, it is only can solve the problem of unauthorized user of electronic data.

Q2. Describe the following terms giving usage of these in the context of computer system :
(a) External Interfaces **[JUN00,Q1(b)]**
(b) Machine Language
(c) Reduced Instruction Set Computers
(d) Modem **[JUN99, Q1(d)][DEC99, Q1(b)]**
(e) Input/Output mechanism

(a) External Interfaces → it is the interface between the i/o module and peripheral device. This interface can be divided in two main categories :
Serial interface - In serial interface only one line is used to transmit data, therefore ,only one bit is transferred at a time. Serial interface is used for serial printers and terminals. In serial interface the i/o devices receives or send bytes one by one in serial fashion e.g.. Key boards a serial interface The most common serial interface is RS-232-C.
Parallel interface - In parallel interface multiple bits can be transferred simultaneously. The parallel interfaces are normally used for high-speed peripherals such as tapes and disks. In this the data is send or received block vise palely such as printer. It is faster than serial interface. A common parallel interface is centralism.

(b) Machine Language → The lowest-level programming language (except for computers that utilize programmable microcode) Machine languages are the only languages understood by computers. While easily understood by computers, machine languages are almost impossible for humans to use because they consist entirely of numbers. Programmers, therefore, use either a high-level programming language or an assembly language. An assembly language contains the same instructions as a machine language, but the instructions and variables have names instead of being just numbers.

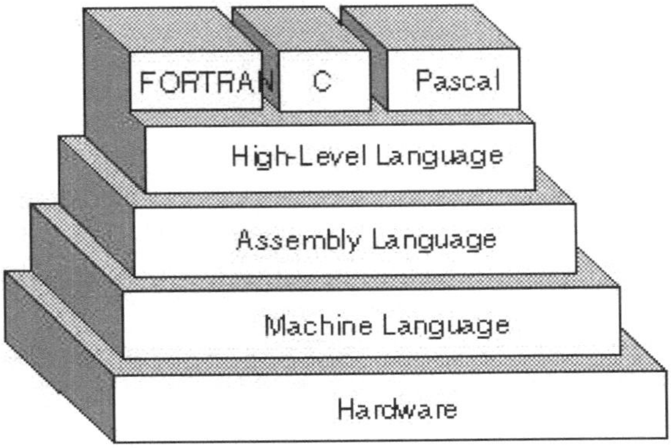

Programs written in high-level languages are translated into assembly language or machine language by a compiler. Assembly language programs are translated into machine language by a program called an assembler.
Every CPU has its own unique machine language. Programs must be rewritten or recompiled, therefore, to run on different types of computers.

(c) Reduced Instruction Set Computers (RISC) → Pronounced risk, acronym for reduced instruction set computer, a type of microprocessor that recognizes a relatively limited number of instructions. Until the mid-1980s, the tendency among computer manufacturers was to build increasingly complex CPUs that had ever-larger sets of instructions. At that time, however, a number of computer manufacturers decided to reverse this trend by building CPUs capable of executing only a very limited set of instructions. One advantage of reduced instruction set computers is that they can execute their instructions very fast because the instructions are so simple. Another, perhaps more important advantage, is that RISC chips require fewer transistors, which makes them cheaper to design and produce. Since the emergence of RISC computers, conventional computers have been referred to as CISCs (complex instruction set computers).

(d) Modem → It stands for Modulator Demodulator, but it's use is much simpler. It enables a computer to "dial-up" to another computer for a variety of purposes including Fax, Gaming, or Internet connections. There is a large variety of modems available now including the original 14.4, 28.8, 33.6, and 56k modems as well as newer ISDN (128k) and ADSL (256k) modems. To use any modem, your Internet Service Provider must support the format (modem, ISDN, or ADSL). Also, new phone lines are needed for ISDN, and ADSL must have support in your area.

(e) Input/Output mechanism → I/O - This means Input/Output. This is the way the computer actually works. They take in information, process it then, give it back out!

✓ **Input** ⇒ Data entered into a computer from a keyboard, voice recognition software, a mouse, another computer, or data storage device such as a disk or tape.

✓ **Output Device** ⇒ Any computer hardware that facilitates the interpretation of computer data. Display monitors, speakers and printers are output devices.

3(a) What is Wide Area Network (WAN)? What are its purposes? What are the possible topologies that may be recommended for a WAN? Which protocol will you suggest for a general purpose WAN? Justify your answer [5]

A **wide area network** or **WAN** is a computer network covering a wide geographical area, involving a vast array of computers. This is different from personal area networks (PANs), metropolitan area networks (MANs) or local area networks (LANs) that are usually limited to a room, building or campus. The best example of a WAN is the Internet. WANs are used to connect local area networks (LANs) together, so that users and computers in one location can communicate with users and computers in other locations. Many WANs are built for one particular organization and are private. Others, built by Internet service providers, provide connections from an organization's LAN to the Internet. WANs are most often built using leased lines. At each end of the leased line, a router connects to the LAN on one side and a hub within the WAN on the other. Network protocols including TCP/IP deliver transport and addressing functions. Protocols including Packet over SONET/SDH, MPLS, ATM and Frame relay are often used by service providers to deliver the links that are used in WANs. X.25 was an important early WAN protocol, and is often considered to be the "grandfather" of Frame Relay as many of the underlying protocols and functions of X.25 are still in use today (with upgrades) by Frame Relay.

✓ **Various topologies which can be recommended for a WAN** ⇒ The topology describes the way the transmission facilities are arranged. Numerous topologies are possible, each one offering a slightly different mix of cost, performance, and scalability.

✓ **Peer-to-Peer Network Topology** ⇒ A peer-to-peer network can be developed using dedicated private lines, or any other transmission facility.
A peer-to-peer WAN constructed with point-to-point transmission facilities can be a simple way to interconnect a small number of sites.
This topology is often the only feasible solution for WANs that contain a small number of internetworked locations. As each location contains only a single link to the rest of the network, static routing can be used.

✓ **Ring Network Topology** ⇒ A ring topology can be developed fairly easily from a peer-to-peer network by adding one transmission facility and an extra port on two routers. This minor increment in cost provides route redundancy that can offer small networks the opportunity to implement dynamic routing protocols. Dynamic routing can automatically detect and recover from adverse changes in the WAN's operating condition.
A ring WAN constructed with point-to-point transmission facilities can be used to interconnect a small number of sites and provide route redundancy at minimal additional cost.
Rings, too, have some basic limitations. First, depending upon the geographic dispersion of the locations, adding an extra transmission facility to complete the ring may be cost prohibitive. In such cases, Frame Relay may be a viable alternative to dedicated leased lines.

✓ **Star Network Topology** ⇒ A variant of the peer-to-peer topology is the star topology, so named for its shape. This topology can also be constructed using almost any dedicated transmission facility, including Frame Relay and point-to-point private lines.
A star topology WAN with point-to-point transmission facilities is much more scalable than a peer-to-peer or ring network. Network-connected devices are a maximum of two hops away from each other.

✓ **Full Mesh** ⇒ At the opposite end of the reliability spectrum, is the full mesh topology. This topology features the ultimate reliability and fault tolerance. Every networked node is directly connected to every other networked node. Full mesh networks can be built with almost any dedicated transmission facility.
A fully meshed WAN topology is readily identified by the complete interconnection of every node with every other node in the network. This approach absolutely minimizes the number of hops between any two network-connected machines, but can be fairly expensive to build and has a finite limit on its scalability.

(b) Define the following terms in the context of computer networks: **[5]**

(i) Transport layer **[JAN01, Q4(b)]**
(ii) Data link layer
(iii) Multiplexer **[JUN99, Q1(d)]**
(iv) Optical fiber **[JAN01, Q4b(i)]**
(v) Half duplex

(i) Transport layer :

Transport Layer (Rx Speed recognition devices on a highway	RESPONSIBLE FOR THE ACCURACY OF THE DATA TRANSMISSION. Ensures reliable delivery of packets. repackages messages, dividing them into smaller packets.

(ii) Data link layer :

Data Link Layer (Rx. Entry ramp/toll booth that allows access onto the highway)	DETERMINES HOW DEVICES CONNECTED WILL GAIN ACCESS. Determines how 1's and 0's are assembled into frames of packets of data. sends data frames from the Network Layer to Physical Layer. Contains the physical address of a device. Like the FROM : and TO: of a envelope.

(iii) Multiplexer → No, this does not refer to a movie theatre with many screens. It is simply a fancy word for the process of taking a single communication channel and dividing it among several different signals. Multiplexing is a technique used in some global navigation satellite receivers to sequence the signals of two or more satellites through a single hardware channel. Multiplexing allows a receiver to track more satellites than the number of hardware channels at the cost of lower effective signal strength. It is the process of weaving multiple signals onto a single channel or communications line. In multiplexing, segments of information from each signal are interleaved and generally separated by time, frequency, or space.

(iv) Optical fiber → Bundled glass rods (fibers) that are extremely thin and flexible and are capable of transmitting voice, video, and data signals in either analog or digital formats. This is accomplished with very little loss in signal quality. A single glass fiber can carry the equivalent of 100 channels of television or 100,000 telephone calls, with even more capacity possible by encasing many fibers within a cable.

(v) Half duplex → Refers to the transmission of data in just one direction at a time. For example, a walkie-talkie is a half-duplex device because only one party can talk at a time. In contrast, a telephone is a full-duplex device because both parties can talk simultaneously. Duplex modes often are used in reference to network data transmissions.

Some modems contain a switch that lets you select between half-duplex and full-duplex modes. The correct choice depends on which program you are using to transmit data through the modem. In half-duplex mode, each character transmitted is immediately displayed on your screen. (For this reason, it is sometimes called local echo -- characters are echoed by the local device). In full-duplex mode, transmitted data is not displayed on your monitor until it has been received and returned (remotely echoed) by the other device. If you are running a communications program and every character appears twice, it probably means that your modem is in half-duplex mode when it should be in full-duplex mode, and every character is being both locally and remotely echoed.

4(a) What is a multiprogramming operating system? How is it related/ different to multitasking and real time system? Is a distributed operating system necessarily multitasking? Justify your answer.

[DEC02, Q2(a)][JUN02, Q4(b)][5]

Multiprogramming Operating System : It denotes and operating system that, in addition to support multitasking, provides sophisticated forms of memory protection and enforces concurrency control when process accesses shared I/O devices & files.

➢ Multi programming operating system usually support multiple users, in which case they are also called multi user Operating System.

➢ Multi user Operating system provides facilities for maintenance of individual users environment, requires user authentication for security and protections & provide per user resource usage accounting.

➢ Multiprogramming implies multiprocessing or multitasking but reverse is not true.

➢ The approach of multiprogramming is such that whenever a program encounter a I/O bound operation it switches to wait state and another program is brought for execution. And keep on executing this process till it encounters an I/O bound operation

➢ No CPU can be utilized more compared to uniprogram operating system.

Multiprogramming	Multitasking
(1) It is capability of Operating System to store more than one program in the same memory	(1) It is used when more than one processes are kept in the state of execution but the processor is one (i.e. uniprocessor)
(2) Multiprocessing implies multitasking	(2) Multitasking does not implies multiprocessing
(3) Multiprogramming operating system is characterized by a multitude of simultaneous active programs which are competing for system resources such as processor, memory and I/O devices	(3) They can do another task easily without waiting for the resources.

Multiprogramming	Real time System
1. Multiprogramming operating system is used when more than one program can be stored in the memory that provides sophisticated forms of memory protection and enforces concurrency control when processes access shared I/O devices.	1. Real time operating system used in environment where a large number of events mostly external to the computer system, must be accepted and processed in short time or within certain deadlines.
2. Memory management is more demanding in multiprogramming.	2. Memory management in Real time operating system is comparatively, less demanding than in multiprogramming operating system.
3. Response time is not quick because shared resources are used.	3. Many processes reside in memory in order to provide the quick response time.

The distributed Operating System is not necessarily a multitasking because in distributed database, the data are distributed over the various sites but they may perform the single task while in multitasking the task is more than so here it is not necessarily that distribution operating system is multitasking.

(b) What is a network operating system? How is it different to distributed operating system? What are the advantages of distributed operating system? [5]

Please Refer, JUNE04, 3(b)

Advantages of Distributed Operating System :

➢ Each user normally works on his own system. Using a different system requires some kind of remote login, instead of having the operating system dynamically allocates processes to CPUs.

➢ Users are not aware of where each of their file is kept. Here file placement is managed by the operating system itself.

➢ Each computer has its own private operating system instead of running part of global system wide operating system.

5(a) Describe the following features of MS Word/Powerpoint : [6]
(i) MailMerge [JUN02, Q5(a)][JUN99, Q2(a)][DEC02, Q4(b)]
(ii) Macro [JUN01, Q5a(ii)][JUN00, Q5(b)]
(iii) Slide transition

(i) MailMerge → A feature supported by many word processors that enables you to generate form letters. To use a mail-merge system, you first store a set of information, like a list of names and addresses, in one file. In another file, you write a letter, substituting special symbols in place of names and addresses (or whatever other information will come from the first file). The power and flexibility of mail merge systems varies considerably from one word processor to another. Some word processors support a full set of logical operators that enable you to specify certain conditions under which information should be merged. Also, some merge systems allow you to merge data from several files at once.

(ii) Macro → This is a program within a program which can carry out a preset complex function with the stroke of one or two keys. You can preset your name and address, for example, and then every time you need to use it, in a particular program, just hit the macro key that you already preset as your name and address, and it will be all printed out for you. Saves time!

(iii) Slide transition → Adding a Transition A transition is a special effect used to introduce a slide during a slide show.

The following steps will show you how to add a transition to a slide.

1. In Slide Sorter View, click the slide you want to add the transition to.
2. Click the Slide Show menu, then click Slide Transition. A Slide Transition dialog box will appear.
3. In the Effect list box, click Checkerboard Across.
4. Click the Medium option button to select a speed for the transition.
5. Click the Apply button. A slide transition icon appears under the slide's left corner, indicating that the transition has been applied.

If you want the same transition to apply to all the slides in your presentation, click the Apply to All button in the Slide Transition dialog box.

(b) What is a worm? How is it related/different to computer virus? How can you prevent computer virus from entering your system?

[JUN02, Q5(b)][JUN99,Q1(e)][4]

A ***worm*** is similar to a virus by its design, and is considered to be a sub-class of a virus. Worms spread from computer to computer, but unlike a virus, it has the ability to travel without any help from a person. A worm takes advantage of file or information transport features on your system, which allows it to travel unaided. The biggest danger with a worm is its ability to replicate itself on your system, so rather than your computer sending out a single worm, it could send out hundreds or thousands of copies of itself, creating a huge devastating effect. One example would be for a worm to send a copy of itself to everyone listed in your e-mail address book. Then, the worm replicates and sends itself out to everyone listed in each of the receiver's address book, and the manifest continues on down the line. Due to the copying nature of a worm and its ability to travel across networks the end result in most cases is that the worm consumes too much system memory (or network bandwidth), causing Web servers, network servers, and individual computers to stop responding. In more recent worm attacks such as the much talked about .Blaster Worm., the worm has been designed to tunnel into your system and allow malicious users to control your computer remotely.

Prevention against viruses entering system :

The first steps to protecting your computer are to ensure your operating system (OS) is up-to-date. This is essential if you are running a Microsoft Windows OS. Secondly, you should have anti-virus software installed on your system and ensure you download updates frequently to ensure your software has the latest fixes for new viruses, worms, and Trojan Horses. Additionally you want to make sure your anti-virus program has the ability to scan e-mail and files as they are downloaded from the Internet. This will help prevent malicious programs from even reaching your computer. If this isn't enough protection, then you may want to consider installing a firewall as well.

A firewall is a system which prevents unauthorized use and access to your computer. A firewall can be either hardware or software. Hardware firewalls provide a strong degree of protection from most forms of attack coming from the outside world and can be purchased as a stand-alone product or in broadband routers. Unfortunately, when battling viruses, worms and Trojans, a hardware firewall may be less effective than a software firewall, as it could possibly ignore embedded worms in out going e-mails and see this as regular network traffic. For individual home users, the most popular firewall choice is a software firewall. A good software firewall will protect your computer from outside attempts to control or gain access your computer, and usually provides additional protection against the most common Trojan programs or e-mail worms. The downside to software firewalls is that they will only protect the computer they are installed on, not a network.

It is important to remember that on its own a firewall is not going to rid you of your computer virus problems, but when used in conjunction with regular operating system updates and a good anti-virus scanning software, it will add some extra security and protection for your computer or network.

CS-611 : COMPUTER FUNDAMENTALS AND PC SOFTWARE
DEC 2003

Note: *There are five questions in this paper. Question 1 is* ***compulsory*** *and carries 30 marks. Attempt any* ***three*** *from the rest.*

1(a) What is an Application Software? Explain various categories of software packages. **[5]**

✓ **Application software** ⇒ application software is written to enable the computer to solve a specific data processing task. A number of powerful software packages, which doesn't require significant programming knowledge, have been developed. These are easy to learn & use as compared to the programming languages. Although these packages can perform many general & special functions, there are applications where these packages are not found adequate. In such cases, application program is written to meet the exact requirements. A user application program is written using one of these packages or a programming language. The most important categories of software packages available are:

- Data Base Management Software
- Spreadsheet Software
- Word Processing desktop Publishing (DTP) & presentation Software Graphics Software
- Data Communication Software.

(b) "User Interface with computer is not complete without an operating system." Do you agree? Give reasons. **[5]**

Operating System is a program that runs on a computer whose purpose is to provide basic services that can be used by applications running on that computer. Such functions might include screen displays, file handling and encryption. MS-DOS and Windows 2000 are examples of operating systems. "Operating System" is the base layer of a computing environment, upon which the application level software (or programs) can be run. Examples of popular operating systems are Macintosh, Windows, and UNIX. Without an operating system, a computer would be unable to work at all, and without application programs, a computer would work but be unable to perform any useful tasks. This is the piece of software on your computer which takes instructions from you, and does the task you desire. They also aid in organisation, and can play a big role in the speed of your computer. Operating systems perform basic tasks, such as recognizing input from the keyboard, sending output to the display screen, keeping track of files and directories on the disk, and controlling peripheral devices such as disk drives and printers. For large systems, the operating system has even greater responsibilities and powers. It is like a traffic cop - it makes sure that different programs and users running at the same time do not interfere with each other. The operating system is also responsible for *security*, ensuring that unauthorized users do not access the system. Now we can conclude that user interface is not complete without an operating sytem or we can say computer is useless machine without an operating system installed on that.

(c) List various secret key algorithms. Explain any one. [5]

A secret key algorithm (sometimes called a symmetric algorithm) is a cryptographic algorithm that uses the same key to encrypt and decrypt data. The best known algorithm is the U.S. Department of Defense's Data Encryption Standard (DES). DES, which was developed at IBM in 1977, was thought to be so difficult to break that the U.S. government restricted its exportation.

A very simple example of how a secret key algorithm might work might be substituting the letter in the alphabet prior to the target letter for each one in a message. The resulting text - "gdkkn," for example - would make no sense to someone who didn't know the algorithm used (x-1), but would be easily understood by the parties involved in the exchange as "hello."

The problem with secret or symmetric keys is how to securely get the secret keys to each end of the exchange and keep them secure after that. For this reason, an asymmetric key system is now often used that is known as the public key infrastructure (PKI).

(d) What are different media for transmission of data? Explain each with an example. [5]

The popular communication media is:

✓ **Coax Cable ⇒** Thin or thick coax cable used in Ethernet networking. This looks similar to cable TV coax but usually has BNC connectors on the ends. It is a round, flexible cable consisting of—from the center outwards—a copper wire, a layer of protective insulation, a braided metal mesh sleeve, and an outer shield, or jacket of PVC or fire-resistant material. Coaxial cable is widely used in networks.

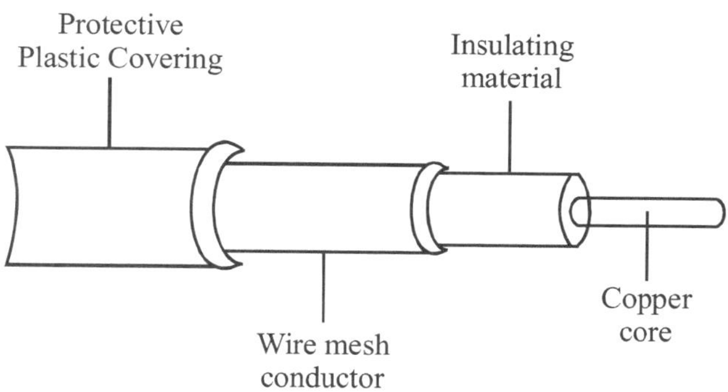

2. TWISTED PAIR CABLING (STP and UTP)

Coaxial and SHIELDED TWISTED PAIR (STP) have a copper braid of foil that offers good resistance to electrical noise, but the extra foil creates a larger, thicker cable, making it difficult to pull the cable through conduit and walls during installation. UNSHIELDED TWISTED PAIR (UTP) does not contain this aluminum shielding and is thinner and therefore easier to install. It offers less resistance to electrical noise.

STP is used in Token Ring, ARCnet and Appletalk networks. UTP is used in Star Topologies.

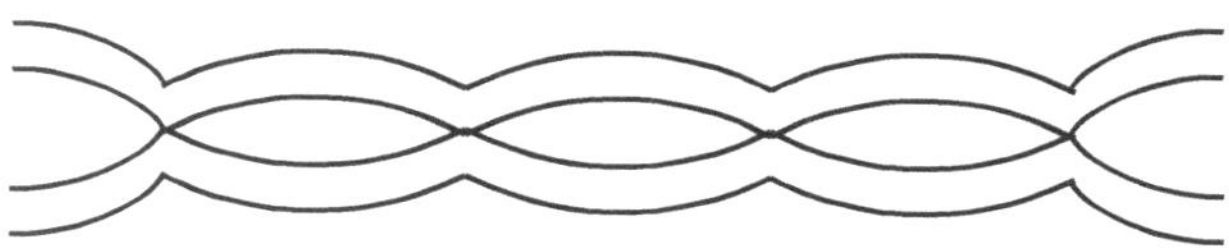

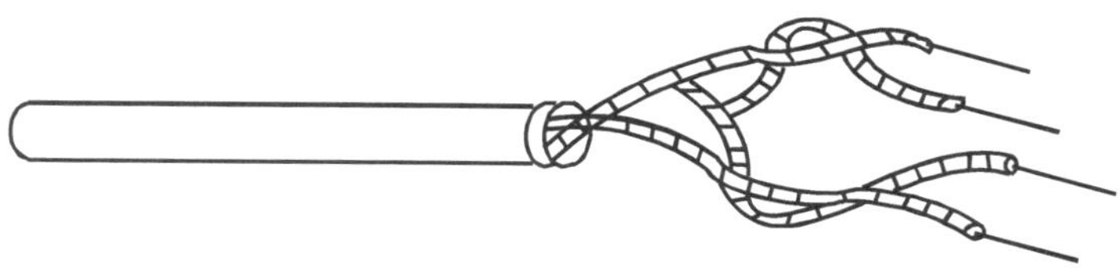

UTP (Unshieded Twisted Pair) is most commonly used in Category Three (CAT3) or Category Five (CAT5). The difference between the ratings is the number of twists per inch. Higher is better. CAT5 is probably the most commonly seen and used. It is inexpensive, reliable, easy to maintain and expand.

✓ **Fiber Optics** ⇒ The use of glass or plastic fibre's for the electronic transmission of data. The technology has several advantages over traditional wire cables in that transmission speed is greatly increased; fiber optics allow for greater bandwidth with no electromagnetic noise; fiber optic cables can carry more data; they transmit the data digitally; and they are lighter and thinner than wire cables.

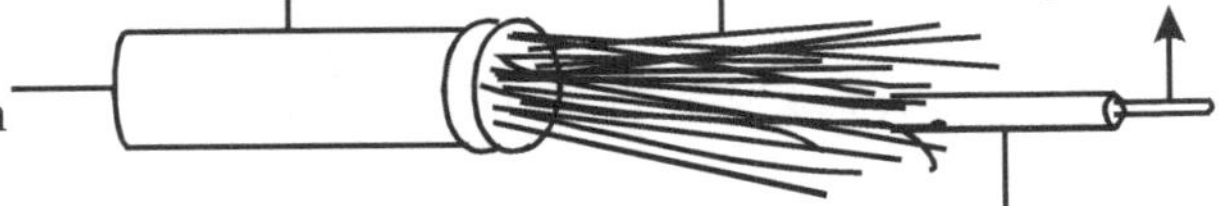

(e) What is the MailMerge feature of word processor? What is its need? [JUN02, Q5(a)][JUN99, Q2(a)][DEC02, Q4(b)][5]

Please Refer DEC01, Q5(a)

(f) What are micro-computers? How do they differ from mini, mainframe and super computers? [DEC02, Q(b)][5]

The processor of a micro computer consists of one chip. The micro computers of today are more powerful than the first mainframes. Micro computers can be classified into two main groups, namely the ordinary desktop PC (Personal Computer) and the portable computer.

Desktop computers

PCs all have the same basic components. PCs can differ widely in their speed, processing power and general ability.

Portable computers

Portable computing describes a whole range of devices ranging from Notebooks and Laptops to PDAs (Personal Digital Assistants).

Micro-computers are different from mini, mainframe and super computers :

The micro-computer mainly differ from all other due to its size and power.

Super computer

The fastest type of computers are supercomputers and they are applied in situations requiring large numbers of mathematical calculations. They are used, for example, in weather forecasting, computer animation and for purposes of scientific research.

✓ **Mainframe computer** ⇒ A mainframe computer is designed to process large amounts of data and to be used by hundreds to thousands of users simultaneously. Mainframes are used by large enterprises to manage payrolls, accounts and for stock control. In scientific institutions mainframes are used to simulate conditions and situations where practical experimentation is difficult or impossible. State and educational bodies use mainframes in instances where fast, accurate and complicated calculations have to be carried out on a large scale. A mainframe computer can almost be said to be more powerful than the supercomputer because it is designed to run more programs simultaneously whilst a supercomputer runs a single program far faster than a mainframe does.

✓ **Mini computer** ⇒ They are smaller and cheaper than mainframe computers, but powerful enough to perform tasks that could only be done by mainframes in the past. The CPU of such a computer consist of more than one chip. These computers are used in factories and scientific laboratories. Mini computers are often used as the server in a LAN (Local Area Network).

2(a) Why are Wide Area Networks also known as Long Hual Networks? How are point to point networks different from broadcast networks? Which topology is most suited for this type of network?

[DEC98, Q4(b)][5]

✓ **Long Haul Network** ⇒ Communications among users on a national or worldwide basis. Compared to tactical communication, long-haul communications are characterized by higher levels of users, such as the National Commands Authority, more stringent performance requirements, such as higher quality circuits, longer switches. So WAN is known as Long Haul Network.

No.	Broad cast Network	Point-to-Point Network
1	A method of sending a signal where multiple parties or nodes may hear a single sender and communicates between them.	A method of communication where one "point" (sender) sends a message to only destination node.
2	All the computers are connected to the same connection medium.	Gateway and router are needed.
3	Good for small number of computers. Cannot handle many computers because many conflicts will occur.	It can handle many computers because sender will directly send a packet to the router/gatway which includes the destination node.

• Point-to-Point topology is more useful and suitable in Wide Area Network (WAN) than Broadcast Network because in Broadcast network the traffic increases and all computers are connected to each other so traffic increases.

(b) Explain optical storage media. [5]

✓ **Storage device** ⇒ A data-holding device, such as a hard disk or CD-ROM.

✓ **Optical storage device** ⇒ A data storage medium that utilises laser technology to read information. CD-ROMs and WORM (Write Once Read Many) are examples of optical disks.

✓ **CD-ROM** ⇒ CD-ROM (Compact Disc, Read-Only-Memory) is an adaptation of the CD that is designed to store computer data in the form of text and graphics, as well as hi-fi stereo sound*):* This is a device that allows you to save data to a CD-ROM. Special CD-Rs are required for this. They also allow you to make backup copies of your CDs. There is a large variety of types, including CD-R or CD-R+RW. The latter has support for rewritable CDs which can be erased and rewritten to, while CD-R only drives can only write to their CDs once. Like CD-ROM drives, burners can be IDE or SCSI. SCSI is definitely preferable when it comes to burners, but a SCSI card is required. Burners are generally quite picky and must have a constant stream of data to work properly. If that stream is interrupted, the burn will fail. This is one reason why SCSI burners tend to be better; SCSI devices can deliver a more reliable stream of data than IDE, while other applications are being run as well.

3(a) Compare and contrast between [5]
(i) CRT, LCDs and Projection Displays
(ii) Volatile and Non volatile memory

(i) Direct-view video displays :- These are video displays in which the light produced by a display device is viewed directly without first bouncing off a screen. All CRT, LCD, and plasma televisions and computer monitors are direct video displays. Direct view displays tend to work best in bright light conditions and have the greatest light output as compared to projection displays.

Projection display systems :- Unlike their direct-view counterparts, a projection display setup relies on the projection of an image onto a screen for viewing purposes. Front and rear projection systems fall within this sub-category; the main difference between these two process is that front projection utilizes a reflective screen surface while rear projection makes use of a transmissive screen surface. Projection displays work best in dimly lit environment. In particular, a front projection setup requires a darkened room - similar to a movie theater - for the best results.

Up to a few years ago, the CRT was the only display technology you could choose for your TV. In reality, you had no choice. You had hundreds of models of TVs on the shelves of big electronic superstores, but inside they were more or less the same - a cathode ray tube as the your Tv display device.

This is no longer true. LCD technology used extensively in laptop screens has now come up to 40 inches and over, while at the larger end, plasma technology is allowing for really big televisions - up to 80 inches diagonal at just 4 inches deep, and which can hang on a wall!

The availability of new direct-view display technologies imply that now you have the possibility to choose the most suitable technology for your requirements. This is however subject to your budget limitations - these new technologies do not come cheap, under certain requirements, a projection tv set-up may be a more appropriate and cheaper alternative worth considering.

Direct-view technology ::

Cathode ray Tube (CRT): (standard) 27" to 40"

Relatively inexpensive up to medium screen size displays; very expensive as you approach big screen sizes

Proven technology: expected half-lifetime: 20,000hrs

Bright crisp pictures - deep blacks and bright whites can be shown simultaneously; can be viewed in bright ambient light conditions.

CRT big screen Tv systems are bulky and very heavy.

LCD Display Panels: (HDTV) 10" to 54"

Clear bright high resolution pictures - with a deeper black than some plasma

Display panel is only a few inches thick

LCD displays tend to exhibit a color shift as the viewing angle changes though new developments are addressing this problem.

Typical expected lamp life: 50,000 to 60,000 hours.

Very expensive in comparison to the image size.

Plasma screens: (HD-ready, HDTV) 32" to 80"

Clear bright high resolution pictures

Display panel is only a few inches thick

Support a viewing angle of up to 170 degrees with no color shift - similar to a CRT.

Reliable technology with an expected half-lifetime of around 30,000hrs.

Very expensive in comparison to the image size.

Projection Display Technology ::

Rear Projection: (standard, HDTV) 42" to 73"

Good picture quality

Easy set-up offering an immediate solution to getting a bigger TV

Relatively bulky and heavy

Affordable - much cheaper than direct-view systems.

Relatively expensive replacement projector lamps costing a few hundred dollars every 2000 to 4000 hours of use.

May exhibit a degradation in picture quality as the viewing angle changes.

Front Projection: Theoretically up to & greater than 150"

Very good picture quality - dependent on type of projection screen.

Projector is small and lightweight.

Affordable - Offer the best dollar to image size ratio.

Relatively expensive replacement projector lamps costing a few hundred dollars every 2000 to 4000 hours of use.

Best when viewed in total darkness

Front projection is the closest you can get to the movie theater magic.

(ii) Volatile and Non volatile memory :- Memory technologies can be divided into two categories, volatile and nonvolatile. Volatile memories lose their contents when power is removed, nonvolatile memories do not. Traditional volatile technologies include SRAM and DRAM. The common factor is they are RAM-based technology, Random Access Memory. The main advantage of RAMs is they are easy to use, read and write operations are similar. The main disadvantage of traditional RAMs is that they can only be used for temporary storage. Traditional nonvolatile technologies are based on ROM-based technology, Read Only Memory. Various improvements to the underlying technology have created Flash and EEPROM memory, these variations of ROM can be written. The process or writing ROM-based memories is difficult and destructive. Traditional ROM based technologies are not suitable for applications requiring many write operations. FRAM is he first nonvolatile RAM. It offers the easy write access of SRAM or DRAM and the nonvolatility of Flash or EEPROM.

(b) What is spooling? What are the benefits obtained by the user from spooling technique? Compare and contrast between spooling and buffering. [JUN01, Q2(a)][JUN00, Q3(a)][JUN99, Q4(a)][5]

✓ **Spooling ⇒** SPOOLING STANDS FOR SIMULTANEOUS PERIPHERAL OPERATIONS ONLINE. To order items or jobs in a queue before sending them to an output device such as a printer. Spooling furnishes a waiting area for documents to pause while waiting for the printer to accommodate each item in the queue. Spooling technique improves system performance by overlapping the input, output and computation of a single job.

✓ **Benefits to the user ⇒** This feature allows you to release a job from your computer while the printer is processing other jobs. With this turned on the job will spool to the printer and wait in line until the printer is available. This allows your computer to run more efficiently without a print job waiting to spool to the printer.

✓ **Compare and contrast between spooling and buffering ⇒** Spooling comes from "Simultaneous Peripheral Operation On-line", which is self-explanatory. Buffering is a general idea which involves using an intermediate entity between two mismatched interacting components in order to reduce the effects of the mismatch. Thus, data buffering uses a storage between two components operating at different speeds to allow both of them to operate without waiting for each other (upto an extent, of course). Buffering is used to implement spooling.

4(a) What are the different approaches to multi-programming operating system? Is it different from network operating system? How? [JUN02, Q3(b)][5]

A multiprogramming operating system is a system that allows more than one active user program (or part of user program) to be stored in main memory simultaneously. Thus, it is evident that a time-sharing system is a multiprogramming system, but note that a multiprogramming system is not necessarily a time-sharing system. A batch or real time operating system could, and indeed usually does, have more than one active user program simultaneously in main storage. Another important, and all too similar, term is 'multiprocessing'.

No, multiprogramming OS is not a NOS because multiprogramming has a significant potential to improve system throughput and resource utilization with very minor differences. While network operating system is a special application that allows computers and other devices on the network the ability to communicate and accept and receive information.

(b) "A bridge is like a smart repeater." Justify the statement with example. [DEC98, Q4b(i)][5]

A bridge is like a smart repeater. Bridges, like repeaters, can connect two network segments, but bridges are a little smarter about the data they transport. Most bridges have the capacity to listen to the network and figure out the address of each computer on both sides of the bridge. The bridge can then inspect each message that comes from one side and broadcast it to the other side of the bridge, if the message is intended for a computer that is on the other side. If the packet's destination is on the same side of the bridge, it is discarded. This creates a more efficient scheme for data transport. The bridge

- Can connect segments that use different cable media types, like 10BaseT(Twister Pair) and 10Base5(Coaxial).
- Cannot connect different transport protocols - like Ethernet and Token Ring networks.

5(a) What is X.25? Explain with example. [5]

✓ **X.25** ⇒ Is an ITU-T standard protocol suite for WAN networks using the phone or ISDN system as the networking hardware. It defines standard physical layer, data link layer and network layers (layers 1 through 3) of the OSI model. The packet switching network was the common name given to the international collection of X.25 providers, typically the various national telephone companies. Their combined network had large global coverage during the 1980s and into the '90s, and it is still in use mainly in transaction systems.

The general concept of X.25 was to create a universal and global packet-switched network on what was then the bit-error prone analog phone system. Much of the X.25 system is a description of the rigorous error correction needed to achieve this, a system known as LAP-B. The X.25 model was based on the concept of establishing "virtual calls" through the network, with "data terminating equipment" (DTE's) providing endpoints to users that looked like point-to-connections X.25 networks are still in use throughout the world, although in dramatic decline, being largely supplanted by newer layer 2 technologies such as frame relay, ISDN, ATM, ADSL, POS, and the ubiquitous layer 3 Internet Protocol.

(b) What is vector processing? Can it be combined with pipelining? How? [DEC02, Q5(b)][5]

Vector processing was first worked on in the early 1960s at Westinghouse in their Solomon project. Solomon's goal was to dramatically increase math performance by using a large number of simple math co-processors (or ALUs) under the control of a single master CPU. The CPU fed a single common instruction to all of the ALUs, one per "cycle", but with a different data point for each one to work on

Today almost all commodity CPU designs include some vector processing instructions, typically known as SIMD. Video game consoles and consumer computer-graphics hardware in particular rely heavily on vector processors in their architecture. The vector instructions were applied between registers, which is much faster than talking to main memory. Vector processor elements have since been added to almost all modern CPU designs, although they are typically referred to as SIMD. In these implementations the vector processor runs beside the main scalar CPU, and is fed data from programs that know it's there.

In order to reduce the amount of time this takes, most modern CPUs use a technique known as in which the instructions pass though several sub-units in turn. The first sub-unit reads the address and decodes it, the next gets the values, and the next does the math. With pipelining the "trick" is to start decoding the next instruction even before the first has left the CPU, in assembly line fashion, so the address decoder is constantly in use. Any particular instruction takes the same amount of time to complete, a time known as the *latency*, but the CPU can process the entire batch much faster than if it did so one at a time.

Vector processors take this concept one step further. Instead of pipelining just the instructions, they also pipeline the data itself. They are fed instructions that say not just to add A to B, but to add all of the numbers "from here to here" to all of the numbers "from there to there". Instead of constantly having to decode instructions and then fetch the data needed to complete them, it reads a single instruction from memory, and "knows" that the next address will be one larger than the last. This allows for significant savings in decoding time. Thus, we can say that vector processing can be combined with pipelining.

CS-611 : COMPUTER FUNDAMENTALS AND PC SOFTWARE
JUNE 2004

Note: *There are five questions in this paper. Question number 1 is* ***compulsory.*** *Attempt any* ***three*** *from the rest.*

1(a) What is memory hierarchy? Why is it needed in a computer? Why do we need Cache and Main Memory, even through faster disks are available? Justify your answer.

✓ **Memory hierarchy** ⇒ The levels of memory in a computer. From fastest to slowest speed, they are:

1. CPU registers
2. L1 cache
3. L2 cache
4. Main memory
5. Virtual memory

The hierarchical arrangement of storage in current computer architectures is called the **memory hierarchy**. Each level of the hierarchy is of higher speed and lower latency, and is of smaller size, than lower levels. Most modern CPUs are so fast that for most program workloads the locality of reference of memory accesses, and the efficiency of the caching and memory transfer between different levels of the hierarchy, is the practical limitation on processing speed. As a result, the CPU spends much of its time idling, waiting for memory I/O to complete.

The memory hierarchy in most computers is as follows:

- **Processor registers** → fastest possible access, only hundreds of bytes

- **Level 1 (L1) cache** → often accessed in just a few cycles, usually tens of kilobytes

- **Level 2 (L2) cache** → higher latency than L1 by 2x to 10x, often 512KB or more

- **Level 3 (L3) cache** → (optional) higher latency than L2, often multiple MB's

Memory Hierarchy

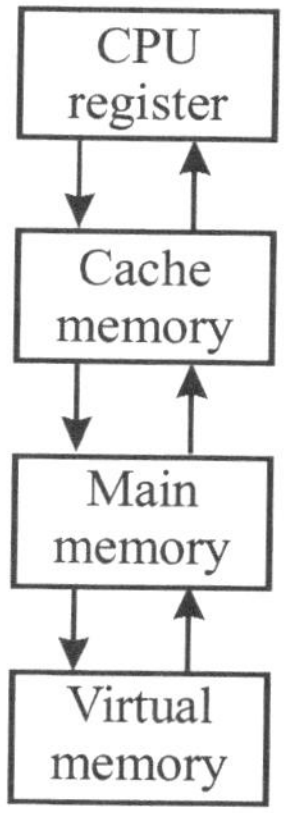

- **Main memory (DRAM)** → may take hundreds of cycles, but can be multiple gigabytes

- **Disk storage** → hundreds of thousands of cycles latency, but very large

Need of cache and Main memory : The above principles suggest that we should try to keep recently accessed items in the fastest memory. Because the smaller memories are more expensive and faster, we want to use smaller memories to try to hold the most recently accessed items close to the CPU and successively larger (and slower, and less expensive) memories as we move away from the CPU. This type of organization is called a memory hierarchy. Two important levels of the memory hierarchy are the cache and virtual memory. Primary storage is used to store data that is likely to be in active use, so it is usually faster than long-term secondary storage. Today, many computers have cache memory located in between the central processing unit and primary storage in order to further increase speed.

A particular location in storage is selected by its physical memory address. That address remains the same, no matter how the particular value stored there changes

Memory hierarchy is required for increased processing speed. This hierarchy permits fetching of instructions and operands at a rate that is high enough to prevent pipeline stalls. A typical hierarchy includes high-speed registers, cache, and/or buffers located on the CPU chip, and complex memory management schemes to support off-chip cache and memory devices.

(b) What is Reduced Instruction Set Computer (RISC)? How is it different from a von Neumann machine?

✓ **RISC ⇒** Reduced Instruction Set Computer. A RISC microprocessor that has fewer, simpler instructions than its CISC counterpart. RISC instructions perform simple, rudimentary functions. The simplicity of these instructions results in a very simple microprocessor design that can execute very fast. RISC instructions are typically characterised by fix length instruction sets (for example, all instructions are 32-bits each).

In a Von Neumann architecture, the instruction has first to be fetched, using the program counter; then it can be executed. Since when the instruction is executed, it may also read or write data, you often cannot load one instruction and execute another at the same time. So the basic sequence in a von-Neuman architecture system is fetch execute. This means that such a system may be *slower*. On the other hand, it has great advantages of *flexibility*, and the efficient use of memory caches can do a great deal to mitigate the apparent slowness of the architecture. In a RISC processor, there are a fairly small number of fairly simple instructions. Each of these instructions does one simple operation, and at most one source value needs to be fetched from memory. In such a processor, the instructions can execute very rapidly. However, some operations require a whole series of instructions: for example, to multiply two eight bit numbers, there is no single instruction; you need a whole list of instructions.

Advantages of RISC : Speed; simple instructions execute faster; if they are carefully chosen, the whole program goes faster. A constant execution rate also simplifies design of a pipeline or cache controller.

Simplicity; RISC processors are easier to design and build; and in some ways they are easier to program, since there are fewer instructions to learn.

High level languages (like C) often do not use many of the specialised instructions; the instructions of a RISC processor are often designed to make a language like C work efficiently; the designers concentrate on instructions which will make C work fast.

(c) Which of the two operating systems, WINDOWS or UNIX is popular among the masses? Give at least two reasons in support of your answer.

MS-WINDOW is the most popular operating system because of the following reasons :

- **GUI →** The main reason of popularity of Windows operating system as compared to Unix is its GUI (Graphical User Interface) as compared to CUI (Character User Interface) in Unix.
- Common look and feel : all window applications have the same basic look and feel. And it is easy to learn.
- Device independence : window provides a device –independent interface to

application.

• Multitasking : windows provide non-pre-emptive multitasking support, users can have several applications in progress at the same time.

• Data sharing : windows allows data transfer between application clipboard. Any type of data can be transferred from one window with the clipboard.

(d) Can an optical fibre be used as a transmission medium for a Wide Area Network? Justify your answer.

Yes, optical fiber can be used as a transmission media for a Wide Area Network because optical fiber has high data rate. Along the long way, a fiber optical carries a signals in the form of fluctuating light in a glass or plastic fiber **cable.** A form of network cabling that transmits signals optically, rather than electrically as do coaxial and twisted-pair cable. The light-conducting heat of a fiber optic cable is a fine glass or plastic fiber called the core. Fiber optic cable can transmit clean signals at speeds as high as 2 Gbps. Because it transmits light, not electricity, it is also immune to eavesdropping.

(e) Do fourth generation languages allow you to create functions or subroutines? Justify your answer.

Subroutines & functions are used to avoid repeated programming of the same calculations, the programmer generally writes these same lines of codes in a function or subroutine and calls them when required. 4GLs are designed to reduce programming effort, the time it takes to develop software, and the cost of software development. They are not always successful in this task, sometimes resulting in inelegant and unmaintainable code. However, given the right problem, the use of an appropriate 4GL can be spectacularly successful.

(f) What is an "ICON"? Where can it be used?

A small graphic image that represents a file or application and when clicked upon produces a programmed result. Use of this mnemonic convention originated at Xerox PARC and was subsequently popularized by the Apple Macintosh. Producing an effective icon is non-trivial because of size and color restraints. A computer icon is a small graphic, usually ranging from 16 pixels by 16 pixels up to 128 pixels by 128 pixels, which represents a file, folder, application or device on a computer system. Icons were first developed as a tool for making computer interfaces easier for novices to grasp in the 1970s at the Xerox Palo Alto Research Center facility. Icon-driven interfaces were later popularized by the Apple Macintosh and Microsoft Windows operating environments.

(g) What is the need of a multi-programming operating system? How is it different from a multi-tasking operating system? Should a real-time

operating system necessarily be multi-programmed? Justify your answer.
Please Refer JUNE03, Q4(a).

(h) Give four ways of protecting your computer against a computer virus attack.

Following are basic ways to protect computer against virus attack.

- Many virus detection programs are available in market. Regularly run these type of softwares in computer and also keep upgrading antivirus software.
- Avoid to copy data from one computer to other computer.
- Whenever any files are downloaded from internet or any other place, first scan those data from antivirus. If data is without virus then only download it.
- Do not download or install any illegal or unauthorized software. Also avoid purchasing pirated softwares.

(i) List two of the networking functions available in Windows. Give the steps involved in performing any one of these.

Two of the networking functions available in window are E-mail and connection to internet. Steps involved in connecting to internet :
there are many ways you can connects to the internet using windows. Two of these are --

1. You choose for the Microsoft Network on-line service.
2. You can check a dial-up-networking connection to an internet access provider.

Steps to follow if you are creating Dial-up Networking connection to an Internet access provider.

1. Letting an internet arrow a
2. Setting up your communications hardware
3. Make sure you have Dial-up Networking installed
4. Install the window 95 TCP/IP protocol
5. Installing TCP/IP information
6. Setting up a connection.
7. Dialling you internet access provider.

(j) List six major advantages of using MS-WORD.

Advantages of MS-Word

One of the main advantages of a MS-word is that a word processor enables you to make changes to a document without retyping the entire document

✓ **Styles** ⇒ Styles allow users to define formats once and then apply them to multiple blocks of text. Microsoft Word supports them.

✓ **Templates** ⇒ Templates are documents saved so that other documents can be based upon them. This is a time-saving idea — but in Word they cause endless problems. In particular, formatting options seems to be stored in both the template and the document. If the information in the template and the document differ, then the document is corrupted and often unusable. This close relationship is further strained by the fact that Word also allows multiple templates to be applied to a document.

✓ **Outlining** ⇒ For document outlines, Microsoft Word uses the Outline view, as the name suggests, the Navigator's main function is to help you jump to key points in a document, such as a heading, a table, or a graphic. From this use, it is a small step to outlining.

✓ **Bulleted and numbered lists** ⇒ Although lists are somewhat more stable in Microsoft Word 2003 than in earlier versions, rearranging list items or nesting lists can quickly corrupt the numbering. Applying lists via a style can make them more stable.

✓ **Headers and footers** ⇒ Microsoft Word has been haunted by a pre-WYSIWYG treatment of headers and footers. In fact, neither is visible until a users selects View > Header and Footer. Once headers and footers are visible, users must turn to an awkward floating window for switching between them or setting up different versions for beginning, right, and left pages.

✓ **Conditional text** ⇒ Conditional text is a block that can be hidden or revealed as needed. This functionality is most often used for maintaining two versions of a document in a single file.

(k) List four main features of MS-PowerPoint. Give reasons for selecting these options.
Please Refer JUNE02, Q5(a).

2(a) "A company has P-4 machine – 1 GHz, having a 32 MB RAM, a 20 GB hard disk drive, a10 Mbps Network Card, a 133 MHz motherboard." What is the meaning of this configuration? It was found that this computer was slow for windows applications. What should be changed in order to make the computer faster? Justify your answer.
Above configuration says that a company is having a machine with Pentium-4 processor of 1GHZ speed. These machines are having 32MB RAM and also 20 GB Hard disk. Network card is capable of passing data with 10Mbps speed

and motherboard's speed is 133 MHz.

Above machine is slow for window application because of less RAM. To speed up the computer, RAM should be increased. 128MB RAM is appropriate to run windows based applications. Because any application which is running needs RAM. So if RAM is increased Application can run faster. And CPU speed is good. Hard disk also has capability of storing huge amount of data. Apart from increasing RAM size we can also upgrade network card to 100 Mbps to speed up exchange of information with other computers over the network.

(b) What are the major utilities available in Windows 95 for correcting disks and access time? Describe the process of using these utilities.

Two major utilities available in window 95 are disk defragmentation and scan disk.

Windows 95 includes a suite of programs designed to optimize your computer's efficiency and access time.

Disk Defragmenter : Disk Defragmenter optimizes the speed with which your programs load and run. With quick startup and shutdown, you can work, play games, and explore the Internet faster and more efficiently. **Using Disk Defragmenter to speed up access to your hard disk**

You can use Disk Defragmenter to rearrange files and unused space on your hard disk so that programs run faster.

✓ **Using ScanDisk** ⇒ You can use ScanDisk to check your hard disk for logical and physical errors. ScanDisk can then repair the damaged areas.

Notes :

- You can start ScanDisk by clicking Start, pointing to Programs, pointing to Accessories, pointing to System Tools, and then clicking ScanDisk

3(a) What are the two major security threats to a computer on a Wide Area Network? How can these threats be controlled? Discuss one such process in detail.

THREATS

✓ **Worm**. In a computer, a worm is a self-replicating virus that does not alter files but resides in active memory and duplicates itself. Worms use parts of an operating system that are automatic, and are usually invisible to the user. Like a virus, worms can be transmitted to a computer through e-mail attachments, downloads, or infected floppy disks or CD's. It is important to have updated antivirus software so that the newest viruses and worms will be detected and halted. A program that enters a computer and replicates itself, often causing damage to the system.

✓ **Virus** ⇒ A virus is a piece of programming code usually disguised as something else that causes some unexpected and usually undesirable event. It is important to have updated antivirus software so that the newest viruses and worms will be detected and halted. A computer program designed to copy itself into other software and spread through multiple computer systems, causing minor damage to completely destroying software systems

✓ **Trojan Horse** ⇒ A program downloaded from the Internet that contains destructive elements to a computer. Unlike a true virus, the Trojan horse does not replicate itself, it simply erases the users hard drive. A Trojan horse can come disguised as a useful application such as a game or even a virus protection program.

✓ **Hacking** ⇒ It is a process of maliciously gaining control of someone computer over WAN / Internet and creating some problem in his/her computer.

✓ **Controlling Virus infection** ⇒ The first steps to protecting your computer are to ensure your operating system (OS) is up-to-date. This is essential if you are running a Microsoft Windows OS. Secondly, you should have anti-virus software installed on your system and ensure you download updates frequently to ensure your software has the latest fixes for new viruses, worms, and Trojan Horses. Additionally you want to make sure your anti-virus program has the ability to scan e-mail and files as they are downloaded from the Internet. This will help prevent malicious programs from even reaching your computer. If this isn't enough protection, then you may want to consider installing a firewall as well.

A firewall is a system which prevents unauthorized use and access to your computer it also protects us from hackers. A firewall can be either hardware or software. Hardware firewalls provide a strong degree of protection from most forms of attack coming from the outside world and can be purchased as a stand-alone product or in broadband routers. Unfortunately, when battling viruses, worms and Trojans, a hardware firewall may be less effective than a software firewall, as it could possibly ignore embedded worms in out going e-mails and see this as regular network traffic. For individual home users, the most popular firewall choice is a software firewall. A good software firewall will protect your computer from outside attempts to control or gain access your computer, and usually provides additional protection against the most common Trojan programs or e-mail worms. The downside to software firewalls is that they will only protect the computer they are installed on, not a network. It is important to remember that on its own a firewall is not going to rid you of your computer virus problems, but when used in conjunction with regular operating system updates and a good anti-virus scanning software, it will add some extra security and protection for your computer or network.

(b) What is network operating system? How is it different from a Distributed operating system? Is Windows 95 a Network operating system? Justify your answer.

✓ **NETWORK OPERATING SYSTEM** ⇒ A special application that allows computers and other devices on the network the ability to communicate and accept and receive information.

Network operating system	Distributed operating system
1. The users are aware of existence of multiple computers and can login to remote machine and copy files from one machine to another machine.	1. Here the user is not aware of the existence of multiple computers, for him it is a single computer he can not know whether he is accessing remote file or its local file.
2. Network operating system may provide remote operations and remote file access.	2. This Operating system dynamically allocates process to CPU if it is not available on local machine no remote login is needed
3. Each computer has its own private operating system.	3. The complete operating system is distributed among the connected system (master/slave)
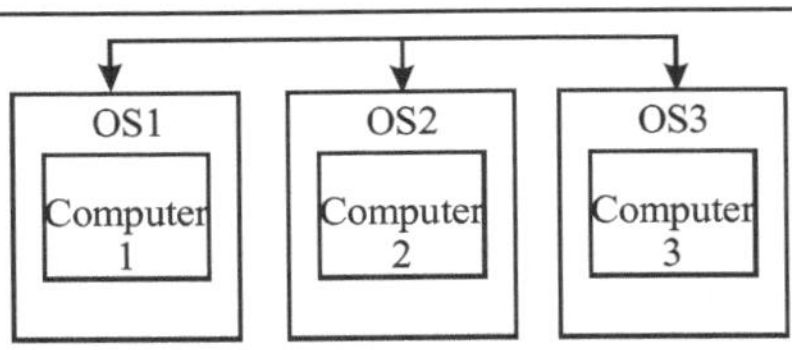 4. Users are typically aware of where each of files are kept and must move file from one system to another with explicit file transfer command.	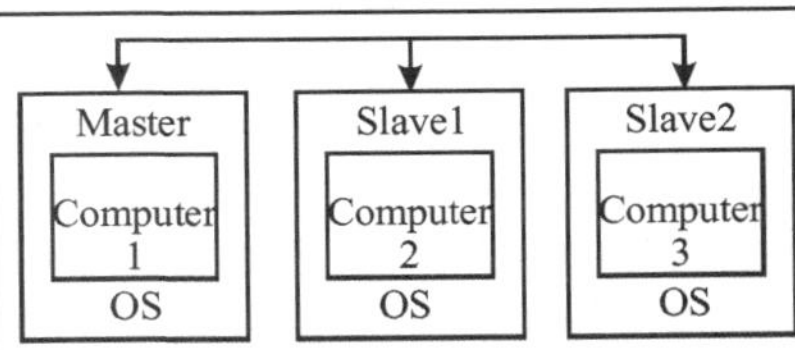 4. Users are not aware of where each of files are kept and must move file from one system to another with explicit transfer command.

No, Windows 95 is not an Network operating system. As it does not provide all the facilities, which a network operating system should provide.

(c) Can you create multimedia-using PowerPoint? Justify your answer.

Yes, we can create multimedia using power point.

We cannot create some very good multimedia file, but power point is having facility to add sound file in the presentation. So, according to slide, one can add some sound file, which will give effect as a multimedia file. So, power point is helpful to create basic multimedia application.

4(a) You want to create a letter of invitation for all your friends. The basic contents of the letters are the same but the name and address in each letter would be different. How would you create these letters using MS-WORD? Describe all the steps involved.

To send same content to many friends main merge feature of MS-WORD is useful.

Following are the steps to be followed to send a letter to friends.

- First open a new document and type a common content format the content as letter.
- Now go to tool mail merge option.
- Now first select current document as a letter.
- Next step is to create a data source.
- Create data source with fields like name, address city, pin etc.
- After creating data source add details of friends in the table.
- Here enter all the list of friends to whom we want to send letter.
- Arrange fields in the main letter.
- Now again click on the mail merge. It will give a new document with many copies.

(b) What are the two basic constructs of a programming language? Describe them with the help of an example each.

Please Refer JUNE01, Q1(c).

Q5. Define the following terms, giving one example of each:

(i) Protocol

Please Refer JUNE01, Q1(d).

(ii) Circuit switching

Please Refer JUNE02, Q3(c).

(iii) Assembly language

Please Refer JUNE02, Q2(b).

(iv) Pipelining

✓ **Pipelining** ⇒ A technique in which memory loads the requested memory contents into a small cache composed of SRAM, then immediately begins fetching the next memory contents. This creates a two-stage pipeline, where data is read from or written to SRAM in one stage, and data is read from or written to memory in the other stage.

(v) Supercomputer

✓ **Supercomputer** ⇒ A very large mainframe computer whose primary activity is carrying out sophisticated and complex calculations. The fastest type of computer in terms of processing speed and use multiprocessing techniques. Supercomputers are very expensive and are employed for specialized applications that require immense amounts of mathematical calculations. For example, weather forecasting requires a supercomputer. Other uses of supercomputers include animated graphics, fluid dynamic calculations, nuclear energy research, and petroleum exploration. In other words, A time dependent term which refers to the class of most powerful computer systems world-wide at the time of reference. Example are CRAY XMP-14. The PARAM Padma, India's newest supercomputer which is more powerful than millions of regular computers put together is being deployed in Russian laboratories to experiment emerging sectors like biotechnology, nanotechnology and weather reporting.

CS-611 : COMPUTER FUNDAMENTALS AND PC SOFTWARE
DEC 2004

Note: *There are five questions in this paper. Question 1 is* ***compulsory*** *and carries 30 marks. Attempt any* ***three*** *from the rest.*

1(a) Explain the functions of the following forms of multiprogramming, with an example of each : [9]
(i) Multitasking
(ii) Multiprocessor
(iii) Multi-user

(i) Multitasking → This refers to a computer's ability to perform different operations simultaneously, such as saving a file while applying a Photoshop filter. In other words it refers to executing many processes on a single processor.. Most operating systems support multitasking, but it can be costly if the need to switch large caches or execution pipelines makes context switching expensive in time.. Multitasking can be either cooperative or preemptive. In the former, the operating system relies on the task to voluntarily cede control to another task; in the latter, the operating system decides which task receives priority multitasking is allowing a user to perform more than one computer task at a time. The operating system is able to keep track of where you are in these tasks and go from one to the other without losing information. Microsoft Windows 2000, IBM's OS/390, and Linux are examples of operating systems that can do multitasking (almost all of today's operating systems can).

(ii) Multi processors → A computer that has two or more processors that have common access to a main storage. Where main storage means (in a computer, program-addressable storage from which instructions and other data may be loaded directly into registers for subsequent execution or processing. *Note 1:* Main storage includes the total program-addressable execution space that may include one or more storage devices. *Note 2: "Main storage"* usually refers to large and intermediate computers, whereas *" memory "* usually refers to microcomputers, minicomputers, and calculators).

(iii) Multi user → allowing simultaneous access to a computer system through two or more terminals. Multi user does not imply multi programming or multi tasking. A dedicated transaction process system such as railway reservation system that supports hundred of terminal sunder control of a single programs an example of multi user operating system.

(b) Explain the methodology of transferring data blocks for the following WAN communication switching techniques : [9]
(i) Circuit switching
(ii) Packet switching
(iii) Message switching.

(i) Circuit Switching → If two processes want to communicate, a permanent physical link is established between them. This link is allocated for the duration of the communication, and no other processes can use that link during this period (even if the two processes are not actively communication for a while). This scheme is similar to that used in the telephone system. Once a communication line has been opened between A and B, no one else can use this circuit, until the communication is terminated explicitly.

(ii) Packet Switching → Messages are generally of variable length. To simplify the system design, we commonly implement communication with fixed length messages called packets, frames or datagrams. One logical message may have to be divided into a number of packets. Each packet may be sent to its destination separately, and therefore must include a source and destination address with its data. Each packet may take a different path through the network. The packets must be reassembled into messages as they arrive.

(iii) Message Switching → If two processes want to communicate, a temporary link is established for the duration of one message transfer. Physical links are allocated dynamically among correspondents as needed, and are allocated for only short periods. Each message is a block of data, with system information (such as the source, the destination and the error correction codes) that allows the communication network to deliver the message to the destination correctly. This scheme is similar to the post office mailing system. Each letter is considered a message that contains both the destination address and source(return) address. Note that many messages (from different users) can be shipped over the same link.

(c) Explain four major features of Microsoft Windows. [6]

Microsoft window is the most popular for personal computers. Window provides an environment that enhances DOS in many ways .the four major features of microsoft windows are-

- **Common look and feel →** All window applications have the same basic look and feel. Once you know one and more two applications, it is easy to learn.
- **Device independence →** Window provides a device –independent interface

to application.

• **Multitasking** → Windows provide non-pre-emptive multitasking support, users can have several applications in progress at the same time each application can be active in separate window

• **Data sharing** → Windows allows data transfer between application clipboard. Any type of data can be transferred from one window with the clipboard.

(d) Discuss the importance of the Mail-Merge feature in WORD. Write a step-by-step procedure to merge labels and envelopes using this feature. [6]

Please Refer JUNE03, 5(a)(i), JUNE04, Q4(a)

2(a) Explain what the memory hierarachy is with the help of a diagram. List any four characteristics of any memory device. [5]

Please Refer JUNE04, Q1(a).

(b) What is a virus? How can it be categorised? Explain what a BOOT infecting virus is. [5]

✓ **Virus** ⇒ A computer virus is a computer program that infects other computer programs and reproduces itself without the knowledge of the PC user. A virus may be destructive, and should never be ignored. Contrary to popular belief, not all viruses are dedicated to performing overt harm on computers that they inhabit. The vast majority of viruses would never perform such fabled destructive behaviour as reformatting the hard drive or spiking the water cooler. There are some nasty ones, though. A virus is a clear example of an area in which it is better to give than to receive

viruses are classified on the basis of their mode of existence and there are three categories of viruses

1. Boot infectors
2. System infectors
3. GENERAL.COM infectors

1. Boot infectors → boot infectors display information originally residing on the location, which they occupy while writing onto the boot sector, the virus ensures that the boot record is not deleted. Once the virus is loaded ,it automatically transfers control to the area where the boot record is available. Boot infectors typically create "BAD SECTORS". Boot infectors are the types which once loaded would stay in the memory until the system is shut off, and until the disk reforms.

3(a) Explain the need for data back-up. Write a step-by-step procedure for taking a back-up in the WINDOWS operating system using MS Back-up utility. [5]

The *Windows* Backup (*Microsoft* Backup) utility helps you create a copy of the information on your hard disk. In the event that the original data on your hard disk is accidentally erased or overwritten, or becomes inaccessible because of a hard disk malfunction, you can use the copy to restore your lost or damaged data. The Windows Backup utility helps you protect data from accidental loss.

The following four steps describe a simple backup operation:

Select files, folders, and drives for backup. Windows Backup provides you with a tree view of the drives, files, and folders that are on your computer, which you can use to select the files and folders that you want to back up. You can use this tree view the same way you use Windows Explorer to open drives and folders and select files.

Select storage media or file location for backed-up data. Windows Backup software provides two options for selecting storage media. You can back up your data to a file on a storage device. A storage device can be a hard disk, a Zip disk, or any type of removable or non-removable media to which you can save a file. This option is always available. You can back up your data to a tape device. This option is available only if you have a tape device installed on your computer or connected to it. If you back up data to a tape device, the media will be managed by Removable Storage.

Set backup options. Windows Backup provides an Options dialog box, which you can use to customize your backup operations. Using the Options dialog box, you can select the type of backup that you want to do. Backup types include: copy, daily, differential, incremental, and normal. Select whether you want a log file to record your backup actions. If you select this option, you can also select whether you want a complete log file or a summary log file. Designate file types that you want to exclude from a backup operation. Select whether you want to verify that the data was backed up correctly.

Start the backup. When you start a backup operation, Windows Backup will prompt you for information about the backup job and give you the opportunity to set advanced backup options. After you have provided the information or changed your backup options, Windows Backup will start backing up the files and folders you selected. If you have scheduled the backup to run unattended, you will still be prompted for information about the backup job. However, after you have provided the information, Windows Backup will not start backing up files, rather, it will add the scheduled backup to the Task Scheduler.

(b) What is Electronic Data Interchange (EDI)? Compare the role of EDI with that of any traditional method in a business scenario. Also mention any two applications of EDI. **[5]**

✓ **Electronic Data Interchange** ⇒ (**EDI**) is the computer-to-computer exchange of structured information, by agreed message standards, from one computer application to another by electronic means and with a minimum of human intervention. In common usage, EDI is understood to mean specific interchange methods agreed upon by national or international standards bodies for the transfer of business transaction data, with one typical application being the automated purchase of goods and services. EDI is still the data format used by the vast majority of electronic commerce transactions in the world. Traditional applications of EDI are purchase orders, bills of lading, invoices, shipping orders and payments. However, the development of standards and the widespread use of computers has encouraged the use of EDI in many new arenas including health care insurance and management, record-keeping, financial services, government procurement, and transactions over the Internet. Organizations adopt EDI for the same reasons they have embraced much of today's modern technology—enhanced efficiency and increased profits.

Benefits of EDI include :

- Administrative cost reduction
- Marketing advantage over competitors who do not use EDI
- Value added to products and services through more rapid and accurate information processing
- Improved inventory control
- Strategic integration of EDI data and information processing, all this clearly states the important role of EDI in traditional business doing way.

Applications of EDI : EDI is not confined to just business data related to trade but encompasses all fields such as medicine (patient records, laboratory results..), transport (container and modal information...), engineering and construction, also it is applied as middleware to exchange information among different applications etc.

4(a) What is Internet? Explain any four services provided by Internet. **[5]**

✓ **Internet** ⇒ A "world-wide" network of information which can be accessed by a modem and communication software through an Internet Service Provider. A global network of computers and computer systems which communicate using the Internet protocol. The Internet is the international network of computers that are linked to each other by a physical data connection and a common communication protocol (TCP/IP). The Internet is not itself a Wide

Area Network, but rather a product of connecting the individual WANs that are contained within it. Four services provided by Internet are :

• **TELNET →** TELNET lets Internet users log in to computers around the world that are connected to the Internet, and to use them as if they were their own.

• **FTP →** "File Transfer Protocol" FTP is the communication protocol dedicated to uploading and downloading files over the Internet. Using a software program called an "FTP client" a user can connect to a designated FTP server over the Internet and send or receive files in real time. The Microsoft Internet Explorer browser has built-in ftp capability

• **FAQ →** "Frequently Asked Questions" This term refers to a collection of questions that have been asked or are likely to be asked about a particular topic. For instance, it is common to find an FAQ section on a given website that addresses essential information about the topic of that site in a question-and-answer format. By presenting information in this manner, the technical experts can spend less time answering the same questions repeatedly and more time with important tasks, such as playing computer games. Many newsgroups, mailing lists and some WWW sites have an FAQ list which is posted regularly. FAQs prevent newsgroup members from having to individually answer common questions.

• **USENET →** The "user's network." A large network connected to the Internet. It contains Newsgroups or discussion areas on almost any topic available. Messages are posted publicly for all to see.

(b) Write the step-by-step procedure to use the following utilities in the WINDOWS operating system: [5]
(i) Drive Space
(ii) Format Disks

(i) DriveSpace

To start DriveSpace.

1. Click the drive you want to compress.
2. On the **Drive** menu, click **Compress**.
3. Click **Start**.
4. If you have not backed up your files, click **Back Up Files**, and then follow the instructions on your screen.

When you are finished, proceed to step 6.

5. Click **Compress Now**.
6. If Windows prompts you to restart your computer, click **Yes**.

Note : You can also open DriveSpace 3 by clicking Start, pointing to Programs, pointing to Accessories, pointing to System Tools, and then clicking Is a virtual device driver claiming a portion of RAM?

(ii) Format disk

Please Refer to JUNE05 Q1(c)(iii)

5(a) List four possible ways to increase memory speed. Also explain how cache memory could be advantageous in increasing the overall speed of memory reference, even though it is a small size memory. [5]

FOUR POSSIBLE WAYS TO INCREASE MEMORY SPEED

1. We must have a separate address and data bus (as well as separate timing and control signals, but these have little impact). Thus, a machine that is to have its program stored in one memory and its data in another would require 59 lines, plus signal lines, for each memory.

2. Primary storage is used to store data that is likely to be in active use, so it is usually faster than long-term secondary storage. Today, many computers have cache memory located in between the central processing unit and primary storage in order to further increase speed.

3. Cache → A cache is a bank of high speed memory that stores the most recently accessed code and data. When the microprocessor requests data that is in the cache, the amount of time to retrieve the data is many times less than the amount of time needed to access main memory. Many microprocessors have a cache inside of the chip itself. In some cases, there is a cache for the cache (known as a 2nd-level cache). A cache may hold code, data, or even recently accessed data on a hard disk. In general, a cache can be created for faster access to any slower device, be it main memory or hard disks.

4. Expansion Card → This is a piece of hardware that is plugged into the main (mother)board of the computer. It expands the capability of your computer, and allows you to add new devices. You can add modems, sound cards, and stuff like that !

HOW CACHE MEMORY COULD BE ADVANTAGEOUS IN INCREASING THE SPEED OF MEMORY

✓ **Cache Memory** ⇒ A small amount (normally less than 1 MB, but todays computers comes up with atleast 1MB) of high-speed memory residing on or close to the CPU. Cache memory supplies the processor with the most frequently requested data and instructions. Level 1 cache (primary cache) is the cache closest to the processor. Level 2 cache (secondary cache) is the cache second closest to the processor and is usually on the motherboard. Cache memory supplies the processor with the most frequently requested data and instructions. Cache memory is a mechanism interposed in the memory hierarchy between main memory and the CPU to improve effective memory transfer rates and raise processor speeds. The name refers to the fact that the mechanism is essentially hidden and appears transparent to the user. Cache memory is the fastest type of RAM available.

(b) What is cryptography? Explain the encryption process with the help of a diagram. [5]

✓ **Cryptography ⇒** Is the field concerned with linguistic and mathematical techniques for securing information, particularly in communications. Historically, cryptography was concerned solely with encryption; that is, means of converting information from its normal, comprehensible form into an incomprehensible format, rendering it unreadable without secret knowledge. Encryption was used primarily to ensure secrecy in important communications, such as those of spies, military leaders, and diplomats. In recent decades, however, the field of cryptography has expanded its remit: modern cryptography provides mechanisms for more than just keeping secrets and has a variety of applications including, for example, authentication, digital signatures, electronic voting and digital cash. Moreover, people without extraordinary needs for secrecy use cryptographic technology, which is often built transparently into much of computing and telecommunications infrastructure.

Encryption process : Encryption (or enciphering) is the process of converting ordinary information (plaintext) into an unreadable form, termed ciphertext, or a cryptogram. Decryption, or deciphering, is the reverse process, recovering the plaintext back from the ciphertext. A cipher (sometimes spelt cypher) is an algorithm for encryption and decryption. The exact operation of a cipher is normally controlled by a key — some secret piece of information that customises how the ciphertext is produced. Cryptographic protocols specify the details of how ciphers (and other cryptographic primitives) are to be used to achieve specific tasks. A suite of protocols, ciphers, key management, user-prescribed actions implemented together as a system constitute a cryptosystem.

Encryption Process

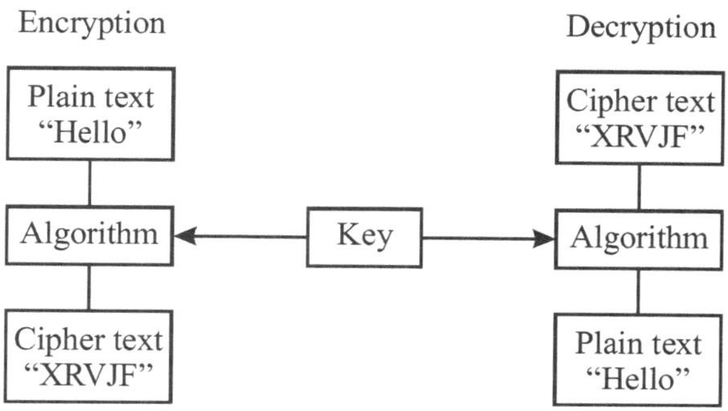

CS-611 : COMPUTER FUNDAMENTALS AND PC SOFTWARE
JUNE 2005

Note: *There are five questions in this paper. Question 1 is* ***compulsory*** *and carries 30 marks. Attempt any* ***three*** *from the rest.*

Q1(a) What is the significance of the mail-merge feature in MS-Word? Write a step-by-step procedure for the following :
(i) To create a data source and a main document.
(ii) To merge the date source with the main document.

✓ **Significance of mailmerge** ⇒ A feature supported by many word processors that enables you to generate form letters. To use a mail-merge system, you first store a set of information, like a list of names and addresses, in one file. In another file, you write a letter, substituting special symbols in place of names and addresses (or whatever other information will come from the first file). The power and flexibility of mail merge systems varies considerably from one word processor to another. Some word processors support a full set of logical operators that enable you to specify certain conditions under which information should be merged. Also, some merge systems allow you to merge data from several files at once.

✓ **Mail Merge** ⇒ Mail merge primarily consists of two files, the Main Document and the Data Source. The Main Document contains the information that will remain the same in each record, and the Data Source contains all the variable information, in the form of *fields*. This is the information that will change in the Main Document when the merge is completed. Along with the information that remains the same, the Main Document also contains merge fields, which are references to the fields in the Data Source.

When the Main Document and Data Source are merged, Microsoft Word replaces each merge field in the` Main Document with the data from the respective field contained in the Data Source. The end result is a third document, a combination of the Main Document and Data Source – although you can also mail merge directly to the printer; (or fax or email) – you don't need to create a merged document on screen; and you can also "preview" the mail merge without actually merging (using the ViewMergedData button).

A step-by-step procedure for the following :

(i) To create a data source and a main document.

(ii) To merge the date source with the main document.

1. If you have an existing file you want to use as the merge document open it now.

2. Start the Mail Merge Helper by going to Tools/Mail Merge.

3. Select the type of Main Document you wish to create.
You will be asked whether you want to use the Active Window or a New Document. To use the document you opened in Step 1, select Active Window. If you select New Document, Word will create a blank document based on the Normal template. For most purposes it is much better to use a template specific to the task in hand rather than the Normal template; so Active Window is usually the better choice.

4. Click Get Data to select your Data Source. There are four methods you can use for your Data Source:
a) Create Data Source
b) Open Data Source
c) Use Address Book
d) Header Options

5. Select Edit Main Document.
Add all text that you want to appear with every record; and insert the appropriate merge fields using the Insert Merge Field button on the Mail Merge Toolbar.

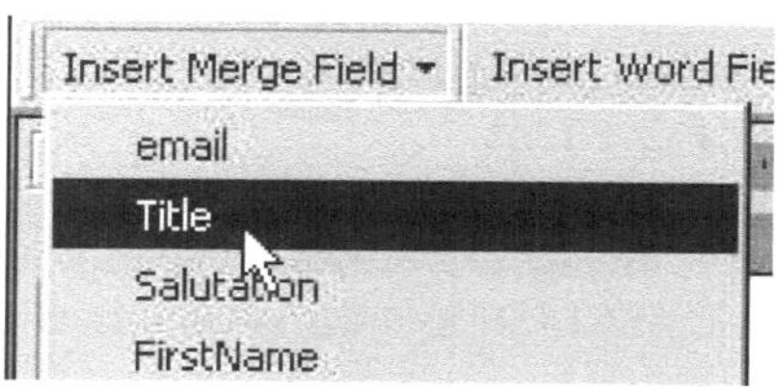

6. You will want to add appropriate punctuation and spaces between the merge fields.

7. As well as the obvious places, such as the address, you may also want to add mail merge fields at strategic points in the main body of the document – "«so-and-so» will be contacting you", etc..

8. You can preview your data prior to performing the merge by clicking the ViewMergedData button on the mail merge toolbar. Doing this is *far* quicker than actually merging, if the Data Source is reasonably large.

You can skip though the records by pressing the Next and Previous buttons. [You can also go to a specific record using the Find button (binoculars). This works fine under Word 2000 but can cause problems if you are using Word 97.

Having proof-read it in this way, you can merge straight to the printer if you want to, *without* having to create a merged document first.

9. You may well need to filter the records, in order to merge only to a subset of your Data Source.

You may also want to change the sort order for the merge without affecting the sort order of the Data Source.

To do this, you can use Mail Merge Query Options

10. Prior to performing the merge, hold <Shift> and then select File/Save All. This will save the Mail Merge Main Document; and if the Data Source is a Word document, it will save that too.

11. Perform the merge. Merge choices are:

Merge to New Document

Merge to Printer

Merge to Email

Merge to Electronic Fax

(b) Explain the role of the following elements in a programming language:
(i) Assignment statement, Print statement
(ii) Conditional statement, Looping statement
(iii) Subroutines and Functions

(i) In programming, a compiler directive that places a value into a variable. For example, counter=0 creates a variable named counter and fills it with zeros. The VARIABLE=VALUE syntax is common among programming languages.

There are four kinds of assignment statements:

1. Arithmetic
2. Logical
3. Statement label (ASSIGN)
4. Character

1 Arithmetic Assignment Statement

The form of an arithmetic assignment statement is:

$v = e$

where: v is the name of a variable or array element of type integer, real, double precision, or complex

- *e* is an arithmetic expression

2 Logical Assignment Statement

The form of a logical assignment statement is:

v = e

- where: *v* is the name of a logical variable or logical array element
- *e* is a logical expression

3 Statement Label Assignment (ASSIGN) Statement

The form of a statement label assignment statement is:

ASSIGN *s* TO *i*

- where: *s* is a statement label
- *i* is an integer variable name

Execution of a statement label assignment statement is the only way that a variable may be defined with a statement label value.

4 Character Assignment Statement

The form of a character assignment statement is:

v = e

- where: *v* is the name of a character variable, character array element, or character substring
- *e* is a character expression

In case of print statement the print option is used to either print a string or constant or the variable i.e. value of the variable. Different language has different statement for printing like in case of BASIC we have

Print "Computer" or Print B.

(ii) A conditional statement, or simply a conditional for short, is an "if-then" statement, written in the form: 'if P, then Q'. Here, 'P' is the *antecedent* (the "if" part of the statement) and 'Q' is the *consequent* (the "then" part). For example, in "If you give me ten dollars, then I will be your best friend," the claim "you give me ten dollars" is the antecedent of the conditional, and "I will be your best friend" is the consequent.

In traditional logic, a statement *if A then B* is true if and only if either *A* is false or *B* is true, or both are false or both A and B are both true. There have been attempts in areas such as modal logic to find a formal definition that is closer to the 'intuitive' meaning: in the traditional logic interpretation *"If it is raining now, then I am a unicorn."* is true provided it is not raining now.

Conditional Statement: Is an "if… then…" statement; for example: *If all girls*

turn into women, then all boys turn into men.
A looping statement that contains the word do followed by a statement (the action), the word while, and an expression in parentheses (the condition). It is used when the same task is to be performed number of times.
(iii) Subroutines &functions are used to avoid repeated programming of the same calculations, the programmer generally writes these same lines of codes in a function or subroutine and calls them when required these are used to get information from files and database and to display to print the information. It contains a query language which is used to answer queries or questions with the data from, database example SQL. All 4GLs are designed to reduce programming effort, the time it takes to develop software, and the cost of software development. They are not always successful in this task, sometimes resulting in inelegant and unmaintainable code. However, given the right problem, the use of an appropriate 4GL can be spectacularly successful.

(c) Write the steps involved in performing the following disk drive utilities:
(i) Disk defragmenter
(ii) Scan disk
(iii) Formatting the disks

(i) DISK DEFRAGMENTER :- Disk Defragmenter is a system utility provided by Windows operating system to speed up access to your hard disk. You can use Disk Defragmenter to rearrange files and unused space on your hard disk so that programs run faster.
To start Disk Defragmenter : You can start Disk Defragmenter by clicking Start, pointing to Programs, pointing to Accessories, pointing to System Tools, and then clicking Disk Defragmenter

(ii) SCANDISK :- You can use ScanDisk to check your hard disk for logical and physical errors. ScanDisk can then repair the damaged areas.
To start ScanDisk : You can start ScanDisk by clicking Start, pointing to Programs, pointing to Accessories, pointing to System Tools and then clicking ScanDisk.

(iii) FORMATTING THE DISKS :- Before storing data on a disk, it must be magnetically mapped so that the computer can go directly to a specific point on the diskette without searching through data. The process of mapping a diskette is called formatting a disk.
To format a disk :
1. If you are formatting a floppy disk, insert the disk into its drive.
2. In **My Computer** or in the right pane of Windows Explorer, click the icon

for the disk you want to format.

3. On the **File** menu, click **Format**.

Notes

- Formatting a disk removes all information from the disk.
- You cannot format a disk if it is open in **My Computer** or Windows Explorer.
- You cannot format a disk if files are open on that disk.
- To format the disk on which Windows 98 is installed,

(d) Mention the difference between synchronous and asynchronous transmission. Also, with the help of a diagram, explain half-duplex and full-duplex communication.

Synchronous Transmission :- In this transmission, bits are transmitted at fixed rate. The transmitter and receiver both the use the same clock signal for synchronisation.

- Allows characters to be sent down the line without start stop bits.
- Allows data to be send as a multiword blocks.
- Uses a group of synchronisation bits which is placed at the beginning and at the end of each block to maintain synchronisation.
- Transmission is faster.
- Synchronous device is more expensive to build.

Asynchronous Transmission :- In this transmission each data word is accompanied by stop (1) and start (0) bits that identify the beginning and ending of the word.

- More reliable as the start and stop bits ensure that the sender and receiver remain in step with one another.
- Transmission is slower as the extra start and stop bits slow down the data transmission.
- Less expensive device is used in this transmission.

Half-duplex	Full-duplex
1. In half-duplex transmission, each station can both transmit and receive, but not at the same time.	**1.**In full-duplex transmission, both stations can transmit and receive simultaneously.
2. It transmission is like a one-lane road with two-directional traffic.	**2.** It transmission is like a two-way street with traffic flowing in both direction at the same time.
3. Example : Walkie-talkies & CB radio.	**3.** Example : Data transmission over Telephone lines.

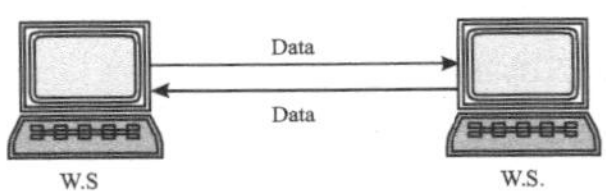

E.g Walkie takies is example of Half duplex

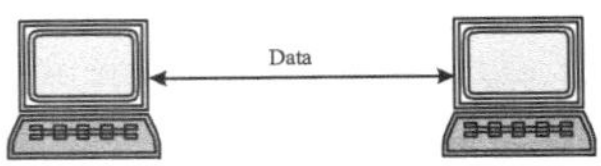

Telephone network is example of Full duplex.

Q2(a) Write the steps involved in changing the following settings in the Windows 95 operating system:
(i) Font setting
(ii) Date and time
(iii) Look of the desktop

(i) Font setting → To change a font type, style or size. Select the text whose format you want to change.
On the Format menu, click font
Clock the option you want.

- You can specify the font for new text by changing the font setting before you begin to type.
- You can change the font for an entire document by clicking the edit menu and then clicking select All before clicking the format menu and then clicking font.

(ii) Insert the current date and time

1. Click where you want to insert the date or time.
2. On the **Insert** menu, click **Date and Time**. Show Me

3. If you want to insert the date or time in a different language format, then click the language in the **Language** box.

The **Language** box includes a list of the enabled editing languages. Additional date and time options may also be available, depending on the language that you selected. For Help on an option, click the question mark and then click the option.

4. In the **Available formats** box, click a date or time format.

5. Do one of the following:

- To insert the date and time as a field that's automatically updated when you open or print the document, select the **Update automatically** check box.

(iii) Look of the Desktop → Click start and then point to setting. Click Control panel and then double click the desktop themes.

- In the Desktop Themes dialog box, click the theme you want in Themes and then click ok.

(b) Write the steps involved in entering TCP/IP information, and, to set up a connection to your access provider.

TCP/IP stands for Transmission Control Protocol/Internet Protocol. This is the protocol that carries data over the Internet. It is actually a set of protocols

- PPP - Point to Point Protocol
- SMPT - Simple Mail Transport
- TCP - Transmission Control Protocol
- IP - Internet Protocol that handles addresses, etc.
- FTP - File Transfer Protocol
- To install the TCP/IP to connect to the Internet, follow steps 1-3, and then in Manufacturers, click Microsoft, and in Network Protocols, click TCP/IP.
- If you have a protocol that is not listed (but is written specifically for Windows 98), click Have Disk, and then follow the instructions on the screen
- To use a different IP or DNS address for a Dial-Up Networking connection.

1. In the Dial-Up Networking window, click the icon for the connection to which you want to assign a new IP or DNS address.
2. On the File menu, click Properties.
3. Click the Server Types tab, and then click TCP/IP Settings.
4. To assign a new IP address, click Specify an IP address.
5. In IP address, type the new IP address.
6. To assign a new DNS address, click Specify name server address.
7. In Primary DNS, type the new DNS address.

Notes

- This setting is useful if you have more than one Internet account and cannot use the same IP address for all of them.

• If you click Server assigned IP address or Server assigned name server addresses, Dial-Up Networking uses the default TCP/IP address information for this connection, as specified in the Network Properties dialog box in Control Panel.

Q3 (a) What is a virus ? List and explain, the categories of the viruses with respect to the sectors infected.

A computer virus is a computer program that infects other computer programs and reproduces itself without the knowledge of the PC user. A virus may be destructive, and should never be ignored. Contrary to popular belief, not all viruses are dedicated to performing overt harm on computers that they inhabit. The vast majority of viruses would never perform such fabled destructive behaviour as reformatting the hard drive or spiking the water cooler. There are some nasty ones, though. A virus is a clear example of an area in which it is better to give than to receive. Viruses are classified on the basis of their mode of existence and there are three categories of viruses :

1. Boot infectors :- boot infectors display information originally residing on the location, which they occupy while writing onto the boot sector, the virus ensures that the boot record is not deleted. Once the virus is loaded, it automatically transfers control to the area where the boot record is available. Boot infectors typically create “BAD SECTORS”. Boot infectors are the types which once loaded would stay in the memory until the system is shut off, and until the disk reforms.

2. System infectors :- This second category of viruses deals with the components of the system itself. All machines without exception require an operating system in order to create an environment in which the operator works. The system infectors attach themselves to a file such as COMMAND.COM.

3. GENERAL.COM Infectors :– These viruses are most dangerous they attach themselves to program files and can spread to almost any executable program in any system. These viruses change the original program instructions into a jumpto.

(b) What is vector processing? Give four reasons for increased complexity in RISC that lead to CISC.

Vector processing is intimately associated with the concept of a

"supercomputer". As with most architectural techniques for achieving high performance, it exploits regularities in the structure of computation, in this case, the fact that many codes contain loops that range over linear arrays of data performing symmetric operations.
The origins of vector architecture lay in trying to address the problem of instruction bandwidth. By the end of the 1960's, it was possible to build multiple pipelined functional units, but the fetch and decode of instructions from memory was too slow to permit them to be fully exploited. Applying a single instruction to multiple data elements (SIMD) is one simple and logical way to leverage limited instruction bandwidth.

These are the four reasons for increased complexity in RISC that lead to CISC
(i) A relatively large number of register in the processor unit.
(ii) Compiler support for efficient translation of high level language programs into machine language programs.
(iii) Efficient instruction pipeline.
(iv) Use of overlapped register windows to speed-up procedure call and return.

Q4(a) Write the function of each layer in an OSI reference model.
OSI MODEL (Open Systems Interconnect)
The seven-layer OSI (Open systems Interconnection) model, created by the ISO (International Standards Organization), defines internetworking environments. It provides a description of how software and hardware interact to permit communication between computers. An *interface* separates each layer from those above and below it; each layer provides services to the layer directly above it.

LAYER	FUNCTION
A application Layer (Rx. the dashboard of your car. The different gauges make you aware of the information that you need to know in order to maintain speed limits and optimal performance for your vehicle.	Allows application processes to access network services. Manages communication between applications. Flow control and error recovery is handled here.
Presentation Layer (RX. the universal sings both on the highway and inside you vehicle.)	**FORMAT** - Function as the network's translator - handles protocol conversion, data translation and encryption, and data compression. The redirector operates here.
Session Layer (Rx. the designated traffic lanes	**TRAFFIC COP.** Provides synchronization between computers, allows applications on two computers to establish a session.
Transport Layer (Rx Speed recognition devices on a highway)	RESPONSIBLE FOR THE ACCURACY OF THE DATA TRANSMISSION. Ensures reliable delivery of packets. Repackages messages. dividing them into smaller packets.

Network Layer (Rx highway exit numbering scheme)	Establishes THE UNIQUE NETWORK ADDRESS AND MANAGES THE TRANSPORT OF INFORMATION PACKETS BETWEEN DIFFERENT NETWORKS. Routes the packets and determines the best route for sending them. Manages network traffic problems, packet switching, routing, and resembling data.
Data Link Layer (Rx. Entry ramp/toll both that allows access onto the highway)	DETERMINES HOW DEVICES CONNECTED WILL GAIN ACCESS. Determines how 1's nd 0's are assembled into frames or packets of data. Sends data frames from the Network Layer to the Physical Layer. Contains the physical address of a device. Like the FROM : and TO : of a envelope.
Physical Layer (Rx. determining if the road infrastructure will be built of concrete or asphalt.)	Transmits data bits between computers, Defines how 1's and 0's are interpreted from the medium. DEFINES CABLES, NETWORK INTERFACE CARDS, AND OTHER PHYSICAL ASPECTS.

(b) What are the minimum requirements for running multimedia applications like audio, video, recording audio in Windows 95 OS?

The minimum requirements for running multimedia application are:

1. CD-ROM Drive :- Reads compact disks in the form of audio or CD-ROM. A CD-ROM holds data (perhaps audio as well). Newer CD-ROM drives will read CD-R (Writable CDs) and CD-RW (ReWritable CDs). The speed of a CD-ROM drive is not usually very important except when installing programs, running games that require use of the CD-ROM drive.

2. Video Card :- This component is used to transfer data to your monitor so that it can be displayed. Today's video cards have a variety of "3D" capabilities. 3D video cards are only needed for playing games though. When playing 3D games, the video card is the most important component.

3. Mouse :- This device is used to move a pointer on your screen, which is a form of navigation. A mouse can be a big help when the operating system you use is based on a GUI (graphical user interface). A mouse is a small handheld pointing device that is used mostly in graphics programs to manipulate what is on the screen. The mouse has two parts: what you can feel and touch (usually having a body and two "buttons"); and the software which is the program that controls the mouse and allows your applications to access it.

4. CPU is also known as the processor or microprocessor. Examples (in roughly ascending order of performance) include Pentium, Pentium with MMX, Cyrix M2, AMD K6, Celeron, K6-2, K6-III, Cyrix III, Pentium II, Celeron-A, Duron, Pentium III, Thunderbird, Athlon. In the Mac market, the Power PC 750 processor (sometimes listed as "G3") is a popular CPU found in iMac computers. And now with P-IV processors realistic sound and video performance can be enjoyed.

5. Memory :- A computer's random-access memory. Memory temporarily holds data and instructions for the CPU. Defined as the internal storage areas of the computer. The most common forms are ROM (Read Only Memory) and RAM (Random Access Memory). This is where the computer stores information as it is working on it. It is temporary storage usually in the form of RAM chips. The computer only works on information in its memory. When it is done, it can be stored to disk. Higher the capacity of RAM easier will be the faster will be the execution of larger programs like playing a large size video file.

6. Super VGA :- Video graphics with higher resolution than VGA. Display monitors receive instructions from a video card that, among other functions, allow for colour display and screen resolution. VGA (Video Gate Array or Video Graphics Adapter) was a standard introduced by IBM in the 1980s that had a maximum resolution of 640x480 pixels with 16 colours. Although SVGA features differ according to individual manufacturers, the standard allows for resolutions of up to 1600x1200 pixels and colour display capabilities from 256 colours to 16 million colours. Standards for video display are reviewed by a number of graphics manufacturers known as the Video Electronics Standards Association (VESA).

Q5(a) Write the working mechanisms of brides and routers.

✓ **Bridge ⇒** A bridge is like a smart repeater. Bridges, like repeaters, can connect two network segments, but bridges are a little smarter about the data they transport. Most bridges have the capacity to listen to the network and figure out the address of each computer on both sides of the bridge. The bridge can then inspect each message that comes from one side and broadcast it to the other side of the bridge, if the message is intended for a computer that is on the other side. If the packet's destination is on the same side of the bridge, it is discarded. This creates a more efficient scheme for data transport. The bridge

- Can connect segments that use different cable media types, like 10BaseT(Twister Pair) and 10Base5(Coaxial).
- Cannot connect different transport protocols - like Ethernet and Token Ring networks.

✓ **Routers** ⇒ A router is like super-intelligent bridge. They can link multiple LANs and look deeper into the data packet to determine its destination. Routers not only know the addresses of the computers on the network but are aware of all the other bridges and routers on the network and can decide the most efficient path in which to send data. The router uses a routing table of network addresses to determine where to forward the packet. When a router receives data, it discards the outer packet or frame or MAC address, repackages the data with network address, and retransmits the signal. By stripping off the outer layers of data before sending a packet, the total number of bits moving across the network is reduced. The router at the receiving end then repackages the data into a packet of frame that is appropriate for its network. There are ROUTABLE and NON-ROUTABLE protocols.

- TCP/IP and IPX/SPX are routable
- NetBEUI is non-routable because it cannot work out of its own subnet

(b) Write two differences between the following :
(i) System Software Vs. Application Software
(ii) Compiler Vs. Interpreter
(iii) Machine language Vs. High level language.

The means of controlling the equipment (Hardware) is called 'Software.

(i) System Software :- It comprises of those programs that control and support the computer system and its data processing applications.
Application Software :- These are written by the programming staff of a computer using organisation to solve a particular problem.

System Software	Application Software
Usually available from the manufacturer.	Available from software vendor not from manufacturer.
It helps the system in its processing application.	It usually solves a particular problem that is unique to that organisation.

(ii) Compiler :- It translates the entire program into machine language before the program is executed. Compiler is most commonly used to translate high level languages.

Interpreter :- It translates program a line at a time as they are being run. Each statement is translated into machine language just before it is executed.

Compiler	Interpreter
It translates the entire program into machine language before the program is executed.	It is less expensive than compiler.
Compilers would be prefened in environment where execution speed is important.	It helps programmers to debug their programs. This boosts programmer productivity.

(iii) A programming language is a language used to write a program, to direct processing steps to be carried out by a computer.

Machine Language :- It is the language of the computer, the only language the computer understand without translation.

High Level Language :- It employs plain English and mathematical expressions and are detached from the machine design.

Machine Language	High Level Language
This language is machine oriented.	This language is detached from computer design.
Writting program in machine language is very difficult.	Programs are cheaper than the low level language in terms of learning & writing but this advantage is offset to an extent by more time on translation.

CS-611 : COMPUTER FUNDAMENTALS AND PC SOFTWARE
DEC-2005

NOTE: *There are five questions in this paper. Question 1 is* ***compulsory*** *and carries 30 marks. Attempt any* ***three*** *from the rest.*

Q1(a). Write four differences between each of the following : 8
(i) Router and Gateway, (ii) Ring topology and Star topology

(i) Following are the four differences between Router and Gateway :

(a) A gateway allows you to access another network. A router can function as a gateway but a gateway is not necessarily a router.

(b) A router operates at the network layer (layer 3) of the OSI model, whereas a gateway operates on, the application layer (layer 7) of the OSI model.

(c) Router can be used to connect networks that may not be similar, while gateways are used to connect two dissimilar LANs.

(d) Gateway is required to convert data packets from one protocol to another before forwarding it, as it connects two dissimilar networks which in router there may be similar networks where no conversion of data packet is required.

ii) Following are the differences between Ring topology and Star topology :

(a) the ring actually consists of a continuous circuit. Signals are passed along the circuit and accessed by stations in sequence. In a star topology the signal is split and sent out simultaneously to all stations.

(b) It is easy to add or remove a node from the network in star. From wiring to installation, it is particularly easy to set up a star topology network. While handling or installation of ring topology is complex.

(c) Failure of one computer will not impact others in star. Failure of one computer may impact others in ring.

(d) Star is the very less expensive as compared to the ring. Most expensive topology is the ring.

(e) Growth of system exerts impact on performance in star as more workload is put on the central hub / computer.

Growth of system has minimal impact on performance in ring.

(b) What are communication channels in Networking? List two transmission media. Further, describe any two such features of each that the other one does not have. 7

Communication Channel : The most basic hardware required for communication is the media through which data is transferred is called as communication channel. There are several types of media, and the choice of the right media depends on many factors such as cost of transmission media, efficiency of data transmission and the transfer rate. Computer communication involves encoding data into some form of energy and sending this across a communication channel.

Following are the two transmission media :

(i) Twisted Pair Cable, (ii) Rodio Channel

Features of both the media as asked : Twisted pair cable are well suited for small distances up to 1 Km. While Radio channel is useless to install for such a small distance. Rodio channel is well suited to cover large gigraphical area. While twisted pair cable is useless to install for such a large distance as it will not be able to transmit data over such a long distance, and will be very very expensive as compared to Radio channel. Data transfer rate is high in radio channel as compared to twisted pair cable.

(c) Write a step-by-step procedure to do the following activities in WINDOWS-95. **9**

(i) Add/Remove applications, (ii) Controlling Access to files/folders

(iii) To record, play and edit sound files

(i) The Windows 95 components, accessories, or other applications can be added or installed, and removed by using the **Add/Remove Programs** utility from the **Control Panel** window. The advantage of using this utility is that Windows 95 maintains control over the installation process by making proper entries into the registry.

To install an application, click on **Install...** button. While installing the application, the wizard helps you to complete the process step-by-step.

To add a program, select it from the displayed list of programs and then click on **Add/Remove** button.

To remove the application, again select it from the displayed list of applications and programs and click on **Add/Remove** button.

(ii) You can control access to your folders by using passwords or by listing names of people you want to have access to these resources.

Following are the steps to control access to a folder :

1. In My Computer, click the shared folder you want to limit access to.

2. On the File menu, click Properties.

3. Click Sharing.

4. If you are using user-level access control, click Add to specify the people you want to be able to use your resources.

5. If you are using share-level access control, type the password you want to use for the folder.

Access file remaining : There are three types of access to a file which can be set by right clicking on the file and choosing properties option, which will further display a property window of the file, there are three option displayed

(i) Read-only : which makes a file read only; one can only see the contents can not change anything to the file.

(ii) Hidden : prevents the file to be displayed or listed when directory is seen.

(iii) Archive : you can see the contents and also perform changes.

(iii) To record, play and edit sound files :

In Win95 or WinNT 4.0, navigate to Start > Programs > Accessories > Multimedia > Sound Recorder.

When the Sound Recorder pops on-screen, you'll notice that it looks a bit like a tape recorder front panel.

· In the center of the window is a flat, green line. As the sound plays or records, this green line oscillates to visually represent the sound.

· To the left is the Position indicator, represented in hundredths of a second.

· To the right is the Length indicator, showing the total duration of the sound file.

· Below these features is a Slide Bar indicator that shows where the sound file is playing, relative to its overall length. You can use the scroll bar to move through the sound file. The bar moves by either sliding it with the mouse or clicking on the right or left arrows.

· Finally, located below the Slide Bar, you'll see the universal symbols (from left to right) for Rewind ◀◀ , Fast Forward ▶▶, Play ▶ , Stop ■ , and Record ● .

Playing a Sound : To play a sound, open the file and click on the Play button.

1. On the File menu, click Open. A dialog box will appear.

2. Navigate to the folder containing the sound file you want to play, select the file and then click Open.

3. Click the play button to start playing the sound.

4. Click the stop button to stop playing the sound.

Recording a Sound : To record and play audio, you'll need a sound card, a microphone and speakers or headphones. If your record button can be activated, your PC is equipped to record. To record your voice, hook the microphone into the audio-in jack on your computer's sound card.

1. Make sure you have a microphone connected to your computer.
2. On the File menu, click New.
3. To begin recording, click and speak into the microphone.
4. To stop recording, click .
5. To continue recording, click and speak into the microphone again.
6. When finished, click to stop recording.
7. On the File menu, click Save As. Type a new name for your file, select the location where it will be saved, and Click the Save button.

You can specify the default sound quality before you record a sound

Editing a File :

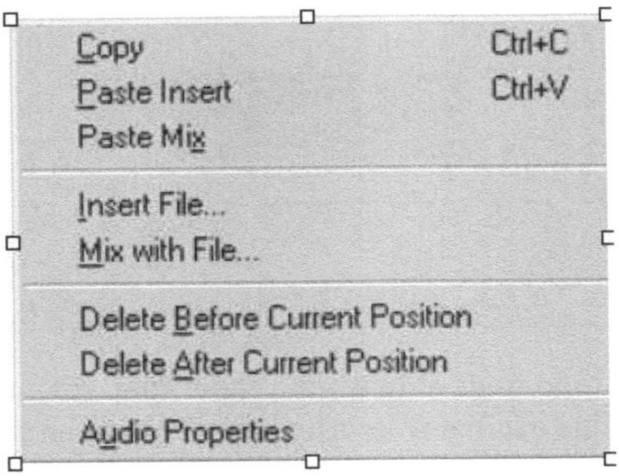

The editing tools are located in Sound Recorder's Edit menu. After you edit a file, click Play to listen to your changes. If you like what you hear, save the file. If you don't approve of the new sound, and you haven't saved the file, choose Revert from the File menu to restore the file to its previous state.

The editing options are:

Insert File, this inserts an entire sound file anywhere in the current file. An inserted file will increase the sound file's length. ***To insert Ding.wav into Chord.wav, you:***

- Scroll to the desired location in the Chord.wav file.
- Select Insert File from the Edit menu. The Insert File dialog box appears.
- Select Ding.wav.
- Click OK.

To listen, click Play. Remember, if you want to save the file, change the name. (You don't want to write over the original Chord.wav file). Mix With File, This mixes a second file with the original file. The sounds in the files will play simultaneously. To mix the Chord.wav file with the Chimes.wav file:

1) Scroll to the desired position in the Chord.wav file.

2) Select Mix With File from the Edit menu. This brings up a dialog box.
3) Select Chimes.wav.
4) Click OK.

Delete Before Cursor Position

This deletes information from the beginning of the file to the current position in the file.

Delete After Current Position

This deletes information from the current position to the end of the file.

(d) Write one feature and one use of each of the following in MS-WORD : 6

(i) Template Wizards, (ii) Macros, (iii) Tab stops

(i) Every Microsoft Word document is based on a template. A template determines the basic structure for a document and contains document settings such as AutoText entries, fonts, key assignments, macros, menus, page layout, special formatting, and styles. You can use any template as it is or tailor it to your specific requirements.

Template wizard is used to make custom templates which later can be used to make documents based on the formatting specifications specified in that format. Feature of template wizard is to provide GUI based template building facility with greater ease to the user.

(ii) If you perform a task repeatedly in Word, you can automate the task by using a macro. A macro is a series of Word commands and instructions that you group together as a single command to accomplish a task automatically. Instead of manually performing a series of time-consuming, repetitive actions in Word, you can create and run a single macro — in effect, a custom command — that accomplishes the task for you.

Here are some typical uses for macros:

- To speed up routine editing and formatting
- To combine multiple commands; for example, inserting a table with a specific size and borders, and with a specific number of rows and columns
- To make an option in a dialog box more accessible
- To automate a complex series of tasks

Macro accomplish a taks automatically and speedly is the main feature of macro for which they are used frequently.

(iii) A stop point for tabbing. In word processing, each line contains a number of tab stops placed at regular intervals (for example, every half inch). They can be changed, however, as MS Word allow you to set tab stops wherever you want. When you press the Tab key, the cursor or insertion point jumps to the next tab stop, which itself is invisible. Although tab stops do not exist in the text file, the word processor keeps track of them so that it can react correctly to the Tab key. Tab key by moving the cursor to the next field or cell. In dialog boxes and menus, pressing the Tab key highlights the next button or option. It is mainly used to format or give a fixed space between different columns. Main feature of tab stop is, it provides uniform space with a single key press, which is faster as compared to pressing spacebar again and again.

Q2(a). Explain two differences between multiprogramming and multitasking. Also give an example each of a multiprogramming and a multitasing operating system. 5

Multiprogramming implies multiprocessing or multitasking operation, but multiprocessing operation(or multitasking) does not imply multiprogramming. Therefore, multitasking operation is one of the mechanism that multiprogramming operating system employs in managing the tatality of computer related resources ike CPU, memory and I/O devices.

The aim of multi-tasking is more sophisticated. Whereas multiprogramming simply aims to maximise the CPU

utilisation, multitasking aims to do this in such a way that intereactive users get a good response.

Example : Real Time OS of multitasking

Example : Time Sharing OS of multiprogramming

(b) What are four measures that one should take to ensure that data does not get corrupted? Also, mention three measures needed for providing physical security to the computer systems. 5

Following are the four measures one should take to ensure that data does not get corrupted :

· IT Planning: the organisation must decide on a policy for introduction of IT. This must be done at the highest level and should address issues such as level of protection for various aspects of information relating to the organisation;

· Selection of technology: keeping in mind obsolescence due to new innovations and necessity for keeping in step;

· Identification of points of exposure of weak links to device means to plug them;

· Physical protection of machine and media.

Following are the three measures needed for providing physical security to the computer systems :

· Physically bolt down the PC to a table so that it cannot be casually lifted and taken away.

· Locate the PC in such a way that it is conveniently accessible to the user, but hidden from casual passers-by;

· Have likeable cupboards for floppies and keep them locked at all times, except when used;

· Keyboard and PC locking devices can be fitted so that the PC cannot be operated unless these locks are opened;

· Keep a record of all floppies in use; do not permit alien floppies into the organisation;

· Use lockable rooms for PCs, specially those handling sensitive data. Make it a practice to lock the room when leaving it for even a short time.

Q3(a). Write a step-by-step procedure to set up a Screen Saver for WINDOWS. Also, mention how to set up a selected wallpaper for the desktop of WINDOWS. **5**

The **screen saver** is set to save the wear and tear of the screen. The screen saver starts if your computer is idle for the number of minutes specified in the Wait box. To clear the screen saver after it has started, move your mouse or press any key. By default, only a limited set of screen savers is installed during Windows Setup. If you assign a password to a screen saver, people who do not know the password cannot clear the screen saver, and therefore cannot easily gain access to your computer.

Following is the step-by-step procedure to set up a Screen Saver for WINDOWS :

1. Right-click on the desktop and select **Properties OR** Choose **Settings** option from the **Start** menu, then select **Control Panel** and choose **Display** from the displayed items.

2. Click on the **Screen Saver** tab.

3. Click on the down-arrow under **Screen Saver** field and browse through the different screen savers.

4. Choose the one that you like.

5. Click on **Settings...** button to customize the way it works.

6. You can set the password by choosing the option **Password Protected**.

7. Set Password... button is activated. Click on it and specify the password.

8. Preview the screen saver and set the timings, so that after the specified time, the screen saver will be activated.

9. Press **OK**.

The looks of Windows include wallpaper and pattern in the background of the desktop, cursor blink rate or item size, color and fonts.

Setting up a selected wallpaper for the desktop of WINDOWS :

In the Pattern or Wallpaper list, click the pattern or wallpaper you want to use.

To cover your entire screen with a small wallpaper image, click Tile.

To center a wallpaper image, click Center.

(b) Write a step-by-step procedure to create a simple presentation using the POWERPOINT package whose slides include a title page (slide), a figure, bulleted text, a bar-graph and an organisation chart. 5

Its very easy to make this type of presentation in Powerpoint software. When you open the new file it asks to select AutoLayout where you can select a title page, a figure, bulleted text, a bar graph and an organisation chart. In detail below is the explanation :

Creating a Title slide

A Title slide is the first slide that will be displayed in your presentation. A Title slide is divided into two parts - the top part for the title and the bottom part for the sub-title or the topic.

To create a Title slide

1. Select **New** from the **File** menu, to display the presentation dialog box.
2. Click the **Blank Presentation**, and than **OK**.
3. Select Title slide from the **AutoLayout** dialog box and click on **OK**.
4. It will display the blank title slide to enter information.
5. Type the title and sub-title.

To add a figure and Bulleted text

Select Text and Figure from AutoLayout and then type the text in the next window displayed. To insert figure select Insert, Picutre, ClipArt (to choose from default pictures available in the Powerpoint software). If you want to select a figure from the hard disk Choose From File instead of ClipArt then browse for the figure.

To create a graph

A graph can be created and viewed in different formats, as a pie, bar, column and so on. Legends, titles and data labels can be added to improve readability.

1. Click on new slide button on the status bar to display AutoLayout dialog box.
2. Select the slide as per your need of placemnet of Bar chart on the page.
3. Click your mouse cursor on the **OK** sign.
4. It will display the blank graph layout slide.
5. Double click on the graph box marked as **"Double click to add graph"** to go in the graph mode. Now you can create and modify the graph. You will see some data also in the **Presentation - Datasheet**. Please do not get disturbed. This is only a default data. You can put the new data i.e. modify the existing data as per your datasheet by taking the mouse cursor and clicking it once.
6. Now click on the chart then choose Chart Type option from the Chart menu and select Bar chart type and click Ok. The chart will be converted to Bar Chart.
7. Whenever you change the values in the datasheet, it will change the graph automatically, displaying backside of the datasheet.

To create Organisation Chart

An organization chart shows the formal structure of a hierarchical group. An organization chart can be used to effectively depict a complex organization scheme as an easily comprehensible visual. These charts are ideal for all types of groups - clubs, companies and governments.

If the hierarchy of an organization is very complex, the Organization Chart that represents this organization may also become complex. In such a situation, it is better to create two organization charts. For example, if you have more than five boxes at the same level, then divide them between two charts and present the charts together. If the organization chart looks too crowded, use abbreviations for the names or titles displayed in the chart. Or, show only the names of people, not their titles.

Steps to create an organization chart

1. Click on **New slide** button on the **status bar** to display AutoLayout dialog box.

2. Select Org Chart layout from the AutoLayout list and than click on OK to display a blank Organization chart presentation slide.

3. Double click on Org. Chart box to display Organization chart window.

4. Click on box to type title and name in the box.

Save and Close a presentation

After creating a slide, now you can save your presentation.

To save a presentation

1. Select **Save** from the File menu to display Save As dialog box.

2. This dialog box displays the current directory and the current drive in respective *directories* and *drives* boxes. Enter the name of the presentation in the *File name* box. No need to give extension because Microsoft PowerPoint automatically adds a .PPT extension to the name.

3. To store the presentation in a different directory, select the directory from the *directories list.*

4. Click **OK** to save presentation file.

To close a presentation

Select **Close** from the File menu to close the current presentation.

Q4(a). Write the characteristics of RISC architecture. **4**

Refer to June02, Q2(d), Page No.-113

(b) What is cryptanalysis? Explain the steps involved in cryptanalysis. Further give one example each of random data and non random data. 6

Cryptanalysis : The interpretation of secret communications without any previous knowledge of the system or the key is called cryptanalysis. In the case of modern cryptosystem, this requires extensive theoretical study, unusual power of observation, inductive and deductive reasoning, great concentration and perseverance. Also necessary are vivid imagination guided by good judgement. This has to be supplemented by a special aptitude and intuition gained from long and varied practical experience.

Following are the steps involved in cryptanalysis :

(a) arrangement and rearrangement of data to disclose non-random characteristics or manifestations (e.g., in frequency counts, repetitions, patterns, and symmetrical phenomena);

(b) an explanation of the non-random characteristics when recognised. The requirements for the first step are experience or ingenuity and time-which may be appreciably reduced by the use of machine aids; for the second step, experience or statistics; and for the third step, experience or imagination, and intelligence.

(c) recognition of the non-random characteristics or manifestations when disclosed;

Example of random data is the data which cannot be predicted by any algorithm in realty there is alway a way to predict the way the random data is produced. John von Neumann wrote in 1951: Anyone who considers arithmetical methods of producing random data is, of course, in a state of sin. However the data produced randomly in the sense that it is not fully predictable without previous knowledge of the file is random data. E.g. radom data about the six coupon numbers 2,9,8,3,0,7 if you donot know the file on the basis of which it is produced. This implies truly random data cannot be produced by computer programs or algorithms, they must be supplied by an external source like human.

Exmple of non random data most typical files.

Q5(a). Write one use each of the following with reference to WINDOWS O/S : 5

(i) Recycle Bin, (ii) Windows Explorer, (iii) Scandisk, (iv) Control Panel (v) My Computer

(i) The Recycle Bin is a temporary storage area used for keeping files until they are either recovered or permanently deleted.

(ii) Windows Explorer is a Windows 95 application that lets you find and view files within their folders and subfolders.

(iii) Scan Disk is an application used to check for errors or damage to a disk.

(iv) The Control Panel is a collection of small applications used for changing settings in the computer system, such as screen colors, fonts, and other features.

(v) My Computer is a folder on the Desktop that provides access to the system?s disk drives and other hardware.

(b) What is Electronic Data Interchange (EDI)? Explain two benefits of EDI. Also list four applications of EDI. 5

Refer to Dec04, Q3(b), Page No.-50

CS-611 : COMPUTER FUNDAMENTALS AND PC SOFTWARE
JUNE-2006

NOTE: *There are five questions in this paper. Question **1** is **compulsory** and carries 30 marks. Attempt any **three** from the rest.*

Q1(a). Explain the steps involved for each of the following in MS-Word: **6**

(i) Changing Document Margins.

Document is the page or work area displayed when we open the new document or file. Margins determine the distance between the text and the page of the paper. In Word, text and graphics are normally printed inside the margins while headers, footers, and page numbers are printed in the margins. Word gives you three ways to set margins. The most straightforward method is to use, the Margins portion of the Page Setup dialog box, reached with the File → Page Setup command.

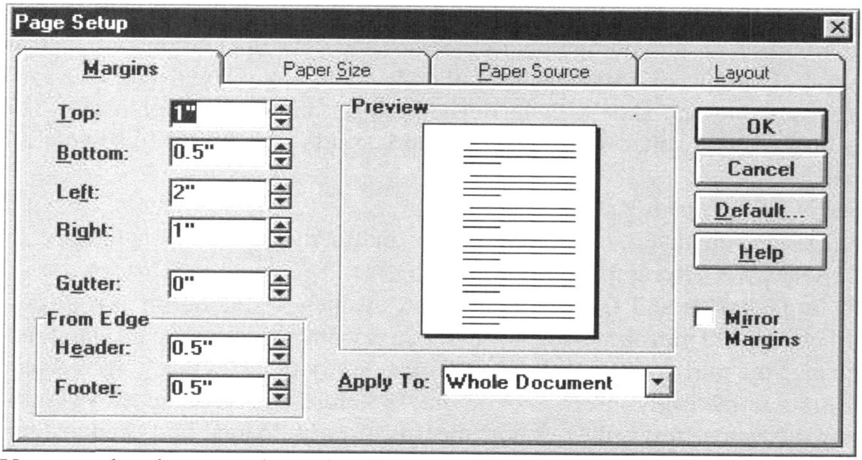

You can also drag margins using the rulers in Print Preview. This lets you see the results of margin changes after a slight repagination delay.

Finally, you can drag new margins with the rulers in Page Layout view. The margin brackets are located on the ruler. Let's look at all three techniques, starting with the dialog box.

Follow these general steps to change margins from within the Page Setup dialog box:

1. Place the insertion point on the page where you want margin settings to be changed (unless you plan to see the Whole Document choice).

2. Choose File → Page Setup.

3. If need be, change paper size and orientation by using the Paper Size tab.

4. Switch to the Margins tab if it is not already displayed.

5. Current settings are shown in the various margin dimension boxes.

6. Type the dimensions you desire, or click the little triangles to increase and decrease settings. The Preview will change as you work.

7. When satisfied, click OK.

Dimensional settings in most of Word dialog boxes can be expressed in inches (in), points (pt), centimeters (cm), picas (pi), and, frequently lines (li). For instance, to set a top margin's height to 12 points, you would type 12 pt in the Top margin box, to set a one-and-one half line top margin, you'd type 1.5 li, etc.

While you can type other measurements, Word will convert them to the default measurement when you close the dialog box. You change the default measurement in the General tab of the Options dialog box (Tools → Options).

(ii) Mirror Margins.

Mirror Margins or Alternate Facing : Select the Mirror Margins feature in the Margins tab of the Page Setup dialog box (File → Page Setup) when you want different left and right margin widths and your final output will be two-sided. Word makes inside margins of odd and even numbered pages the same size; and does the same with the outside margins of odd and even pages. This is how you get white space on the appropriate side of even and odd, two-sided pages.

Setting mirror margins :

1. On the **File** menu, click **Page Setup**, and then click the **Margins** tab.

2. Select the **Mirror margins** check box.

3. In the **Inside** and **Outside** boxes, enter values for the mirror margins.

To change the mirror margins for part of a document, select the text, and then change the mirror margins as usual. In the **Apply to** box, click **Selected text**. Word automatically inserts section breaks before and after the text with the new margin settings. If your document is already divided into sections, you can click in a section or select multiple sections, and then change the margins.

(iii) Setting Page Margins.

Page margins : Page margins are the blank space around the edges of the page. In general, you insert text and graphics in the printable area inside the margins. However, you can position some items in the margins — for example, headers, footers, and page numbers.

Word offers several page margin options. We can use the default page margins or specify our own.

Changing the page margins :

Switch to print layout view.

Point to a margin boundary on the horizontal ruler or vertical ruler. When the pointer changes to a double-headed arrow, drag the margin boundary.

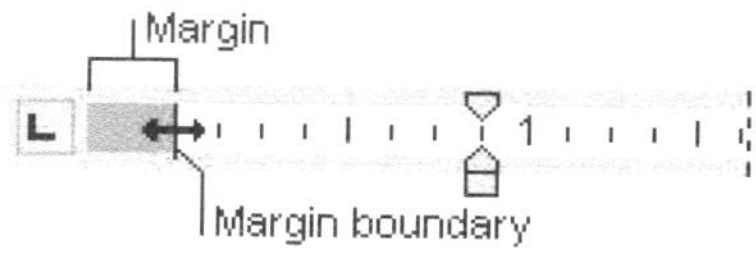

· To specify exact margin measurements, hold down ALT as you drag the margin boundary; the ruler displays the measurements of the margins. If you prefer to type the measurements, click **Page Setup** on the **File** menu, and then click the **Margins** tab.

· To change the margins for part of a document, select the text, click **Page Setup** on the **File** menu, click the **Margins** tab, and then set the margins you want. In the **Apply to** box, click **Selected text**. Word automatically inserts section breaks before and after the text with the new margin settings. If your document is already divided into sections, you can click in a section or select multiple sections, and then change the margins.

(b) What is Circuit Switching? How is it different from Message Switching? **4**

Refer to June02, Q3(c), Page No.-115

CIRCUIT SWITCHING VS. MESSAGE SWITCHING

(i) In **Circuit Switching** establishment of an end-to-end connection between users of a network happens. The associated facilities are dedicated to the particular connection for the duration of the call.

While **Message Switching** is the practice of transporting complete messages from a source to a destination in non-real time and without interaction between the source and destination or without an end-to-end connection, usually in a store-and-forward fashion.

(ii) In **Circuit Switching** networks, when establishing a call a set of resources is allocated for this call. These resources are dedicated for this call, and can't be used by any of the other calls. Circuit Switching is ideal when data must be transmitted quickly, must arrive in sequencing order and at a constant arrival rate. Therefore when transmitting real time data, such as audio and video, Circuit Switching networks will be used.

In **Message Switching**, different messages can use the same network resources within the same time period. Since network resources are not dedicated to a certain session the protocol avoid from waste of resources when no data is transmitted in the session. Message Switching is more efficient and robust for data that is burst in its nature, and can withstand delays in transmission, such as e-mail messages, and Web pages.

(iii) Circuit switching were used in the public switched telephone network (PSTN) while Message switching was used in public (and private) switched data networks.

(c) Explain five resources used to manage windows and user-defined objects. 10

Resources

Following are the Five Resources used to manage windows and user-defined objects : MS-Windows provides nine kinds of resources to application developers. These resources are : icons, cursors, menus dialog boxes, fonts, bitmaps, char strings, user-defined resources, and keyboard accelerators. From these we have explained most of them for the knowledge.

1. Icons and cursors: Windows defines a few types of icons and cursors. An icon or a cursor is essentially a bit-mapped region that is used to represent and symbolise a window or cursor. A developer can also define an original icon or cursor using the ICONEDIT utility.

2. Menus : Each window can have its own menu bar. A menu item can be a character string or **a** bitmap. Each item of a menu bar in turn can have a pop-up menu presenting a list of options. Currently, Windows does not support nesting of pop-up menus within other pop-up menus. (Windows 3.0 provides this functionality). But a pop-up menu can invoke a dialog box.

3. Dialog boxes : These provide another mechanism besides pop-up menu and menu bars to obtain information from the end-user. Dialog boxes are much more flexible than menu bars **or** pop-up menus. Dialog boxes usually contain a group of child windows such -as buttons, scroll bars, and editable fields. Just like windows, dialog boxes have a function that is used to process **messages** received from the user upon selection of options

4. Fonts : Windows provides a few families of fonts with different sizes and shapes : modem, roman, Swiss, Helvetica, and script. Application processors and desktop publishing can define additional fonts as needed. Fonts can be installed other than default fonts available in windows.

5. Bitmaps : They are used to represent icons, cursors, or draw picture on the screen. Both mono and colour bitmaps can be defined.

6. Character Strings : Character strings are handled as resources mainly to provide a manageable solution to internationalisation of a window application.

7. User-Defined Resources : These can be used for any purpose and support any user-defined data type. Any arbitrary data can be managed as a user-defined resource.

(d) Explain access modes and access time with reference to memory.

Also write the three types of access modes. **5**

Access Modes: A memory is considered to consist of various memory locations. The information from these memory locations can be accessed in the following ways:

· **Random Access Memory (RAM):** It is the mode in which and memory location can be accessed in any order in the same amount of time. Ferrite and Semiconductor memories, which generally constitute main memory, are of this nature. The storage locations can be accessed independently and there exist separate access mechanism for each location.

· **Sequential Access**: On the other hand we have memories, which can be accessed in a pre-defined sequence for example, the songs stored on a cassette can be accessed only one by one. The example of sequential access memory is Magnetic Tape. Here the access mechanism need to be shared among different locations. Thus, either the location or the read/write head or both should be moved to access the desired location.

· **Direct Access:** In certain cases the information is neither accessed randomly nor in sequence but something in between. In direct access, a separate read/ write head exist for a track and on a track the information can be accessed serially. This semi-random mode of operations exists in magnetic disks.

Access Time: The time a program or device takes to locate a single piece of information and make it available to the computer for processing. DRAM (dynamic random access memory) chips for personal computers have access times of 50 to 150 nanoseconds (billionths of a second). Static RAM (SRAM) has access times as low as 10 nanoseconds. Ideally, the access time of memory should be fast enough to keep up with the CPU. If not, the CPU will waste a certain number of clock cycles, which makes it slower.

Permanence of Storage:

Some memories loose information over a period of time. For example, there can be some memories where the stored data bit value 1 looses its strength to become 0 over a period of time. These kinds of memories require refreshing. The memories, which require refreshing, are termed as dynamic memories. In contrast, the memories, which do not require refreshing, are called static memories. Another factor, which can destroy the contents, is the presence and absence of electricity. The memories, which looses their content on failure of power are termed as **volatile** memories, those, which do not are called **non-volatile.** Magnetic memories are non-volatile and semi-conductor main memories are volatile in nature.

Physical Characteristics:

In this respect the memory devices can be categorised into four main categories viz., electronic, magnetic, mechanical and optical. One of the requirements for a storage device is that it should exhibit two well-defined physical states, such that 0 and 1 can be represented in those two states. The Data transfer rate of the memory depends on the how quickly the state can be recognised and altered. The following table lists some of the memory technologies along with their physical and other important characteristics.

Technology	Access time (in seconds)	Access mode	Performance of storage	Physical nature of storage medium	Average cost (Rs/bit) (Approx.)
Semiconductor memories	10^{-8}	Random	Volatile	Electronic	10^{-2}
Magnetic disk	10^{-2}	Direct	Non-Volatile	Magnetic	10^{-5}
Magnetic tape	10^{-1}	Sequential	Non-Volatile	Magnetic	10^{-7}
Compact disk ROM	Approx. 10^{-1}	Direct	Non-Volatile	Optical	10^{-5}

The physical size of memories should be small and it must consume less power. Higher power consumption may result in more costly equipment for internal cooling of computer. The storage devices, which require mechanical motion e.g. hard disks are more prone to failure rather than the semiconductors memories which are totally electronic in nature. Very high speed semiconductor memories are also prone to failure as technology is moving towards its limits.

(e) What is Boot Infector? Explain how it affects the system file. Also, explain how it can be prevented. 5

Boot Sector Infector

Every logical drive, both hard disk and floppy, contains a boot sector. This is true even of disks that are not bootable. These boot sectors usually contain specific information relating to the formatting of the disk and a small program - the boot code (which starts loading the system files of the active OS on that drive). The boot code is what displays the 'Non-system Disk or Disk Error' message familiar to those who have left a 'non-bootable' diskette in the A: drive of a PC when it booted. As well as these system boot sectors, hard drives also have a special boot sector known as a master boot sector or master boot record. As the boot code is a program, it can also be infected by a computer virus. Boot sector infections normally start from leaving an infected diskette in a PC's floppy drive and rebooting the machine. When the viral boot code is read from the boot sector and executed, the virus copies itself to a 'safe' place in memory, hooks disk I/O functions, infects the hard drive and remains resident, lying in wait for uninfected boot sectors to present themselves (these will usually be on diskettes accessed in the floppy drives). The safe memory location used by most boot viruses (and many file infectors too) is at the 'top of memory'. Brain - the first PC virus - was also the first PC boot sector infector. Although Brain was limited to diskette boot sectors, most boot viruses since typically infect the system boot sectors of floppy disks and the MBRs of hard drives. Perhaps the main advantage of this strategy is that the virus' code will always be the first to run, whichever drive type is booted from. Stoned was the first virus to implement this and in many ways remains the classic example of the technique. A few boot viruses, such as Form (which is perhaps most notable for its perseverance), infect the system boot sectors of both diskettes and hard drives. Some multipartite viruses have boot sector components that only infect MBRs while others have boot sector parts that only infect diskette or hard drive system boot sectors.

PREVENTION TECHNIQUES :

Prevention can be divided into two areas:

1) safe user practices and

2) anti-viral tools.

90% of all virus infections, or the damaging results of infection, can be easily prevented by following safe usage guidelines. Most of the other 10% of infections, or damaging results, can be avoided by the use of anti-viral software or hardware tools.

Safe user practices:

1. !! NEVER BOOT FROM ANY FLOPPY OTHER THAN !!
!! THE ORIGINAL WRITE PROTECTED DISKETTE !!
!! FROM THE ORIGINAL DISTRIBUTION PACKAGE !!

The above recommendation is extremely important. Most of the boot sector infector viruses can ONLY infect your system if you boot from an infected floppy diskette. Booting from borrowed, unknown or multiple diskettes greatly increases the opportunity for infection.

2. One and only one boot diskette should be assigned to each and every floppy based PC (systems without a fixed disk), and that diskette should be CLEARLY labeled as the boot diskette for that system.

3. If you have a system with a fixed disk - NEVER boot from a floppy drive. The only exceptions to this involve recovering from a viral infection.

4. Create meaningful volume labels on all fixed and floppy disks at format time. Develop a habit of checking volume labels each time a DIR command is executed. Keep a look out for changes in the volume labels.

5. Watch for changes in the pattern of your system's activities.

Do program loads take longer than normal? Do disk accesses seem excessive for simple tasks? Do unusual error messages occur with regularity? Do access rights on any of the system devices turn on when there should be no activity on that device? Do you have less system memory available than usual? Do programs or files disappear mysteriously? Do you suddenly notice a reduction in available disk space? Any of these signs can be indicative of viral infections.

Q2(a). What is Multimedia ? Explain three multimedia tools available with Windows-95. **5**

Multimedia tools available in Windows 95 are available under accessories option which can be selected by following the given steps:

1. Open the **Start** menu.
2. Select **Programs** from the menu.
3. From the cascading menu, click on **Accessories**.
4. Then click on **Multimedia** from the cascading menu of Accessories.

The options of the Multimedia menu are – (i) CD player, (ii) Media Player, (iii) Sound Recorder, and Volume Control. Each of these is discussed below :

(i) CD Player

You can use CD Player to play audio compact discs from a CD-ROM drive connected to your computer. To use CD Player, you also need a sound card.

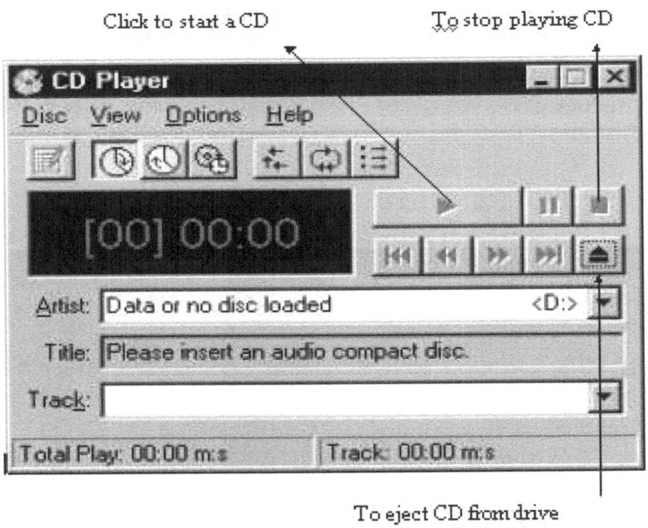

Before playing a CD make sure it is in the CD-ROM drive, and then click the start button as shown in Figure. Your CD continues to play even if you minimise CD Player.

(ii) Media Player

You can use Media Player to play audio, video, or animation files, and to control the settings for multimedia hardware devices. To use Media Player also, you should have a sound card.

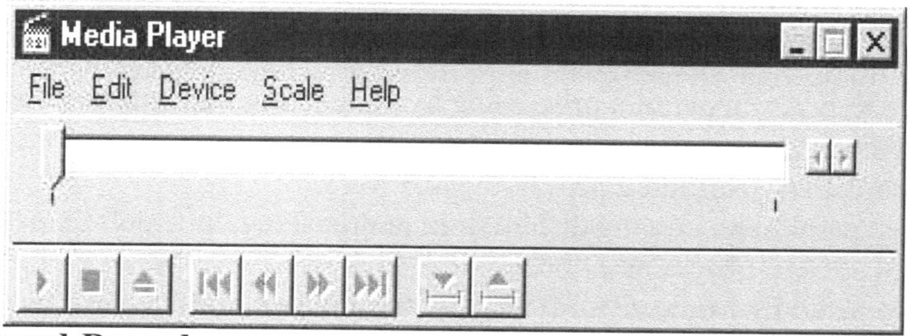

(iii) Sound Recorder

The Sound Recorder is a handy but somewhat limited digital recorder. Using Sound Recorder you can record, play, and edit sound files. To use Sound Recorder, you must have a sound card and speakers installed on your computer. If you want to record live sound, you also need a microphone. This multimedia utility can be used to create recorded messages and include them in files or include them in electronic mail messages that you send to other users.

Refer to Dec05, Q1(c). Page No.-156

(b) What is a dial-up network ? Explain how it is different from cable network. **5**

(1) The switched telephone network that can be accessed remotely via analog modems or ISDN and regulated by government and administered by common carriers. Also called "plain old telephone network" (POTS) and "public switched telephone network" (PSTN).

Difference: The dial-up network requires a connection through an analog line to the modem pool prior to accessing the Internet. Whereas cable network works with a modem called cable modem(A cable modem is a device that allows computers to communicate over the cable network and access the Internet. It provides high-speed access to the Internet by taking advantage of the huge information-carrying capacity of the cable TV infrastructure). Cable network accepts the digital signal from the cable modem, which always remains on. Dial-up connections are generally in the 56K range whereas cable connections can be considerably faster.

Q3(a). What is parallel processing ? Also explain the categories of Flynn's classification. **5**

The simultaneous use of more than one CPU to execute a program. Ideally, parallel processing makes a program run faster because there are more engines (CPUs) running it. In practice, it is often difficult to divide a program in such a way that separate CPUs can execute different portions without interfering with each other.

Most computers have just one CPU, but some models have several. There are even computers with thousands of CPUs. With single-CPU computers, it is possible to perform parallel processing by connecting the computers in a network. However, this type of parallel processing requires very sophisticated software called distributed processing software.

Note that parallel processing differs from multitasking, in which a single CPU executes several programs at once.

First proposed by Michael J. Flynn in 1966, Flynn's did the classification of parallel computer architectures that are based on the number of concurrent instruction (single or multiple) and data streams (single or multiple) available in the architecture. The four categories in Flynn's taxonomy are the following:

(i) (SISD) single instruction, single data : A single processor executes a single instruction stream, to operate on data stored in a single memory. There is often a central controller that broadcasts the instruction stream to all the processing elements.

(ii) (MISD) multiple instruction, single data : Each processor owns its control unit and its local memory, making them more powerful than those used in SIMD computers. Each processor operates under the control of an instruction stream issued by its control unit: therefore the processors are potentially all executing different programs on different data while solving different sub-problems of a single problem. This means that the processors usually operate asynchronously.

(iii) (SIMD) single instruction, multiple data : A single computer instruction perform the same identical action (retrieve, calculate, or store) simultaneously on two or more pieces of data. Typically this consists of many simple processors, each with a local memory in which it keeps the data which it will work on. Each processor simultaneously performs the same instruction on its local data progressing through the instructions in lock-step, with the instructions issued by the controller processor. The processors can communicate with each other in order to perform shifts and other array operations.

(iv) (MIMD) multiple instruction, multiple data : Multiple computer instructions, which may or may not be the same, and which may or may not be synchronized with each other, perform actions simultaneously on two or more pieces of data. The class of distributed memory MIMD machines is the fastest growing segment of the family of high-performance computers.

(b) What are the steps for recording a macro in MS-Word? How does one run a recorded macro? 5

It's easy to create a Macro: you start the Word macro recorder and record a sequence of actions, then stop the recorder and edit the macro if needed. The macro recorder cannot record mouse actions in document text. You must use the keyboard when recording such actions as moving the insertion point and selecting text. However, you can use the mouse to choose commands and select options when you're recording a macro.

There are three ways to start the macro recorder: **Double-click REC on the status bar. Select Tools→Macro, then click the Record button in the Macro dialog box.**

Click the Record button on the Macro toolbar.

Following are the steps to Record a Macro :

1. Start the macro recorder by selecting any of the three options described earlier. The Record Macro dialog box appears.

2. Enter a name for the Macro in the Record Macro Name box. If you don't give your macro a name, Word will name it Macro1, Macro2 and so on. No spaces, commas, or period allowed in the name.

3. Enter a description of what the macro does in the Description box. This is optional and you can use upto 255 characters.

4. To assign a macro to a toolbar, a menu or a keyboard shortcut, click the appropriate button.

5. If the current document is attached to a template other than the Normal template, select either that template or Normal in the Make Macro Available to box. If the current document is attached to the Normal template the macro is automatically stored in the Normal template.

6. Choose OK, then perform the actions you want to record.

7. To stop recording the macro, do one of following:

· Double-click REC on the status bar.

· Click the stop button on the Macro Recorder toolbar.

Running A Macro : Once you have recorded your macro, you can assign it to a toolbar, a menu or a shortcut key combination. You can then run it as you would a normal Word command or feature.

If you don't want to assign a macro to a toolbar, or key combination-perhaps you simply have too many macros, or use some of them too seldom, - you can also run a macro by choosing ToolsMacro, selecting the macro name in the Macro dialog box, and clicking the Run button.

If you've got everything right, your macro will perform the actions you taught it to do. If something is wrong, you can edit it any point of time.

Q4(a). What is Network security ? Explain two measures that can be adopted for Network security. **5**

The networks are computer networks, both public and private, that are used every day to conduct transactions and communications among businesses, government agencies and individuals. The networks are comprised of "nodes", which are "client" terminals (individual user PCs) and one or more "servers" and/or "host" computers. They are linked by communication systems, some of which might be private, such as within a company, and others which might be open to public access. The obvious example of a network system that is open to public access is the Internet, but many private networks also utilize publicly-accessible communications. Today, most companies' host computers can be accessed by their employees whether in their offices over a private communications network, or from their homes or hotel rooms while on the road through normal telephone lines.

Network security involves all activities that organizations, enterprises, and institutions undertake to protect the value and ongoing usability of assets and the integrity and continuity of operations. An effective network security strategy requires identifying threats and then choosing the most effective set of tools to combat them.

✓ **Threats to network security include:**

Viruses : Computer programs written by devious programmers and designed to replicate themselves and infect computers when triggered by a specific event

Trojan horse programs : Delivery vehicles for destructive code, which appear to be harmless or useful software programs such as games

Vandals : Software applications or applets that cause destruction

Attacks : Including reconnaissance attacks (information-gathering activities to collect data that is later used to compromise networks); access attacks (which exploit network vulnerabilities in order to gain entry to e-mail, databases, or the corporate network); and denial-of-service attacks (which prevent access to part or all of a computer system)

Data interception : Involves eavesdropping on communications or altering data packets being transmitted

Social engineering : Obtaining confidential network security information through nontechnical means, such as posing as a technical support person and asking for people's passwords.

Measures adopted to reduce the risk of being attacked by computer virus:

Antivirus software packages : These packages counter most virus threats if regularly updated and correctly maintained.

Secure network infrastructure : Switches and routers have hardware and software features that support secure connectivity, perimeter security, intrusion protection, identity services, and security management. Dedicated network security hardware and software-Tools such as firewalls and intrusion detection systems provide protection for all areas of the network and enable secure connections.

Virtual private networks : These networks provide access control and data encryption between two different computers on a network. This allows remote workers to connect to the network without the risk of a hacker or thief intercepting data.

Identity services : These services help to identify users and control their activities and transactions on the network. Services include passwords, digital certificates, and digital authentication keys.

Encryption : Encryption ensures that messages cannot be intercepted or read by anyone other than the authorized recipient.

Security management : This is the glue that holds together the other building blocks of a strong security solution.

None of these approaches alone will be sufficient to protect a network, but when they are layered together, they can be highly effective in keeping a network safe from attacks and other threats to security. In addition, well-thought-out corporate policies are critical to determine and control access to various parts of the network.

(b) What is a magnetic disk? Define 'optical disk'. List three advantages of an erasable optical disk over a magnetic disk. 5

A magnetic disk is a memory device, such as a floppy disk, a hard disk, or a removable cartridge, that is covered with a magnetic coating on which digital information is stored in the form of microscopically small, magnetized needles. Optical disk is a plastic-coated disk that stores digital data, such as music or text, as tiny pits etched into the surface and is read with a laser scanning the surface. Also called laser disk.

Erasable Optical Disks: This is an optical disk that can be erased and written on repeatedly. An erasable optical disk has a great deal of data capacity. It can store up to 4.6 GB. An erasable optical disk functions like a magnetic disk and has huge capacity, so it will replace the magnetic disk in the future. And it is very cheap as compared to magnetic disk. Moreover, Optical disk does not spin, does not need to move access arms and read/write heads, because a laser beam can be moved electronically. The capacity of the storage is considerably greater than their magnetic disk counterparts, and optical disk storage may eventually replace all magnetic tape and disk storage.

Q5(a). What is Mail Merge ? Explain its advantages using an example. 5

Mail merge is an extremely useful application whereby a 'standard letter' can be sent out to an extremely large number of recipients, but which appears to be written to them personally. This method is used a lot by companies that advertise products and services through the post. To manually type each of several thousand letters to individual people would be both a time-consuming and tedious exercise, not to mention the possibility of creating typing errors in the process. And let's face it – nobody in their right mind would want to spend their entire working life typing out the same letter over and over again.

For mail merge to work, all you need is a template, which consists of the 'standard letter' containing blank 'fields' into which the required 'personal' data will be inserted. This data is usually held in a database file and can be updated as necessary. Having typed the 'standard letter' and having checked it thoroughly for mistakes, the mail merger is run and it takes information sequentially from the data file, inserting it into the blank spaces and printing off the letters, one at a time.

The **advantages of mail merge** are that thousands of letters can be printed out very quickly. You don't have to waste time creating thousands of identical letters. Every letter will be identical (apart from the personal details). With clever formatting (very easy using modern word processors), the printed letter can look as if it were created personally for the recipient.

The **disadvantages** are that the letter will actually be quite impersonal even though it at first doesn't appear to be so. Also, if the data in the database is inaccurate, the recipient may receive a mailshot which is totally inappropriate, e.g. if they are down on the database as male instead of female, they may get sent a letter for a totally inappropriate product! In addition, mail merging encourages the sending out of thousands of tons of junk mail each year, which is not very environmentally conscious.

(b) What is data communication? Explain two differences between synchronous and Asynchronous transmission. **5**

Data Communication : The transfer of information between functional units by means of data transmission according to a protocol. Note: Data are transferred from one or more sources to one or more sinks over one or more data links.

The difference between synchronous and asynchronous data communication is that asynchronous data blocks can be sent and received at **any time,** while synchronous datablock have to be **"clocked".** The asynchronous datablocks have startbits and stopbits so that the receiving computer can recognize the datablocks as such. In contrast, the synchronous datablocks come at regular intervals, so long as there is something to be sent.

Both sender and receiver know about these intervals and how long they are, and because they can do **without** those startbits and stopbits that are needed in asynchronous communication, they can maximize throughput to the highest rate of sent/received datablocks that they can safely handle.

CS-611 : COMPUTER FUNDAMENTALS AND PC SOFTWARE
December -2006

Note: Question number 1 is **compulsory**. Attempt any **three** questions from the rest.

Q1(a). Differentiate between Microcomputers, Minicomputers and Mainframes. *6*

Ans. Refer to Dec-2003, Q.No.-1(f), Page No.-69

(b) Draw and explain the structure of Von-Neumann machine. Also, explain the key features of a Von –Neumann machine. *8*

Ans. Refer to June 2001, Q.No.-1(a), Page No.-142

(c) Explain five types of media through which data may be communicated. *10*

Ans. First : Refer to Chapter-5, Page No.-19, Q.No.3

(iv) Microwave Systems

They use very high frequency radio signals transmitting data through space. Data may be transmitted along a ground route by repeater stations, usually located about 25 miles apart. Each station receives the data, amplifies it and again retransmits it. The microwave signals may also be passed on to the communications satellite that acts as a reflector accepting signals from one point on earth and returning the same to some other point on earth.

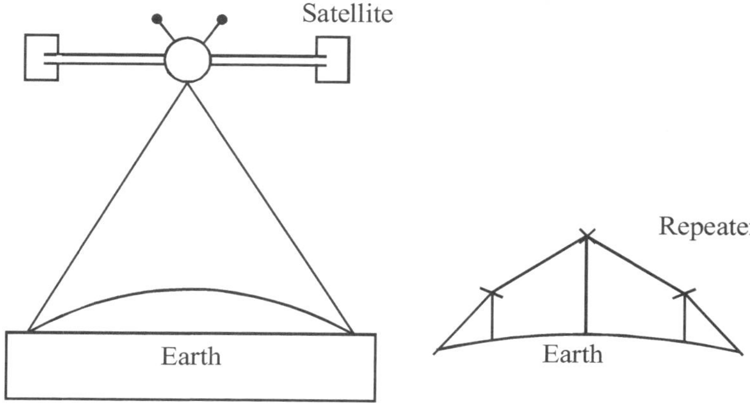

Figure : (a) Transmission through satellite
(b) Transmission through repeaters

(v) Radio Wave

To use the radio waves as the communication media, the authority has to get the frequency allocated. The transmission and reception is done at this particular frequency. It is illegal to use a frequency that has not been allocated.

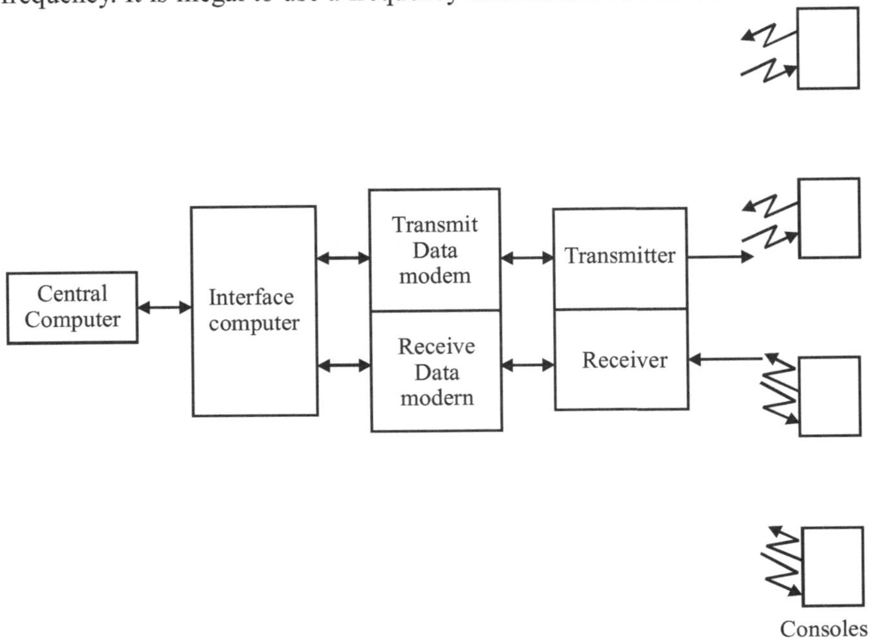

Figure : Radio Wave

(d) What is a Screen Saver ? How can we protect a Screen Saver using a password ? *6*

Ans. The screen saver is set to save the wear and tear of the screen. The screen saver starts if your computer is idle for the number of minutes specified in the Wait box. To clear the screen saver after it has started, move your mouse or press any key.

By default, only a limited set of screen savers is installed during Windows Setup. If you assign a password to a screen saver, people who do not know the password cannot clear the screen saver, and therefore cannot easily gain access to your computer.

To set–up the screen saver protect it using a password follow the steps given below : -

1. Right–click on the desktop and select **Properties** OR Choose **Settings** option from the Start menu, then select **Control Panel** and choose **Display** from the displayed items.

2. Click on the **Screen Saver** tab.

3. Click on the down–arrow under Screen Saver field and browse through the different screen savers.
4. Choose the one that you like.
5. Click on **Setting...** button to customize the way it works.
6. You can set the password by choosing the option **Password Protected.**
7. Set Password... button is activated. Click on it and specify the password.
8. Preview the screen saver and set the timings, so that after the specified time, the screen saver will be activated.
9. Press **OK.**

2(a) What do you mean by Normal view and page layout view of a document ? How do they differ from each ether? *5*

Ans. Normal View

Normal view is the best view for most of your typing & editing. This is the word's default view. Normal view shows breaks, fonts & other character attributes. Page breaks (shown as dotted lines), & optionally the names of paragraph styles are shown the area outside the text body the area containing headers, footers, footnotes, page numbers, margin spacing etc. does not appear. Images are also not shown in normal view however the cursor movement is fastest in normal view. To switch to normal view. Click the normal view button on the horizontal scroll bar or click view menu >> normal or press Alt + Ctrl + N keys.

Normal view has following 3 advantages : –

1) You can see the section breaks. If you have more than 1 section in a document, you should seriously consider working in normal view when formatting or entering text.

2) You can see style names for all paragraphs. Normally this area is hidden to make it visible choose tools >> option. Click the view tab & enter the width in style area width box enter or press OK.

3) Because it doesn't attempt to place pictures, normal view runs considerably faster than print layout view. On slower machines or with large complex files that contain many graphics, the difference in scrolling speed can be considerable.

Page Layout view : Page Layout view is the most accurate of all the views available in word. The main benefit of page layout view is that it is true WYSIWYG. The view shows the vertical ruler along the left side of the document. It enables the user to see all the elements of documents on the page as it will be printed. You can see page beaks, headers & footers, footnotes, page numbers & margin spacing.

The trade-off is that print layout view is slower because word, windows &

your computer must all work to continually display these elements accurately

To switch to page layout view : -

1) Click the page layout view button on the horizontal scroll bar or click view menu >> page layout or Press Alt + Ctrl + P keys together.

(b) Define the term Parallel Processor. Explain the four categories of parallel processor. *5*

Ans. Refer to June-2006, Q.No-3(a), Page 173

Q3(a). Draw and explain any three topologies of a LAN. *6*

Ans. (1) Star Topology : In a star topology, each device has a dedicated point-to-point link only to a central controller, usually called a hub. The devices are not linked to each other. Unlike a mesh topology, a star topology does not allow direct traffic between devices. The controller acts as an exchange: if one device wants to send data to another, it sends to the controller, which then relays the data to the other connected devices.

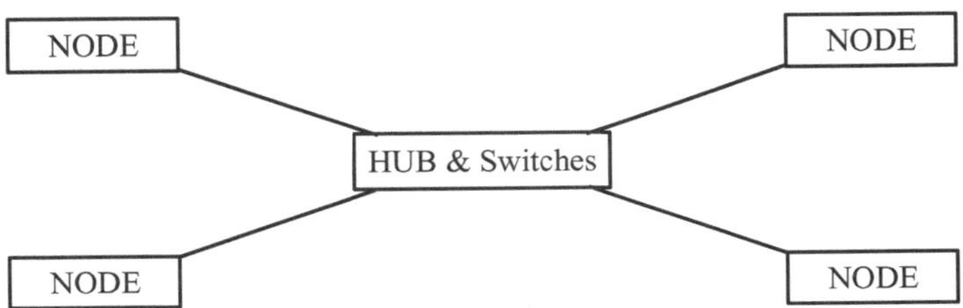

Star Topology

Advantage

1) On any node failure, rest keep working.

2) Scalable

3) Can work as logical bus

Disadvantage

1) If hub or switch fails network can go down.

(2) Bus Topology : All stations are connected to a single communication line. This single communication line is referred as to a bus information frames originating at a station are propagated away from the station in both directions on the bus. Each station on the bus interrogates the information and name destination address field for its own address. If the destination field does not match. The station's address, the station discards the station discards the information frame back onto the bus. If the destination address matches the station address, it accepts the information frame and processes the frame. An extension to bus topology is tree topology. Tree topology extends the branches of bus topology allowing more stations to access the bus.

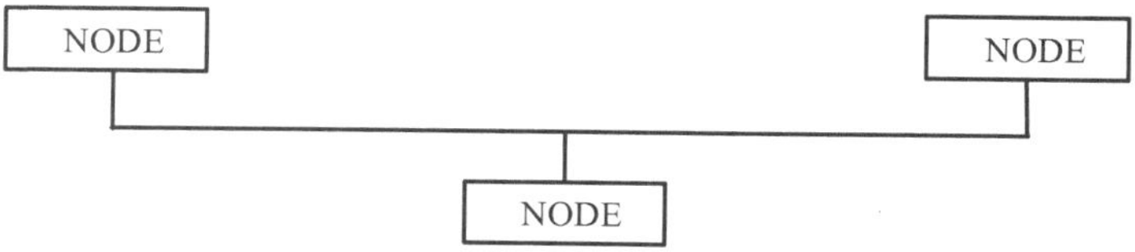

Bus Topology

Advantage

1) Easy to install

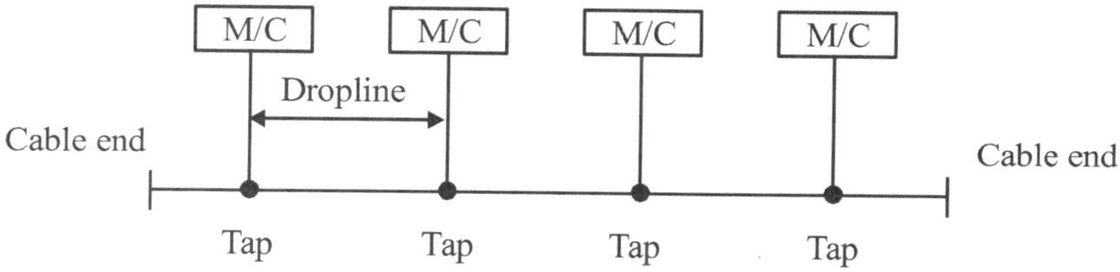

2) Backbone cable can be laid among the most efficient path.

3) Less cable length required than mesh, star or tree topologies.

Disadvantage

1) Difficult reconfiguration

2) Difficult fault isolation

3) New devices cannot be easily added.

4) Signal reflection at taps can degrade quality of service.

5) Adding or modifying devices requires redesigning or backbone.

6) A fault in the bus cable stops all transmission.

7) In case of bus cable fault the damaged area such signals back to origin, creating noise.

(3) Ring Topology : LAN that have each station attached to an adjacent using point to point links from a physical ring. The ring itself is circular and the information travels in one direction. Each station attached and active to the right the information frame, then retransmits the information travels in one direction.

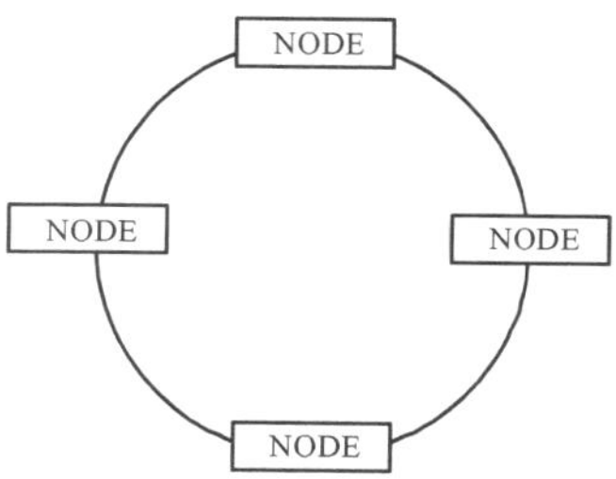

Ring Topology

If UNIX system is connected to a network, it is most likely one of the two types broadcast or token passing. The topology (the wiring scheme) would be bus, ring or star. The most commonly used networking hardware are Ethernet, Token Ring, FDDI.

Advantage

1) Relatively easy to configure and install.

2) To add or delete a device requires moving only two cable connections.

3) Fault isolation is easy.

Disadvantages

1) Unidirectional traffic can be a disadvantage. A break in a simple ring can put entire network out of use.

(b) Write the process of creating a folder in Windows. How can you copy the files in an existing folder to the newly created folder? *4*

Ans. You can create a new folder directly on the desktop, at the root level of a disk drive, or within another folder.

To create a new folder, follow the steps given below :

1. In My Computer or Windows Explorer, open the folder in which you want to create a new folder.

2. On the File menu, point to New, and then click Folder. The new folder appears with a temporary name.

3. Type a name for the new folder, and then press ENTER.

The name can contain up to 255 characters, including spaces. But, it cannot contain any of the following characters: \ / : * ? < > |

To copy a file, follow the given steps :-

1. In my Computer or Windows Explorer, click the file you want to copy. To select more than one file to copy, hold down CTRL key, and then click the items you want.

2. On the Edit menu, click Copy.

3. Open the folder or disk where you want to put the copy.

4. On the Edit menu, click Paste.

Q4(a). Explain the terms Soft page break and Hard page break in MS-Word. *5*

Ans. Word uses "Soft" and "Hard" page breaks to indicate when one page ends and another begins. Then are two categories of page breaks.

a) Soft Page Break

Soft Page Break are automatically inserted by Word, when text reaches the bottom of the page and are represented by a dotted line across the document. The text beneath it will appear on the second page if we print this document. This position of Soft Page Breaks in a document automatically change when text is added or deleted to reflect the new page boundaries.

b) Hard Page Break

You insert Hard Page Breaks when you want to end one page and begin another. This is done via the "Break" command in the Insert menu, or by pressing the "CTRL+ENTER".

Hard Page Breaks appear with the words "Page Break" on the line. They remain at the exact same spot in the document regardless of any text changes you make.

(b) Explain the four categories of programming languages. Also, indicate the category that is Perceived to be the hardest to program. *5*

Ans. We can choose any language for writing a program according to the need. But a computer executes programs only after they are represented internally in binary form (sequences of 1s and 0s). Programs written in any other language must be translated to the binary representation of the instructions before the computer can execute those. Programs written for a computer may be in one of the following categories of languages.

(1) Machine Language : This is a sequence of instructions written in the form of binary number consisting of 1s, 0s to which the computer responds directly. The machine language was initially referred to as code, although now the term code is used more broadly to refer to any program text. Machine language is considered to be the first generation language.

Advantage of Machine Language :

It is faster in execution since the computer directly starts executing it.

Disadvantages of Machine Language :

It is difficult to understand and develop a program using machine language. Anybody going through this program for checking will have a difficult task understanding what will be achieved when this program is executed. Nevertheless, the computer hardware recognizes only this type of instruction code.

(2) Assembly Language : When we employ symbols (letter, digits or special characters) for the operation part, the address part and other parts of the instruction code, this representation is called an assembly language program. This is considered to be the second–generation language. Machine and Assembly languages are referred to as low level languages since the coding for a problem is at the individual instruction level. Each machine has got its own assembly language, which is dependent upon the internal architecture of the processor. As assembler is a translator, which takes its input in the form of an assembly language program and produces machine language code as its output.

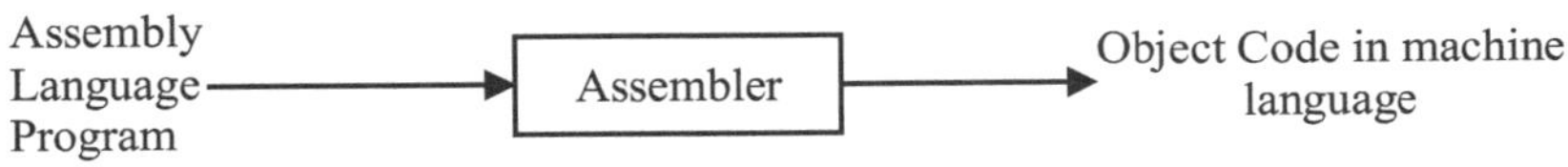

Assembler

e.g. ADD <a> <b>; is an instruction to add values of two registers.

Advantage of Assembly Language :

Writing a program in assembly language is more convenient than in machine language. Instead of binary sequence, as in machine language, it is written in the form of symbolic instructions. Therefore, it gives a little more readability.

Disadvantages of Assembly Language :

Assembly Language (program) is specific to particular machine architecture. Assembly languages are designed for specific make and model of a microprocessor. It means that assembly language programs written for one processor will not work on a different processor if it is architecturally different. That is why the assembly language program is not portable.

Assembly language program is not as fast as machine language. It has to be first translated into machine (binary) language code.

(3) High–level Language : Programming languages like COBOL, FORTRAN and BASIC are called high level programming languages.

The time and cost of creating machine and assembly languages was quite high. And this was the prime motivation for the development of high level languages.

Since a high level source program must be translated first into the form the machine can understand, this is done by a software called Compiler which takes the source code as input and produces as output the machine language code of the machine on which it is to be executed.

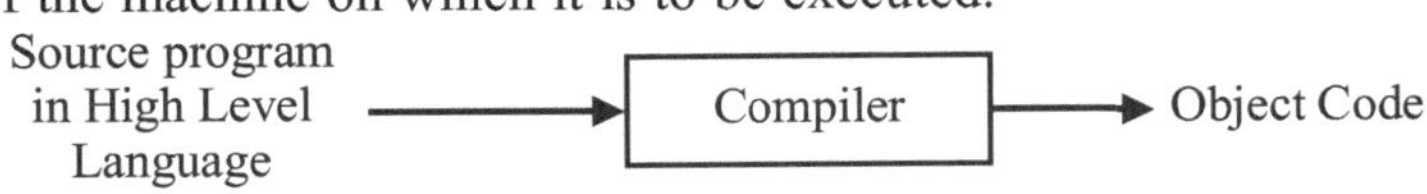

Compiler

During the process of translation, the Compiler reads the source programs statements–wise and checks the syntax (grammatical) errors. If there is any error, the computer generates a printout of the errors it has detected. This action is known as diagnostics. There is another type of software, which also does the translation. This is called an Interpreter.

Advantages of High–level Programming language :

(1) Readability : Programs written in these languages are more readable than assembly and machine language.

(2) Portability : Programs could be run on different machines with little or no change. We can, therefore, exchanges software leading to creation of program libraries.

(3) Easy debugging : Errors could easily be removed (debugged).

(4) Easy Software development : Software could easily be developed. Commands of programming language are similar to natural languages (English).

(4) Fourth Generation Language.

The fourth generation of programming languages is not as clearly defined as are the other earlier generations. Most people feel that a fourth generation language, commonly referred to as 4GL is a high level language that requires significantly fewer instructions to accomplish a particular task than a third generation language.

Most third generation languages are procedural languages. This means that the programmer must specify the steps, that is the procedure, the computer has to follow in a program. By contrast, most generation languages are non–procedural languages. The programmer does not have to give the details of procedure in the program, but instead, specifies what is wanted.

Major fourth generation languages are used to get information from files and databases, and to display or print the information. These fourth generation languages contain a query language which, is used to answer queries or questions with data from a database. For example the following figure shows a query in a common query language SQL.

```
SELECT ADDRESS FROM PERSONNEL
WHERE NAME = "SANJAY"
```

It is most difficult to understand and develop a program using machine languages it is written in the form of binary numbers consisting of 1 s and 0 's

Q5(a). Define the term Virus. Explain the features of at least four prevalent viruses in the computer industry. ***5***

Ans. Computer Viruses are computer programs which are a collection of coded instructions. Computer virus is a broad term in itself and includes not only viruses, but also worms and Trojans. The basic difference between a normal program and virus is that viruses are self–replicating, they have the capability of executing themselves without being asked for.

Type of Virus

Some of the most commonly prevalent viruses in the computer industry.

1. Scores Virus : These viruses are prevalent in Macintosh machines. Scores virus has a built in time trigger that activities at two, four and seven days after the disk has became infected. The consequences are varied raging from printing problems, systems clashes and malfunctioning of disk operations. Data files are not directly affected by this virus, but erasure of this virus requires deletion of all files.

2. Brain Virus : This is one of the first viruses that came into being. Also known as the Pakistani virus, it was developed by the Pakistani brothers to keep track of low cost software that were sold out of their outlet in Lahore. The virus pops up a screen saying "Welcome to the Dungeon". This virus is known to destroy data and are highly contiguous.

3. Lehigh Virus : This virus originated at the Lehigh University Computer Centre. This virus stays in the stack space of COMMAND.COM. With the booting of a PC from an infected disk, the virus is spread through commands such as COPY, TYPE, DIR etc. On any other disk with COMMAND.COM the virus code gets copied to the other disk and a counter is incremented on the parent. When the counter reaches a value of 4, all files of the disk gets erased. The boot sector gets ruined and also the FAT.

4. Friday the 13th : This virus attacks not only the COMMAND.COM but also other executable files. When a .COM or .EXE file is executed for the first time after booting, the virus captures a specific interrupt and inserts its own code; after which, whenever any .EXE file is executed, the virus code is written to the end of the file resulting in increase in size of the file by 1808 bytes. In .COM files the virus code is written to the beginning of the file.

(b) Define the term Multimedia. Explain any four Multimedia tools. *5*

Ans. Multimedia is the term for different media like graphics, animation, sound, and video all wrapped in one interactive package. The basic idea is to manage and coordinate the various devices of communication and electronics with the PC as a central controller. Multimedia brings dazzle to presentations, actions to games, and fun to learning. It promises to play an important role in the communication systems of the future.

Now - Refer to June-2006, Q.No.-2(a), Page No.-172

We also have volume control as the multimedia tool present in window 95.

Volume Control : If you have a sound card, you can use volume control to control the volume and speaker balance when you play audio files.

To adjust the volume for multimedia devices, open the multimedia properties dialog box. In the playback or Recording area, drag the volume slider.

CS-611 : COMPUTER FUNDAMENTALS AND PC SOFTWARE
June, 2007

Note : Question number 1 is **compulsory**. Attempt any **three** questions from the rest.

1. (a) Explain the Von Neumann architecture of a computer with the help of a diagram. *5*

Ans. Refer to Jan 2001, Q.No.-1(a), Page No.-142

(b) Define computer virus. How do they infect and spread in a computer system? Explain at least three categories of viruses on the basis of their mode of existence. Give three examples of computer viruses. *8*

Ans. First - Refer to June-2005, Q.No.-3(a), Page No.-39

The Process of Infection

On booting, the system carries out the ROM instructions, the first being the power on Self Test (POST) which is followed by the bootstrap process of reading the boot record and loading of the Disk operating system. In MS-DOS, it involves the loading of IBMDOS.COM IBMBIO.COM and COMMAND.COM along with some optional files like CONFIG.SYS and AUTOEXEC.BAT. The booting process culminates into the systems prompt displayed on the VDU.

The infection may begin as soon as a computer system boots from a contaminated disk or executes infected program. Whatever viruses are present gets activated, which immediately begin to spread throughout the system.

All input/output activities on a PC are carried out by interrupts. The interrupt mechanism in itself is very complex. User wishes to save his program and presses CTRL+S (a wordstar command) on the key board. This treated as an interrupt. The main memory has specific routines to handle these user requests. One such set of routines exists in the ROM–BIOS and the another is in the DOS program in the memory, loaded from IBMBIO.COM. The routine that services the interrupt requests are termed as Interrupt Service Routines (ISR's) and are located in the memory with their addresses. Then interrupt request activates a number and not the routine address, thus, there exists a table with the interrupt numbers and the corresponding routine address. When an interrupt request is made, the CPU looks up the table, performs the required routines and transfers the control back to the program.

The contents of ISR address table being in the RAM is vulnerable to modification by user programs and that is what a virus does-modifying the ISR's.

Viruses are classified on the basis of their mode of existence and there are three categories of viruses which are as follows :

1. BOOT Infectors

As the name suggests, they are characterised by the fact that they physically reside in the boot sector [0 (zero)] sector of the disk. A system infected by such a virus will have the virus residing in a particular area of the disk rather than in a program file. These viruses get loaded soon after the Power on Self Test. They sometimes have the capability to trap soft booting (i.e. CTRL+ ALT+DEL) and remain in control even if the system is booted from a non-infected floppy, thereby contaminating the clean floppy.

Boot infectors displaces information originally residing on the location, which they occupy. While writing onto the boot sector, the virus ensures that the boot record is not deleted. Once the virus is loaded, it automatically transfers control to the area where the boot record is available. The reason behind doing this is that the boot record contains instructions to read IBMBIO.COM and IBMDOS.COM and if these files are not readable, access to the disk is not possible, and so the virus becomes ineffective.

Boot infectors typically create "Bad sectors". Boot infectors are the types, which once loaded would stay in the memory until the system is shut off, and until the disk reformats.

2. SYSTEM Infectors

This second category of viruses deals with the components of the system itself. All machines without exception require an operating system in order to create an environment in which the operator works. In MS-DOS, COMMAND.COM contains all the internal commands. If no such command file exists, commands such as COPY, DIR etc. are not loaded onto the memory when the machine is booted. The System Infectors attach themselves to a file such as COMMAND.COM or other memory resident files and manipulate these files.

System infectors differ from Boot infectors in the sense that system infectors gain control after the computer is booted and infects the hard disk or bootable floppies, which contain the appropriate system files only. They have another peculiarity that they may activate after a given period of time or may instantly begin subtle modifications in system processing such as, increasing the time to perform system functions, scrambling of data, or modification of systems error messages or information messages.

3. GENERAL .COM or .EXE Infectors

From the infection point of view, these viruses are most dangerous and devastating of the three classes of viruses. They attach themselves to program files and can spread to almost any executable program in any system. These viruses change the original program instructions into a "jump" to its own code and follows that code with a return to the original program. As a result, whenever the program is executed, the virus gets loaded and executed first and then allows the original program to proceed. It remains memory resident and infects each and every program that is loaded for execution.

By attaching themselves to EXE or COM files, they alter the file size and sometimes multiple infections renders program files too large to be accommodated in the memory.

Example of computer virus are :

(1) Scores Virus

(2) Brain Virus

(3) Lehigh Virus

(c) What are Screen Savers? Write steps to set-up a screen saver for your computer. *5*

Ans. Refer to Dec-2005, Q.No.-3(a), Page No.-161

(d) What are Macros? Mention the uses of macros. Write steps for recording and running a macro with the help of an example. *6*

Ans. A Macro is a series of Word commands grouped together as a single document to make everyday tasks easier. It can be assigned to a toolbar, a menu, a shortcut key and run it by simply clicking a button, selecting a menu choice or pressing a key combination. Macros are instructions in Word's macros language Word Basic.

Some typical uses of Macros are :

- To speed up routing, editing and formatting
- To combine more than one command
- To make an option in a dialog box more accessible
- To automate a complex series of tasks.

Recording a Macro

It's easy to create a Macro: you start the Word macro recorder and record a sequence of actions, then stop the recorder and edit the macro if needed. You can then run the macro whenever you need to perform that same set of actions. For example if you often need to display as much of a document as possible, you can record a macro that maximizes the document window and then hides the horizontal ruler, toolbars and scroll bars.

The macros recorder cannot record mouse actions in document text. You must use the keyboard when recording such actions as moving the insertion point and selecting text. However, you can use the mouse to choose commands and select options when you're recording a macro.

There are three ways to start the macro recorder:

- Double-click REC on the status bar.
- Select Tools–Macro, then click the Record button in the Macro dialog box.

• Click the Record button on the Macro toolbar.

To Record A Macro

1. Start the macro recorder by selecting any of the three options described earlier. The Record Macro dialog box appears.

2. Enter a name for the Macro in the Record Macro Name box. If you don't give your macro a name, Word will name it Macro 1, Macro 2, and so on. No spaces, commas, or periods allowed in the name.

3. Enter a description of what the macro does in the Description box. This is optional and you can use upto 255 characters.

4. To assign a macro to a toolbar, a menu or a keyboard shortcut, click the appropriate button.

5. If the current document is attached to a template other than the Normal template, select either that template or Normal in the Make available to box. If the current document is attached to the Normal template the macro is automatically stored in the Normal template.

6. Choose OK, then perform the actions you want to record.

7. To stop recording the macro, do one of following :

• Double–click REC on the status bar.

• Click the stop button on the Macro Recorder toolbar.

Running A Macro

Once you have recorded your macro, you can assign it to a toolbar, a menu or a shortcut key combination. You can then run it as you would a normal Word command or feature.

If you don't want to assign a macro to a toolbar, or key combination-perhaps you simply have too many macros, or use some of them too seldom to merit having them available all the time, you can also run a macro by choosing Tools–Macro, selecting the macro name in the Macro dialog box, and clicking the Run button.

If you've got everything right, your macro will perform the actions you taught it to do. If something is wrong, you may have to edit it.

(e) Write the steps involved in creating a presentation using Powerpoint to include the following tasks and by selecting the corresponding slide layout(s): *6*

(i) To include a title for the presentation

Ans. To include a title for the presentation

A title slide is the first slide that will be displayed in your presentation. A title slide is divided into two parts – the top part for the title and the bottom part for the sub–title or the topic.

To create a title slide

1) Select New from the file menu, to display the presentation dialog box.

2) Click the blank presentation, and then OK

3) Select title slide from the auto layout dialog box and click on OK.

4) It will display the blank title slide to enter information.

5) Type the title and sub–title.

(ii) To include a chart and text on the same slide

Ans. To include a chart and text on the same slide.

A chart or graph can be created and viewed in different formats, as a pie, bar, column and so on. Legends, titles and data tables can be added to improve readability.

To include a chart

1) Click on the new slide button on the status bar to display auto layout dialog box.

2) Select a slide layout which can include both chart and text.

3) Click on the OK button.

4) It will display the blank graph layout slide.

5) Double click on the graph box marked as "Double click to add graph" to go in the graph mode. Now you can create and modify the graph.

(iii) Bulleted lists

Ans. Bulleted Lists

(1) Select the text or paragraphs you want to add bullet.

(2) Click the format menu and choose Bullets and Numbering. The bullets and Numbering dialog box appears.

(3) Click the Bulleted tab.

(4) Select the bullet.

(5) In the size: spin box, enter the bullet size you want as a percentage of the text size.

(6) In the color : spin box, choose the color of the bullet you want.

(iv) Media clip and some text

Ans. Media clip

(1) Select the slide where you want to add a picture or media clip.

(2) On the drawing toolbar, click Insert Clip art. The Insert Clip Art dialog box appears.

(3) Click the pictures tab or sounds tab or motion clips tab and then from the category choose the descried clip.

(4) After selecting the clip, click the picture and then choose insert clip. Alternatively right click the mouse and choose insert.

(5) When you are finished using the clip gallery, click the close button on the clipart gallery title bar.

(v) Text over some objects

Ans. Text over some objects

You can place text anywhere on a slide without being restricted to using a placeholders.

(1) On the Drawing toolbar, click text box.

(2) Position mouse pointer at the place where you want to add text and then click it. A new text box appears.

(3) Enter the text you want to add. The text box expands to accommodate the new text.

(4) When finish typing the text, click anywhere on the blank slide.

(vi) Text in the form of columns

Ans. Text in the form of columns

Tables are used to display text in a columnar form

To create a table

(1) Click on new slide button on the status bar to display auto layout dialog box.

(2) Select table layout from the Autolayout list and then click on OK to display a blank table presentation slide. From where you can add table.

(3) Double click on table box to display Insert table dialog box.

(4) Type number of columns and number of rows in respective boxes of your requirement and click on OK to go in word table (rows and columns) form.

(5) And lastly type your information in the cells.

2. (a) What are Document Templates? List their uses. Explain the format of at least three commonly used document templates and write the steps to use them in your document. ***5***

Ans. Every Microsoft word document is based on a template. A template determines the basic structure for a document and contains document settings such as Autotext entries, fonts, key assignments, macros, menus, page layout, special formatting, and styles.

Global templates, including the normal template, contain settings that are available to all documents.

Document templates, such as the memo or fax templates in the templates dialog box, contain settings that are available only to documents based on that template.

Templates can help you do work faster on a particular type of documents. Word provides documents templates, such as memos, reports, business letters, fax form invoices etc. You can use any of the document template as it is or tailor it to your specific requirements. Template avoid the routine repetitive work of creating new documents.

Steps to create a document from a document template :

(1) When you select new from file menu, you are shown templates from which you can choose.

(2) When you pick a template and create a new document based on that template, the template remains "attached" to the document.

(3) Any text that is in the template will be the start of your new document.

(4) All styles in the template used in the document will become defined in the document.

(5) Autotext entries, Macros, Keyboard, customizations and toolbars in the template are available to the document.

Commonly used document templates are :

(1) Wed page template : – It provides you a template to create a elegant web page. Ready made wed pages of various designs are present.

(2) Fax template : – Allows you to create a fax without repetitive work.

(3) Letters template : – Provides a boilerplate for a new letters. It is basically a detailed documents with preset text and formatting on which a new document can be based by amending them according to our requirements.

(b) What do you understand by formatting a disk? Write steps for formatting a disk and explain the various options for formatting a disk. *5*

Ans. Formatting a disk means establishing the tracks and sectors on the disk where files will be stored. Beware that formatting a disk removes all information from the disk, you cannot format a disk if there are file open on that disk. If the disk has been compressed, use DriveSpace, or other compression software, to format the disk.

To format a disk

1. If the disk you want to format is a floppy disk, insert it into its drive. Otherwise, go to step 2.

2. Double–click the My Computer icon, and then click the icon for the disk you want to format. Be sure not to double–click the disk icon, because you cannot format a disk if it is open in My Computer or Windows Explorer.

3. On the File menu, click format.

The various options for formatting disks are :

Capacity	It could be low–density or high–density.
Format Type : Quick (erase)	Formats the disk without checking for errors.
Format Type : Full	Checks for the disk errors and then reformats it.
Format Type : Copy System files Only	Copies the system files to the formatted disk to make it bootable.
Label	Type the label name for the disk.
No Label	This option is selected if you do not require the label name for the disk after formatting it.
Display Summary when finished	To get information about the bad sectors (if any) after the disk is formatted.
Copy System Files	Copies the system files during the formatting process.

3. (a) Differentiate the following: *5*

(i) Volatile and Non-volatile memory

Ans. Refer to Dec-2003, Q.No.-3(a)(ii), Page No.-73

(ii) Magnetic disk and Magnetic tape

Ans. Magnetic disk & tape

Magnetic disk & tape are primary computer storage media. The choice depends on accessing requirements. Disk is direct; tape is sequential. Locating a program or data on disk takes a fraction of a second. On tape, it can take several seconds or even minutes.

Tapes have traditionally been used for backup and archival storage, and tape libraries with robotic mechanisms are common in large enterprises. For a while, single tape drives were popular for desktop computers, but were eclipsed by Zip disks, CD-Rs, CD-RWs and other removable magnetic disk media .

(b) List all the layers in OSI reference model. Also, explain the functions and services offered by each and every layer. *5*

Ans. The Open Systems Interconnection Basic Reference Model (OSI Reference Model or OSI Model for short) is a layered, abstract description for communications and computer network protocol design, developed as part of Open Systems Interconnection initiative. It is also called the OSI seven layer model.

Description of OSI layers

OSI Model			
	Data unit	**Layer**	**Function**
Host layers	Data	**Application**	Network process to application
		Presentation	Data representation and encryption
		Session	Interhost communication
	Segments	**Transport**	End-of-end conditions and reliability (TCP)
Media Layers	Packets	**Network**	Path determination and logical addressing (IP)
	Frames	**Data link**	Physical addressing (MAC & LLC)
	Bits	**Physical**	Media, signal and binary transmission

Layer 7: Application layer : The application layer is the seventh level of the seven-layer OSI model. It interfaces directly to and performs common application services for the application processes; it also issues requests to the presentation layer. The common application layer services provide semantic conversion between associated application processes.

Layer 6: Presentation layer : The Presentation layer transforms data to provide a standard interface for the Application layer. MIME encoding, data encryption and similar manipulation of the presentation is done at this layer to present the data as a service or protocol developer sees fit..

Layer 5: Session layer : The Session layer controls the dialogues/connections (sessions) between computers. It establishes, manages and terminates the connections between the local and remote application. It provides for either full-duplex or half-duplex operation, and establishes checkpointing, adjournment, termination, and restart procedures. The OSI model made this layer responsible for "graceful close" of sessions, which is a property of TCP, and also for session checkpointing and recovery, which is not usually used in the Internet protocols suite.

Layer 4: Transport layer : The Transport layer provides transparent transfer of data between end users, thus relieving the upper layers from any concern while providing reliable data transfer. The transport layer controls the reliability of a given link through flow control, segmentation/desegmentation, and error control. Some protocols are state and connection oriented. This means that the transport layer can keep track of the packets and retransmit those that fail. The best known example of a layer 4 protocol is the Transmission Control Protocol (TCP).

Layer 3: Network layer : The Network layer provides the functional and procedural means of transferring variable length data sequences from a source to a destination via one or more networks while maintaining the quality of service requested by the Transport layer. The Network layer performs network routing functions, and might also perform segmentation/desegmentation, and report delivery errors. Routers operate at this layer—sending data throughout the extended network and making the Internet possible. This is a logical addressing scheme – values are chosen by the network engineer. The addressing scheme is hierarchical. The best known example of a layer 3 protocol is the Internet Protocol (IP).

Layer 2: Data Link layer : The Data Link layer provides the functional and procedural means to transfer data between network entities and to detect and possibly correct errors that may occur in the Physical layer. The best known example of this is Ethernet. Other examples of data link protocols are HDLC and ADCCP for point-to-point or packet-switched networks and Aloha for local area networks. It arranges bits from physical layer into logical chunks of data, known as frames.

This is the layer at which the bridges and switches operate

Layer 1: Physical layer : The Physical layer defines all the electrical and physical specifications for devices. This includes the layout of pins, voltages, and cable specifications. Hubs, repeaters, network adapters and Host Bus Adapters (HBAs used in Storage Area Networks) are physical-layer devices. The major functions and services performed by the physical layer are:

(1) Establishment and termination of a connection to a communications medium.

(2) Participation in the process whereby the communication resources are effectively shared among multiple users. For example, contention resolution and flow control.

(3) Modulation, or conversion between the representation of digital data in user equipment and the corresponding signals transmitted over a communications channel. These are signals operating over the physical cabling (such as copper and fiber optic) or over a radio link.

4. (a) What is an operating system? Mention the types of operating systems and explain any two of them in detail. *5*

Ans. Overview of Operating System : An Operating System is a master software that acts as an intermediary between the users of a computer and the computer hardware. It is considered as the brains of a computer system. It controls the internal activities of the computer hardware and provides user interface. In fact, it can be looked upon as enveloping the hardware.

One of the primary jobs of an Operating System is to work as an interface between the user and the hardware. This interface enables a user to utilize hardware resources very efficiently.

Types of Operating Systems : Operating Systems may be classified into the following types:

(a) Single-use Operating System

(b) Multiuser Operating System

(c) Single-tasking Operating System

(d) Multitasking Operating System

(e) Real–time Operating System

(f) Network Operating System

(g) Distributed Operating System

Single-user Operating System : Operating System which allows only one user to work on a computer at a time is known as single user Operating system. Examples include MS–DOS, Windows 9x etc.

Multiuser Operating System : A Multiuser operating system allows a number of users to work together on a single computer. UNIX is a multiuser operating system. It is not that all users will bump on a computer at the same time. Each user will be provided with a terminal and all such terminals will be connected to the single computer.

Single-tasking Operating System : Operating system which can execute a single job at a time is known as Single-tasking operating system. For example, MS–DOS is a single tasking operating system because you can open and run only one application in DOS, at one time.

Multitasking Operating System : Multitasking operating system allows the user to perform more than one job at the same time on a computer. Most of today's operating systems such as Windows 9X, OS/2, UNIX, LINUX etc. support multitasking. For example, when you open MS-Word and Internet Explorer at the same time, the Windows operating system is doing multitasking.

Real-time Operating System : Real-time Operating System work towards providing immediate processing and also responding user's commands in a very short time. Such a operating system is more commonly used in chemical industry for process control and scientific processing like airplane control and space vehicle control operations. Success of a real time system does not depend only on the correctness of the result, but also on the timeliness of the result. A correct answer obtained after the expiration of time limit is a bad as a wrong answer. Some examples of real time operating systems are HP–RT and VTWorks.

Network Operating System (NOS) : Network Operating System (NOS) is an operating system specifically designed to support interconnection of several computers. NOS provides support for multiuser operations as well as administrative, security and network management functions. Some examples of NOSs are Novell's Netware, Microsoft's Windows NT, and Artisoft LANtastic etc.

Distributed Operating System : A Distributed Operating System hides the existence of multiple computers (interconnected by a network) from the user. That is, the user remains unaware of the fact that many computers are being used to process the data. These computers may be located at many places around the globe. Distributed Operating System provides single-system image to its users. Each computer in a distributed computing system processes a part of the global distributed operating system. All these computers work in close coordination with each other. Processes and system resources are managed globally, and controlled from specific locations.

User view the complete system as a "virtual uniprocessor" and not as a collection of machines. The distributed operating system works towards generating this illusion.

(b) Explain the two different ways by which you can connect to the network. *3*

Ans. There are different ways by which we can connect to the network : –

(i) Dial up connection

(ii) ISDN, ADSL and leased line connections

(iii) Satellite Connections

Dial up connections : To access the Internet via a phone line, the concept is : connect your commuter to the telephone system using a regular phone line (with a modem). To start work, you run a communication program to dial the phone and establish a connection with a remote Internet host. Once the connection is established, you log in to the serves by typing your username and password.

ISDN and Leased Line Connections : This is a permanent connection, which can be set up over a telephone line using a modem or a router. These are best suited for larger organisations. ISDN and ADSL allow the user to connect to another computer at a speed which is much faster than even the fastest modem because it is digital.

(c) Explain any two different ways of protecting the Word-document. *2*

Ans. Protecting Documents

Protecting a document implies saving it from being changed either accidentally by some other user. A document can be protected in two ways:

1. Opening document as read only.

When a document is opened a read–only, the user cannot make any changes to the document. This can be achieved by selecting the read–only check box in the Open dialog box. This read–only option will not allow any changes in the document to be saved.

2. Protecting a document with a password.

The other way to protect a document is to use the Protection Password, which is typed in the Protection Password box. In this way, the users who know the password can only open the document. These passwords can be changed and deleted too.

5. (a) Explain the measures to be taken to provide network security. *4*

Ans. The protection required for networked systems is much more extensive as physical security measures are totally inadequate; it is also extremely difficult to know who, when and how someone is accessing your data; in LANs, generally there would be one server which holds the shareable data on network and services the requests of various nodes; the normal method used is password identity for permitting access; the measures that can be adopted for additional security are:

(a) Keep the servers away and limit physical access to them.

(b) Run servers in the background mode; thus the server can be booked on, for use in the network, but, for direct use of the server, a separate password would be necessary.

(c) Some networks provide auditing facilities, which can be used to advantage.

(d) Be aware that the network cables can be taped, so try and shield or conceal them to prevent easy access; if possible use optical fibre;

(e) Use codes and ciphers in data communication; remember, however, that this would impose considerable overheads on your resources;

(f) Use fibre-optic cables for highly sensitive networks as they are difficult to tap; however, here too it may be possible to steal data through sensing the perturbations of the fibre itself;

(g) Prohibit the use of passwords embedded in communication access scripts; if this is unavoidable, use encryption for passwords;
(h) Consider the use of see-through devices for any system accessed through networks or through dial up.

(b) What is the function of the Briefcase in Windows 95? Explain the steps to use the Briefcase. *3*

Ans. Briefcase : Briefcase is designed for mobile users who carry portable computers with them while travelling. These users work at home and while travelling on the road, therefore they can use Briefcase to help keep the various copies of the files updated.
The principle behind Briefcase is that, the user has multiple copies of files on different systems. The Briefcase keeps track of which files are the most recent and update the files that do not have the most recent data.
To use Briefcase, follow the steps given below:
1. Drag files from shared folders on your computer to the Briefcase icon on your portable computer.
2. After you finish working on the files on the portable computer, reconnect to your main computer.
3. Click Update All in Briefcase to automatically replace the unmodified files on your main computer with the modified files in your Briefcase. The files on your main computer are automatically revised; you do not need to move the files you worked on out of Briefcase or delete the existing copies.
When you are copying files from your main computer into Briefcase, the two computers must be connected, either over a network or by a cable.
If you don't see a Briefcase icon on your desktop, follow the step given below:
1. Click on Settings from the Start menu, then click on Control Panel, and finally double–click on Add/Remove programs objects to open the Add/Remove Programs dialog box.
2. Click Accessories, and then click Details.
3. Click the check box for Briefcase to mark it for installation, and then click OK.

(c) With the help of a diagram, explain the synchronous and asynchronous mode of transmission. *3*

Ans. Modes of Data Transmission : There are two methods of timing control for reception of bits. The transmission modes corresponding to these two methods are called asynchronous transmission and synchronous transmission.
Asynchronous Transmission : Asynchronous transmission refers to the case when the sending end commences transmission of bytes at any instant of time. Only one byte is sent at a time and there is no time relation between consecutive bytes, i.e., after sending a byte, the next byte can be sent after arbitrary delay. In the idle state, when no byte is being transmitted, the polarity of the electrical signal corresponds to "1".

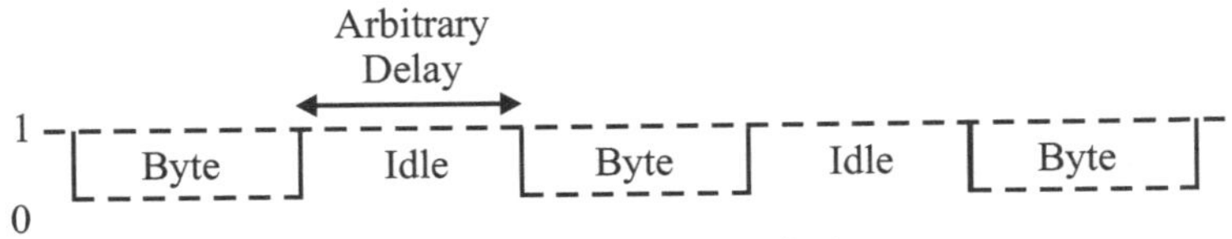

Asynchronous Transmission

Due to the arbitrary delay between consecutive bytes, the time occurrences of the clock pulses at the receiving end need to be synchronized repeatedly for each byte. This is achieved by providing two extra bits, a start bit at the beginning and a stop bit at the end of a byte. The start bit is always "0" and is prefixed to each byte. The stop bit is always "1" and is suffixed to each byte and is usually 1, 1.5, or 2 bits.

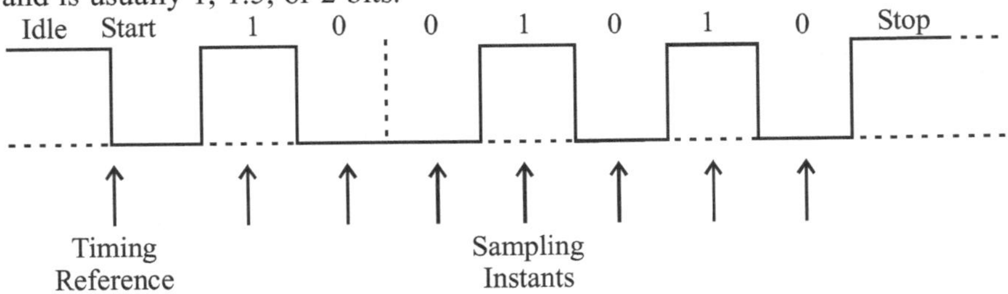

Start and Stop Bits

Synchronous Transmission : A synchronous action, unlike an asynchronous action, is carried out under the control of a timing source. In synchronous transmission, bits are always synchronized to a reference clock irrespective of the bytes they belong to. Either the receiver clock is derived by the modem from the transmitted signal or a separate clock signal must accompany the data from the transmitter to the receiver. There is no start or stop bit. Bytes are transmitted as a block (group of bytes) in a continuous stream of bits. Even the inter block idle time is filled with idle characters.

Continuous transmission of bits enables the receiver to extract the clock from the incoming electrical signal. As this clock is inherently synchronized to the bits, the job of the receiver becomes simpler.

There is, however, still one problem. The bytes lose their identity and their boundaries need to be identified. Therefore, a unique sequence of fixed number of bits, called flag, is prefixed to each block. The flag identifies the start of a block. The receiver first detects the flag and then identifies the boundaries of different bytes using counter. Just after the flag there is first bit of the first byte.

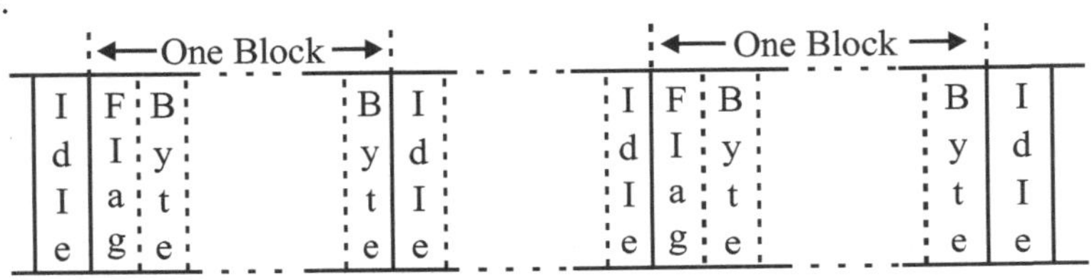

Synchronous Transmission

CS – 611: COMPUTER FUNDAMENTALS AND PC SOFTWARE
Dec, 2007

Note: *Question number 1 is* ***compulsory****. Attempt any* ***three*** *questions from the rest.*

Q1. (a) Explain the hierarchical memory system of a computer system.
Ans. Memory hierarchy ⇒ The levels of memory in a computer. From fastest to slowest speed, they are:
1. CPU registers
2. L1 cache
3. L2 cache
4. Main memory
5. Virtual memory

The hierarch arrangement of storage is current computer architectures is called the memory hierarchy. Each level of the hierarchy is of higher speed and lower latency, and is of smaller size, than lower levels. Most modern CPUs are so fast that for most program workloads the locality of reference of memory accesses, and the efficiency of the caching and memory transfer between different levels of the hierarchy, is the practical limitation on processing speed. As a result, the CPU spends much of its time idling waiting for memory I/O to complete.

The memory hierarchy in most computers is as follows:
Processor register → fastest possible access, only hundreds of bytes
Level 1 (L1) cache → often accessed in just a few cycles, usually tens of Kilobytes
Level 2 (L2) cachehigher latency than L1 by 2x to 10, often 512KB or more.
Level 3 (L3) cache(optional) higher latency than L2, often multiple MB's

Memory Hierarchy

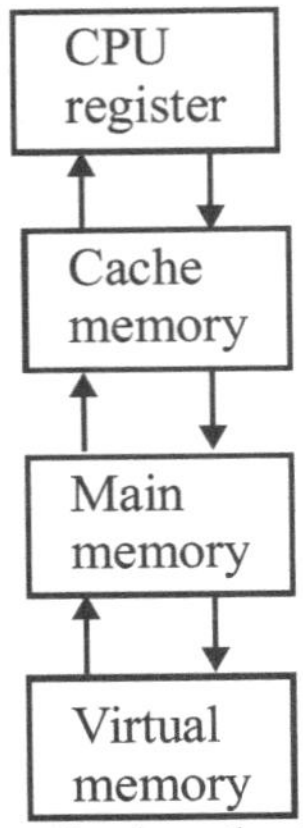

•**Main memory (DRAM)** may take hundreds of cycles, but can be multiple gigabytes

•**Disk storage**hundreds of thousands of cycles latency, but very large

Need of cache and Main memory: The above principles suggest that we should try to keep recently accessed items in the fastest memory. Because the smaller memories are more expensive and faster, we want to use smaller memories to try to hold the most recently accessed items close to the CPU and successively larger (and slower, and less expensive) memories as we move away from the CPU. This type of organization is called a memory hierarchy. Two important levels of the memory hierarchy are the cache and virtual memory. Primary storage is used to store data that is likely to be in active use, so it is usually faster than long-term secondary storage. Today, many computers have cache memory located in between the central processing unit and primary storage in order to further increase speed. A particular location in storage is selected by its physical memory address. That address remains the same, no matter how the particular value stored there changes

Memory hierarchy is required for increased processing speed. This hierarchy permits fetching of instructions and operands at a rate that is high enough to prevent pipeline stalls. A typical hierarchy includes high-speed registers, cache, and/or buffers located on the CPU chip, and complex memory management schemes to support off-chip cache and memory devices.

(b) Explain the functioning of the following computer devices in brief:
(i) Liquid crystal display (LCD) monitor

Ans. A liquid crystal display (LCD) is a thin, flat display device made up of any number of color or monochrome pixels arrayed in front of a light source or reflector. It is often utilized in battery-powered electronic devices because it uses very small amounts of electric power.

Functioning: Each pixel of an LCD typically consists of a layer of molecules aligned between two transparent electrodes, and two polarizing filters, the axes of transmission of which are (in most of the cases) perpendicular to each other. With no liquid crystal between the polarizing filters, light passing through the first filter would be blocked by the second (crossed) polarizer.

The surface of the electrodes that are in contact with the liquid crystal material are treated so as to align the liquid crystal molecules in a particular direction. This treatment typically consists of a thin polymer layer that is unidirectionally rubbed using, for example, a cloth. The direction of the liquid crystal alignment is then defined by the direction of rubbing. Electrodes are made of a transparent conductor called "ITO" or Indium Tin Oxide.

Before applying an electric field, the orientation of the liquid crystal molecules is determined by the alignment at the surface. In a twisted nematic device (still the most common liquid crystal device), the surface alignment directions at the two electrodes are perpendicular to each other, and so the molecules arrange themselves in a helical structure, or twist. Because the liquid crystal material is birefringent, light passing through on e polarizing filter is rotated by the liquid crystal helix as it passes through the liquid crystal layer, allowing it to pass through the second polarized filter. Half of the incident light is absorbed by the first polarizing filter, but otherwise the entire assembly is transparent.

When a voltage is applied across the electrodes, a torque acts to align the liquid crystal molecules parallel to the electric field, distorting the helical structure (this is resisted by elastic forces since the molecules are constrained at the surfaces). This reduces the rotation of the polarization of the incident light, and the device appears gray. If the applied voltage is large enough, the liquid crystal molecules in the center of the layer are almost completely untwisted and the polarization of the incident light is not rotated as it passes through the liquid crystal layer. This light will then be mainly polarized perpendicular to the second crystal layer. This light will then be mainly polarized perpendicular to the second filter, and thus be blocked and the pixel will appear appear black. By controlling the voltage applied across the liquid crystal layer in each pixel, light can be allowed to pass through in varying amounts thus constituting different levels of gray.

(ii) Projection display

Ans. Projection display systems:- Unlike their direct-view counterparts, a projection display setup relies on the projection of an image onto a screen for viewing purposes. Front and rear projection systems fall within this sub-category; the main difference between these two process is that front projection utilizes a reflective screen surface while rear projection makes use of a transmissive screen surface. Projection displays work best in dimly lit environment. In particular, a front projection setup requires a darkened room-similar to a movie theater - for the best results.

UP to a few years ago, the CRT was the only display technology you could choose for your TV. In reality, you had no choice. You had hundreds of models of TVs on the shelves of big electronic superstores, but inside they were more or less the same - a cathode ray tube as the your TV display device.

This is no longer true. LCD technology used extensively in laptop screens has now come up to 40 inches and over, while at the larger end, plasma technology is allowing for really big televisions - up to 80 inches diagonal at just 4 inches deep, and which can hang on a wall!

The availability of new direct-view display technologies imply that now you have the possibility to choose the most suitable technology for your requirements. This is however subject to your budget limitations - these new technologies do not come cheap, under certain requirements, a projection tv set-up may be a more appropriate and cheaper alternative worth considering.

(iii) Inkjet printer

Ans. Inkjet Printer ⇒ A printer that creates characters and images by spraying fine streams of ink onto paper at high speeds. Inkjet printers are relatively inexpensive and produce high quality text and graphics in both black and white and colour. Inkjet printers are the most common type of computer printer; and industry and commerce also use them extensively for special-purpose applications. For example, many ATMs, stock control systems, and cash registers use an inkjets are usually inexpensive, quiet, reasonably fast, and many models can produce high quality output Compared to earlier consumer-oriented printers, ink jets have a number of advantages. They can print finer, smoother details through higher print head resolution, and many ink jets with photorealistic-quality color printing are widely available.

Difference between inkjet or Dotmatrix printer:

- **Quality of type**The output produced by printers is said to be either letter quality (as good as a type writer), near letter quality, or draft quality., ink-jet printers produce letter-quality type. Some dot-matrix printers claim letter-quality print, but if you look closely, you can see the difference.

•Impact or non-Impact → Impact printers include all printers that work by striking an ink ribbon. dot-matrix, printers are impact printers. Non-impact printers include ink-jet printers. The important difference between impact and non-impact printers is that impact printers are much noisier.

•fronts → Some printers, notably dot-matrix printers, are limited to one or a few fonts. In contrast, and ink-jet printers are capable of printing an almost unlimited variety of fonts.

•Price → dot matrix printers are relatively cheaper than inkjet printers

(c) Explain the usage of the following hardware devices in LAN:

(i) BridgeA bridge is like a smart repeater. Bridges, like repeaters, can connect two network segments, but bridges are a little smarter about the data they transport. Most bridges have the capacity to listen to the network and figure out the address of each computer on both sides of the bridge. The bridge can the inspect each message that comes from one side and broadcast it to the other side of the bridge, if the message is intended for a computer that is on the other side. If the packet's destination is on the same side of the bridge, it is discarded. This creates a more efficient scheme for data transport. The bridge

• Can connect segments that use different cable media types, like 10BaseT (Twister Pair) and 10Base5 (Coaxial).

•Cannot connect different transport protocols - like Ethernet and Token Ring networks.

(ii) Routers

Ans. Routers ⇒ A router is like super-intelligent bridge. The can link multiple LANs and look deeper into the data packet to determine its destination. Routers not only know the addresses of the computers on the network but are aware off all the other bridges and routers on the network and can decide the most efficient path in which to sent data. The router uses a routing table of network addresses to determine where to forward the packet. When a router receives data, it discards the outer packet or frame or MAC address, repackages the data with network address, and retransmits the signal. By stripping off the outer layers of data before sending a packet, the total number of bits moving across the network is reduced. The router at the receiving end then repackages the data into a packet of frame that is appropriate for its network. There are ROUTABLE and NON-ROUTABLE products.

• TCP/IP and IPX/SPX are routable

• Net BEUI is non-routable because it cannot work out of its own subnet

(iii) Gateways

Ans. Gateways ⇒ A gateway is like a super-intelligent router. Gateways are designed to connect radically different networks. Although slower than a bridge or router, a gateway has its own processor and memory to perform complex functions such as interpreting between computers that speak different languages through both protocol and bandwidth conversion. A gateway can convert a TCP/IP packet to a NetWare IPX packet and vice versa. An example of a gateway is a messaging gateway, which converts messages between different protocols.

(d) List the minimum hardware requirements for running multimedia applications in Windows 95.

Ans. The minimum requirements for running multimedia applications are:

1. CD-ROM Drive :- Reads compact disks in the form of audio or CD-ROM. A CD-ROM holds data (perhaps audio as well). Newer CD-ROM drives will read CD-R (Writable CDs) and CD-RW (RE Writable CDs). The speed of a CD-ROM drive is not usually very important except when installing programs, running games that require use of the CD-ROM drive.

2. Video Card :-This component is used to transfer data to your monitor so that is can be displayed. Today's video cards have a variety of "3D" capabilities. 3D video cards are only needed for playing games though. When playing 3D games, the video card is the most important component.

3. Mouse:-This device is used to move a pointer on your screen, which is a form of navigation. A mouse can be a big help when the operating system you sued is based on a GUI (graphical used interface). A mouse is a small handheld pointing device that is used mostly in graphics programs to manipulate what is on the screen. The mouse has two parts: what you can feel and touch (usually have a body and two "buttons"); and the software which is the program that controls the mouse and allows your applications to access it.

4. CPU is also known as the processor or microprocessor. Examples (in roughly ascending order of performance) include Pentium, Pentium with MMX, Cyrix M2, AMD K6, Celeron, K6-III, Pentium II, Celeron-A, Duron, Pentium III, Thunderbird, Athlon. IN the Mac market, the Power PC 750 processor (sometimes listed as "G3") is a popular CPU found in IMac computers. And now with P-IV processors realistic sound and video performance can be enjoyed.

5. Memory:- A computer's random-access memory. Memory temporarily holds data and instructions for the CPU. Defined as the internal storage areas of the computer. The most common forms are ROM (Read Only Memory) and RAM (Random Access Memory). This is where the computer stores information as it is working on it. It is temporary storage usually in the form of RAM chips. The computer only works on information in its memory. When it is done, it can be stored to disk. Higher the capacity of RAM easier will be the faster will be the execution of larger programs like playing a large size video file.

6. Super VGA :-Video graphics with higher resolution than VGA. Display monitors receive instructions from a video card that, among other functions, allow for colour display and screen resolution. VGA (Video Gate Array or Video Graphics Adapter) was a standard introduced by IBM in the 1980s that had a maximum resolution of 640×480 pixels with 16 colours. Although SVGA features differ according to individual manufactures, the standard allows for resolutions of up to 1600 ×1200 pixels and colour display capabilities from 256 colours to 16 million colours. Standards for video display are reviewed by a number of graphic manufactures known as the Video Electronics Standards Association (VESA).

(e) List the three basic steps involved in cryptanalysis.

Ans. Cryptanalysis: The interpretation of secret communications without any previous knowledge of the system or the key is called cryptanalysis. In the case of modern cryptosystem, this requires extensive theoretical study, unusual power of observation, inductive and deductive reasoning, great concentration and perseverance. Also necessary are vivid imagination guided by good judgement. This has to be supplemented by a special aptitude and intuition gained from long and varied practical experience.

Following are the steps involved in cryptanalysis:

(a) arrangement and rearrangement of data to disclose non-random characteristics or manifestations (e.g., in frequency counts, repetitions, patterns, and symmetrical phenomena);

(b) an explanation of the non-random characteristics when recognised. The requirements for the first step are experience or ingenuity and time-which may be appreciably reduced by the use of machine aids; for the second step, experience or statistics; and for the third step, experience or imagination, and intelligence.

(c) recognition of the non-random characteristics or manifestations when disclosed;

Q2. (a) How does the GUI make the use of software easy? List and explain any three MS WORD editing and proofing tools.

Ans. GUI"Graphical User Interface" Though the use of a GUI, one may operate a computer by interacting with pictures and menus on the screen, as opposed to entering commands directly through the keyboard. The use of a

GUI requires an input device in addition to the keyboard (such as a mouse, trackball, touchscreen, or stylus pad). The term GUI is usually pronounced "gooey", which makes it particularly fun to slip into conversation. It makes easy the use of software through the use of its components.

(i) Windowing System → It allows programs to display multiple applications at the same time. Windowing system include programming tools for building movable and resizable windows, menus, dialog boxes and other items on the display. Some GUI contain properly windowing system such as Macintosh. Other uses the common windowing system such as X windows or simple X.

(ii) An imaging Model → The imaging model defines how fonts and graphics are created on the screen. Imaging model handle for example, typeface and size in a word processor or curve and lines in a drawing program.

This component of the system environment has taken on increasing sophistication as application incorporate complex curves, colors, shading and dimensions.

(iii) An Application program interface → API is a set of programming language functions that allow the programmer to specify how the actual application will control the menus scrollbars and icons that appear on the screen.

- Linking windowing models.
- APIs align with particular GUIs.
- Its feature varies from package to package .

Microsoft Word Editing and Proofing Tools are a collection of editing technologies that enable users to proof documents. The tools include spelling and grammar checkers, AutoCorrect lists, AutoSummarize capabilities for Microsoft Word, and more. Also included are language-specific tools such as Input Method Editors (IMEs) for inputting text in Japanese, Korean and Chinese; Word Breakers for highlighting words in Japanese and Chinese; Korean features including a Hanja dictionary and Hanja/Hangul converter; and, additional fonts for Arabic, Chinese, Hebrew, Japanese and Korean.

Spelling Checker

The spelling checker identifies possible misspellings in a text file by comparing the contents of the file with a database of accepted spellings, and is one of the most frequently used features of Microsoft Word. But spellers can perform more sophisticated tasks then simply comparing terms from a database. For some languages, inflectional information (i.e. variations of a word) is introduced in algorithms to fine-tune the output; this is the case for highly inflectional languages such as Swedish and Romanian.

Grammar and Style Checker

The grammar checker corrects sentences using a system of rules that defines the grammatical structure of a language. Microsoft Word integrates this tool and runs it in the background, making corrections automatically.

Thesaurus

The basic function of a thesaurus is to look up synonyms for a particular word. But the thesauri in Proofing Tools perform more sophisticated tasks than simply retrieving direct synonyms for a given term from a database. Special algorithms in thesauri extract inflectional information (i.e. variations of a word) from a stem word (i.e. base word) to provide a series of synonyms with the same inflection. For example, looking up the word running, would yield the possible synonym jogging.

Auto Correct

AutoCorrect automatically detects and corrects typos, misspelled words, grammatical errors, and incorrect capitalization. For example, if you type the plus a space, then Auto Correct replaces what you have typed with "the." You can also use AutoCorrect to quickly insert text, graphics, or symbols. For example, type (c) to insert "C", or type act to insert "Acme Corporation."

Hyphenation

Hyphenation helps eliminate gaps or in justified text, and helps maintain even line lengths in narrow columns. The hyphenation tool allows a user to connect (as two words) or divide (as a word at the end of a line of print) two or more terms with a hyphen. Languages vary in their flexibility on hyphenation rules.

AutoSummarize

AutoSummarize identities the key points in a document for you to share with others or quickly scan. The tool determines key points by analyzing a document and assigning a score to each sentence. Sentences that contain words used frequently in the document are given a higher score. You can then choose a percentage of the highest-scoring sentences to display in the summary. AutoSummarize works best on well-structured documents such as reports, articles, and scientific papers.

Input Method Editors

An Input Method Editor (IME) works with the operating system to allow you to enter Asian text in Windows and enabled application - including Office 2003 - by converting your keystrokes into Asian characters. Often the only visual indication that an IME is installed on a computer is a floating toolbar for controlling the conversions, and an indicator on the Windows taskbar. Different Asian languages require different IMEs — for example, to enter Japanese text, us the Japanese IME.

(b) Write the RSA approach to encryption.

Ans. RSA approach to encryption → RSA is an Internet encryption and authentication system that uses an algorithm developed in 1977 by Ron Rivest, Adi Shamir, and Leonard Adleman. The RSA algorithm is the most commonly used encryption and authentication algorithm and is included as part of the Web browsers from Microsof and Netscape. It's also part of Lotus Notes, Intuit's Quicken, and many other products. The encryption system is owned by RSA Security. The company licenses the algorithm technologies and also sells development kits. The technologies are part of existing or proposed Web, Internet, and computing standards.

Q3. (a) Define a macro in MS WORD. With the help of an example, write the steps for creating a macro of your own choice.

Ans. Macro This is a program within a program which can carry out a preset complex function with the stroke of one or two keys. You can preset your name and address, for example, and then every time you need to use it, in a particular program, just hit the macro key that you already preset as your name and address, and it will be all printed out for you. Saves time!

It's easy to create a Macro: you start the Word macro recorder and record a sequence of actions, then stop the recorder and edit the macro if needed. The macro recorder cannot record mouse actions in document text. You must use the keyboard when recording such actions as moving the insertion point and selecting text. However, you can use the mouse to choose commands and select options when you're recording a macro.

There are three ways to start the macro recorder: Double-click REC on the status bar. Select Tools Macro, then click the Record button in the Macro dialog box.

Click the Record button on the Macro toolbar.

Following are the steps to Record a Macro:

1. Start the macro recorder by selecting any of the three options described earlier. The Record Macro dialog box appears.

2. Enter a name for the Macro in the Record Macro Name box. If you don't give your macro a name, Word will name it Macro 1, Macro 2 and so on. No spaces, commas, or period allowed in the name.

3. Enter a description of what the macro does in the Description box. This is optional and you can use upto 255 characters.

4. To assign a macro to a toolbar, a menu or a keyboard shortcut, click the appropriate button.

5. If the current document is attached to a template other than the Normal template, select either that template or Normal in the Make Macro Available to

box. If the current document is attached to the Normal template the macro is automatically stored in the Normal template.

6. Choose OK, then perform the actions you want to record.

7. To stop recording the macro, do one of following:

• Double-click REC on the status bar.

•Click the stop button on the Macro Recorder toolbar.

Running A Macro : Once you have recorded your macro, you can assign it to a toolbar. a menu or a shortcut key combination. You can then run it as you would a normal Word command or feature.

If you don't want to assign a macro to a tool bar, or key combination-perhaps you simple have too many macros, or use some of them too seldom, - you can also run a macro by choosing Tools Macro, selecting the macro name in the Macro dialog box, and clicking the Run button.

If you've got everything right, your macro will perform the actions you taught it to do. If something is wrong, you can edit it any point of time.

(b) List the steps followed to find a specific text in a given document.

Ans. MS-WORD provides some excellent features as Find and Replace, which may be used for a number of tasks with flexibility. Using these features it is possible to find a specific text in a document, search for a particular pattern of text etc. To find a particular text in a document, choose the EDIT ~ Find Option. A dialog box appears which is used to specify the text to be found. The text found by this option can be changed, by clicking the mouse at the position required in the document. The dialog box can be reused to fetch the next instance of the text.

Following steps are to followed to execute Find and Replace command.

1. Type the text to be searched in the find dialog box.

2. Click on Find Next (only to Find)

3. Click at replace on the top left hand corner (for Find & Replace). You will find another box where you can type text which has to be replaced by the found text.

4. Type the text which will replace the text.

5. Click on Replace or Replace All as per requirement.

6. Click on Close to resume editiong.

Q4. (a) Explain the following services provided by the Internet:

(i) Global Internet mail

(ii) Usenet views and news

(iii) Telnet

(i) Global Internet mail

Ans. Global Internet Mail is a personal e-mail program available to all service members that can be used from any computer with Internet access, including government systems.

While official government e-mail accounts are the most secure fonn of e-mail communication, messages sent between GI Mail accounts are more secure than those sent between public e-mail accounts.

"GI Mail offers an added layer of 'protection' to military service members and is the Department of Defense preferred alternative to commercial e-mail services.

Commercial e-mail services, such as yahoo, hotmail and AOL are outside of the DoD's control, and the confidentiality of forwarded e-mails cannot be guaranteed. GI Mail is the only DoD-approved morale Web mail service.

"These services are hosted on non-Air Force systems and could be compromised without the knowledge of military users. "On the other hand, GI Mail offers similar services and functionality as commercial programs but with the advantage of being placed inside the government network behind a firewall at Scott Air Force Base, Ill." GI Mail is sponsored and maintained by the U. S. Air Force.

(ii) Usenet views and news

Ans. Usenet Views, a Windows Forms program for viewing and analyzing Usenet statistics, they are generic in nature and can be used in a wide range of applications to show a variety of data.

Usenet news : Usenet is the set of machines that exchange articles or news tagged with one or more universally-recognized labels, called newsgroups (or "groups" for short). (Note that the tenn newsgroup is correct.)

(iii) Telnet

Ans. A terminal emulation program for TCPIIP networks such as the Internet. The Telnet program runs on your computer and connects your PC to a server on the network. You can then enter commands through the Telnet program and they will be executed as if you were entering them directly on the server console. This enables you to control the server and communicate with other servers on the network. To start a Telnet session, you must log in to a server by entering a valid username and password. Telnet is a common way to remotely control Web servers.

(b) What is the functioning ofEDI? Discuss the application-to-application EDI.

Ans. Any organization using ED! communicates with their Trading partners, in one of the two ways: (i) Exchange of date with several trading partners directly. (ii) Interaction with multiple companies through a central information clearing house. In the latter case, all transaction takes place through a third *party's computer* system, which then sends them to the appropriate receiver's computer. This enables the sender to communicate with an unlimited number of trading partners without worrying about the proprietary system audit trails, variables transmission speeds, and general computer compatibility. EDI Works in the Following Manner:

• Prior to any computer work, representatives of two companies interested in exchanging data electronically meet to specify the application in the EDI standards, which they will implement.

• The two companies exchange data electronically in the standard formats.

• Each company-adds EDI program to its computer to translate the company data into standard formats for transmission, and for the reverse translation in the data it receives. The sender transmits the database formatted in the EDI standards to the receiver who then translates the formatted message to a computer record to be processed and used internally. All transmission is checked both electronically and functionally and the protocol includes procedure for the error detection and correction. Once a company has established standardized communications with another company, it is now in a position to communicate with any other company that is also using the EDI standards. The Flow of Information in EDI is as Follows

• Collection of data for its own operational or statistical requirements, which is edited to be added to its own database.

• Extraction of Pertinent information by the company from its database, summarized if necessary and constructed into EDI transaction sets, and finally it is transmitted to the company or organization requiring it for valid reasons.

Application-to-application EDI: In EDI, in the place of traditional methods for the transmission e.g. a purchase order between a buyer and a seller, data isentered into the buyer's computer system, the same data is electronically sent into to the seller's computer system without the need for rekeying or reentry. This is normally referred to as application EDI. When EDI is fully integrated with application programs, not only does data flow electronically between trading partners without the need for rekeying, but data also flows electronically between internal applications of each of the trading partners.

5. (a) Write the steps involved in creating a PowerPoint presentation to include the following tasks:
(i) to include a title for the presentation
(ii) to include 4 bulleted lists
(iii) to include an image
(iv) to include a table with 3 rows and 4 columns

Ans. It very easy to make this type of presentation in Power point software. When you open the new file it asks to select Auto Layout where you can select a title page, a figure, bulleted text, a bar graph and an organization chart. In detail below is the explanation :

Creating a Title slide

A Title slide is the first slide that will be displayed in your presentation. A Title slide is divided into two parts- the top part for the title and the bottom part for the sub-title or the topic.

To create a Title slide

1. Select New from the File menu, to display the presentation dialog box.
2. Click the Blank Presentation, and than OK.
3. Select Title slide from the Auto Layout dialog box and click on OK.
4. It will display the blank title slide to enter information.
5. Type the title and sub-title.

To include 4 bulleted lists

1. Go to format menu
2. Select the bullets and numbering, then choose the format in which you want to include the list.

To include an image

1. Insert Menu select picture option

Then you can choose clipart, or insert from a file option.

To include a table with 3 rows and 4 columns

I. Go to insert menu, then select table. Dialogue box will appear, then enter 3 in rows and 4 in columns.

To close a presentation

Select Close from the File menu to close the current presentation.

(b) Write the essential difference between Spooling and Buffering.

Ans. Spooling => SPOOLING STANDS FOR SIMULTANEOL PERIPHERAL OPERATIONS ONLINE. Buffering and Spooling are t,., methods to increase the system performance in case of batch processing.

Buffering	Spooling
(i) It is a method of overlapping input, output and processing of a Single job. (ii) If the CPU is much faster than an input device, buffering will be a little use. iii) A holding area for data shared by devices that operate at different speeds or have different priorities. *A* buffer allows a device to operate without the delays that other devices impose.	(i) To order items or jobs in a queue before sending them to an output device such as a printer. (ii) Since it allows overlapping of more than one job, it is better approach than buffering. ((iii) Spooling is more sophisticated form of buffering and allows overlapping of input, output of more than one job.

Compare and contrast between spooling and buffering=> Spooling comes from "Simultaneous Peripheral Operation On-line", which is self-explanatory. Buffering is a general idea which involves using an intermediate entity between two mismatched interacting components in order to reduce the effects of the mismatch. Thus, data buffering uses a storage between two components operating at different speeds to allow both of them to operate without waiting for each other (upto an extent, of course). Buffering is used to implement spooling.

Feedback is the breakfast of Champions.

Ken Blanchard

You can Help other students.
"Inform any error or mistake in this book."

We and Universe
will reward you for Your Kind act.

Email at : feedback@gullybaba.com
or
WhatsApp on 9350849407

CS – 611: COMPUTER FUNDAMENTALS AND PC SOFTWARE
June, 2008

Note: *Question number 1 is* ***compulsory****. Attempt any* ***three*** *questions from the rest.*

Q1. (a) Define a Computer. Draw its Von Neumann Architecture, briefly explaining its various components.

Ans. A computer is a machine that manipulates data according to a list of instructions. The ability to store and execute lists of instructions called programs makes computers extremely versatile and distinguishes them from calculators. The Church–Turing thesis is a mathematical statement of this versatility: any computer with a certain minimum capability is, in principle, capable of performing the same tasks that any other computer can perform. Therefore, computers with capability and complexity ranging from that of a personal digital assistant to a supercomputer are all able to perform the same computational tasks given enough time and storage capacity.

Now Refer : Jan-2001, Q.No.-1(a), Page No.-142

(b) Elaborate the term "Breach of Security" and explain at least eight ways that can lead to data loss.

Ans. SECURITY: "Data or information security is the protection of data against accidental or intentional, destruction, disclosure or modification". Computer data security refers to the technological safeguards and managerial procedure, which can be applied to computer hardware, software and data to ensure that organizational assets and individual privacy are protected.

The "New Scientist" in its issue of 7 July 83 warned: "New PC users beware! PCs are the biggest threat to Computer Security. Micros are left in unguarded offices or at home, where data snoopers may steal confidential files or data, if not the machine itself".

Breaches of Security:

1. Theft of PC and Media: May sound preposterous but it is a distinct possibility. A smart person with a false calling card can take away the PC for repairs and of course never show his face again! However, electronic media like floppies and CD-ROMs are slightly safe as it is far easier to lock up floppies in a safer place.

2. Damage due to Breakage: Floppies are easily breakable. It is hard to visualize dropping PCs but it can happen if they are shifted from one place to another. More likely is that something may get dropped on the PC resulting in damage. Damage can also occur due to natural causes such as storms or floods or due to electrical or other fires.

3. Environmental Damage: The manufacturer recommends some environmental conditions like temperature and humidity ranges, voltage limits, dust micron limits etc. If the conditions in your office remain outside – these limits the PC and media are likely to get damaged.

4. Inadvertent Corruption/Loss: This can occur due to:

(i) Usage of Inferior Media: If sub-standard media is used, as it would be generally cheaper, after using it for some time it may develop faults and data held on it may become unusable. One hears about frequent corruption of data on inferior floppies.

(ii) Erasure of Files: Files may get erased from the media due to incorrect actions by the operator. Corruption may occur due to the PC being subjected to frequent power failures, wrong programming techniques or defective software.

5. Environmental losses: Excessive dust or humidity can result in corruption of disc surfaces or read/write heads resulting in loss of data.

6. Malicious damage/Leakage: We now turn to the real problem of computer installations, be they stand alone PCs or large main frames with hundred of terminals. It is not necessary that outsiders would do this; it is equally possible that some unhappy or impish insiders may wreck havoc.

7. Unauthorised Access: As the saying goes "Curiosity killed that Cat", but it does not stop the human from trying to look at things they should not or need not. Information on personnel, finance, products or assets can be accessed and copied for malafide use.

8. Modifications Erasures etc.: The person accessing data files may be authorized to read the data only, but he would like to alter, modify or erase the data by writing into that file.

(c) Differentiate between files and folders in Windows. Write steps for creating files and folders and controlling access to them.

Ans. All the data on your hard drive consists of files and folders. The basic difference between the two is that files store data, while folders store files and other folders. The folders, often referred to as directories, are used to organize files on your computer. The folders themselves take up virtually no space on the hard drive. Files, on the other hand, can range from a few bytes to several gigabytes. They can be documents, programs, libraries, and other compilations of data.

Now Refer to Dec-2006, Q.No.-3(b)
Now Refer to Dec-2005, Q.No.-5(c)(ii)

(d) What are Business Graphics? Explain the various types of Business Graphics, with examples.

Ans. Business Graphics: A picture is worth a thousand words. We live in a visual world and the human mind can comprehend and retain concepts learnt through visual depiction for longer time. In today's world, it is very critical for a person to put across ideas effectively, whether it is business or not. One way of putting across ideas effectively, is the use of visual images. And the best form of visual images is graphics and pictures. Graphics if used to convey ideas in business situations are known as Business Graphics.

Types of Business Graphics: There are three types of Business Graphics. They are:

1. Presentation Graphics,
2. Analytic Graphics, and
3. Design Graphics.

1. Presentation Graphics: Convincing the audience about an idea and putting your views across is the aim of any presentation. The main goal of presentation graphics is to get a message across. Example of presentation graphics tools include Harvard Graphics, PowerPoint etc.

2. Analytic Graphics: Analytic Graphics presents the data and information in such a way that it helps in people analyzing it. Its aim is to show relationships in data and information.

Analytic Graphics need not have a very high quality. They are used to produce graphics from the data stored in database management systems like MS-Access and electronic spreadsheets like MS-Excel. They help in analyzing the data and taking a decision thereby. Graphics provided by spreadsheet packages like *Lotus 1-2-3, MS-Excel* are examples of analytic graphics.

3. Design Graphics: Design Graphics are used to create visual images of products, models, etc. Computer Aided Design (CAD) is an example of design graphic tool.

(e) What is a LAN? Explain any four LAN Topologies.

Refer to Page No.-22
Now Refer to Dec-2006, Q.No.-3(a)

Q2. (a) What are the advantages of using Optical Memories over the traditional magnetic memories? Explain any two optical memories.

Ans. An optical memory suitable for storing optical signals from a set of predetermined wavelengths is demonstrated. This memory is random access, allowing a controller to read the stored data at any point in time.

Now Refer to Dec-2003, Q.No.-2(b)
Now Refer to June-2006, Q.No.-4(b)

(b) What is EDI? Explain its benefits over the traditional methods of information flow. Support your answer with a diagram.

Refer to Dec-2004, Q.No.-3(b), Page-50

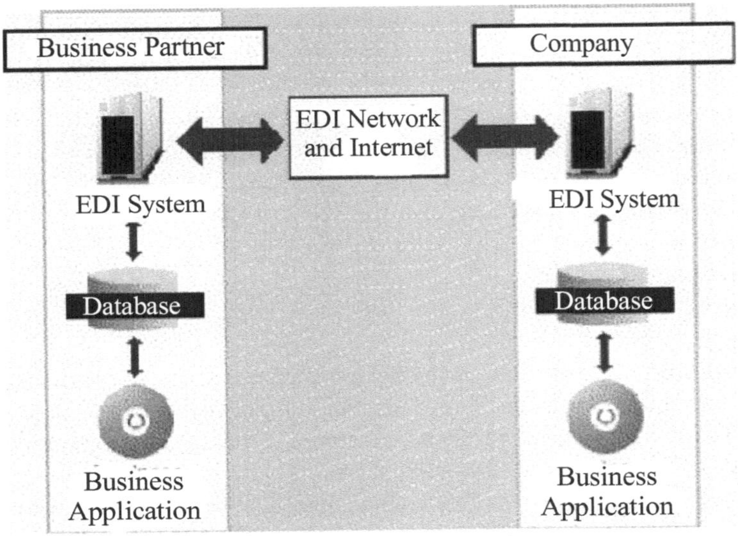

Figure: How EDI Words

Q3. (a) What is a Dialog Box in Windows? How do we move within a dialog box and what are the operations available for supplying information in a dialog box?

Ans. Working with a Dialog Box: A *dialog box* supplies additional information to a command, required for the completion of a task. An ellipsis (…) after a menu command indicates that a dialog box will appear on choosing this command. Most dialog boxes contain options that can be selected. After specifying the options, one can choose a command button to carry out the command. Some other dialog boxes may display information, warnings or error messages. Moving a dialog box is just like moving a window – by dragging the title bar or using the Move command on the Control menu.

Types of Options: One may need to select one or more options within a dialog box and for this one need to move from one option to another. To move within a dialog box:

One can either click that option or press TAB to move to the next option and SHIFT + TAB to the previous option.

The currently selected option is marked by the selection cursor, which appears as a dotted rectangle, a highlight or both. The types of dialog box options are as follows:

Command Button: A Command Button initiates an immediate action, such as carrying out or canceling a command. The OK, Cancel and Help buttons are common command buttons. They are often located along the bottom or on the right side of the dialog box. Some command buttons are marked with greater-than signs (>>) which expands the active dialog box. A command button containing an ellipsis (...) opens another dialog box.

Text Box: A text box is used to type information. On moving to an empty text box, an insertion point appears to its far left side.

List Box: A list box displays a list of choices. If there are more choices than can fit in the box, scroll bars are provided to move quickly through the list. Usually only one item can be selected in a list box and in some cases, more than one item can also be selected.

Drop-Down List Box: A drop-down list box appears initially as a rectangular box containing the current selection. On selecting the down arrow in the square box at the right, a list of available choices appears. If there are more choices than can fit in the box, scroll bars are provided.

Option Buttons: Option buttons represent a group of mutually exclusive options. Only one option can be selected at a time. The selected option button contains a black dot. If one operation is already selected, then the current option replaces it.

Check Box: A check box presents non-exclusive options, that is, more than one option can be selected at a time. Selected check boxes contain an X.

(b) What is Cryptography? Explain with the help of a diagram the Encryption and Decryption Process. Explain with an example, transposition and substitution.

Ans. Refer to Dec-2004, Q.No.-5(b)

Substitution and Transposition Ciphers are two categories of ciphers used in classical cryptography. Substitution and Transposition differ in how chunks of the message are handled by the encryption process.

A more complex substitution cipher would be created if, instead of incrementing each character by three, we used a more complex key. This table shows a simple substitution cipher with a key of "123".

Plaintext	V	O	Y	A	G	E	R
Key	+1	+2	+3	+1	+2	+3	+1
Ciphertext	W	Q	B	B	I	H	S

An even more complex substitution cipher can be made by having each character of the alphabet correspond to a different letter of the alphabet, without a set pattern.

Plaintext	A	B	C	D	E	F	G	H	I	J	K	L	M	N	O	P	Q	R	S	T	U	V	W	X	Y	Z
Key	T	O	E	U	N	Z	I	A	G	X	P	Q	Y	R	H	V	S	M	D	F	C	J	W	B	K	L

Using this substitution cipher to encrypt VOYAGER would give us these results:

Plaintext	V	O	Y	A	G	E	R
Ciphertext	J	H	K	T	X	N	M

The Vernam Cipher, or one time pad, is a simple substitution cipher where the key length equals the message length.
ROT-13 is a simple substitution cipher used to encode messages on Usenet.
Transposition ciphers
Transposition ciphers encrypt plaintext by moving small pieces of the message around. Anagrams are a primitive transposition cipher.
This table shows "VOYAGER" being encrypted with a primitive transposition cipher where every two letters are switched with each other:

V	O	Y	A	G	E	R
O	V	A	Y	E	G	R

Q4. (a) What are Tables? How can we include tables in a PowerPoint presentation? Write steps for setting the borders and shading for a table.
Ans. Tables: Word's Tables feature, enables you to arrange columns of numbers and text in a document without using tabs. It helps you to organize complex columnar information.
Tables also provide a convenient way to present text in side-by-side paragraphs as in a resume or to arrange text beside graphics. You can use them to create such diverse documents as forms, television scripts, financial reports, parts catalog and resumes. You can insert tables anywhere you need them in Word documents. Word's table feature and the terminology used to describe it, reminds you of a spreadsheet. Word tables consist of horizontal rows and vertical columns. You do the typing in areas called cells. Cells can contain text, numbers or graphics. The text in cells in edited and embellished as usual with Word's formatting toolbar and ruler.

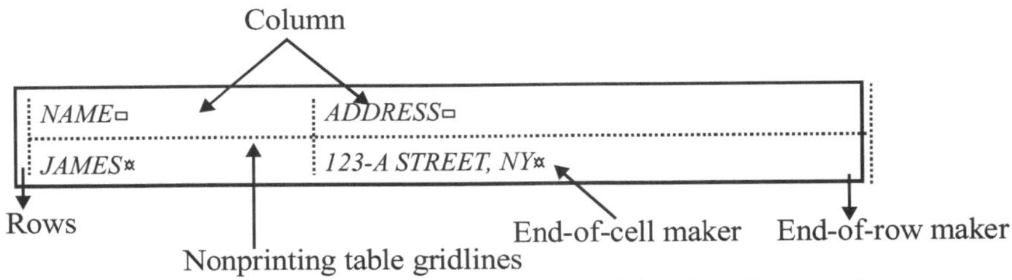

A number of table specific features let you control the size, shape and appearance of cells. Border and Shading features are available. It is also easy to insert and delete rows and columns.

They can be created from existing text without needless retyping. Also the table feature can be used to organize information and then convert your table to text.

Another feature, Table Wizard, helps you automate table creation. The dotted lines around each cell represent nonprinting table gridlines.

Format → Borders and Shading command can be used to add printing borders.

Creating Tables: Tables are used to display data in a columnar form.

To create a Table:

1. Click on New slide button on the status bar to display AutoLayout dialog box.

2. Select Table layout from the AutoLayout list and then click on OK to display a blank Table presentation slide. From where you can add table.

3. Double click on Table box to display Insert table dialog box.

4. Type number of columns and number of rows in respective boxes of your requirement and click on OK to go in word table (rows and columns) form.

5. And lastly type your information in the cells.

(b) Why do we use looping and conditional statements in a program? Explain with an example any three looping and conditional statements w.r.t. 'C' language.

Ans. First Refer : June-2005, Q.No.-1(b)(ii)

Conditional branching:

```
if (condition) statement ;  /* basic form of if statement */

if (condition) statement ;
 else statement_2 ;          /* optional  else  clause */

if (condition_1)
    if ( condition_2 ) statement ;
    else statement_2 ;        /* else  belongs to closest previous if */
```

Looping statements

```
for ( initialization ; condition ; increment ) statement ;
                         /* The flow sequence is :            */
                          /*   initialization              */
                          /*   test condition and exit if false */
                          /*   statement                  */
                          /*   increment                  */
                          /*   loop back to test condition     */
```

```
while ( condition ) statement ; /* keep repeating statement until the */
                                /* condition is false, zero. This is */
                                /* classical C thinking, rather than saying*/
                                /* keep repeating while condition is true*/

do                              /* another form of the 'while statement'*/
{                               /* always execute once before testing   */
   statement_sequence
}  while ( condition ) ;        /* test for finished at the end, all    */
                                /* other loops test first              */
```

Q5. Write short notes on the following :

(a) RISC

Refer to Page-113, Q.No.-2(d)

(b) Viruses

Refer to Page No.-39

(c) ISDN

Ans. Integrated Services Digital Network: ISDN is basically used for Communication of both data and voice. ISDN was first launched in Singapore in 1990. It has the following features:

(a) Transmission and processing of digital data

(b) Processing of various types of information data, voice, video etc.

(c) Electronic mail box

(d) Tele-conferencing

(e) Telefax, videofax etc.

(d) Disk Fragmentation

Ans. Refers to the condition of a disk in which files are divided into pieces scattered around the disk. Disk Fragmentation occurs naturally when you use a disk frequently, creating, deleting, and modifying files. At some point, the operating system needs to store parts of a file in noncontiguous clusters. This is entirely invisible to users, but it can slow down the speed at which data is accessed because the disk drive must search through different parts of the disk to put together a single file. In DOS 6.0 and later systems, you can defragment a disk with the DEFRAG command. You can also buy software utilities, called disk optimizers or defragmenters, that defragment a disk.

CS – 611: COMPUTER FUNDAMENTALS AND PC SOFTWARE
Dec, 2008

Note: *Question number 1 is* ***compulsory****. Attempt any* ***three*** *questions from the rest.*

Q1. (a) List the differences between system software and application software. What are the salient features of Data Base Management Software?

Refer to Page No.-44., Q.No.-5(b) (I)

The salient features of Database Management Software are as follows:

1. DBMS reduces data redundancy.
2. DBMS provides greater query flexibility.
3. DBMS solves data integrity (inconsistency) problem.
4. DBMS makes data independent of the application programs. That is, fields can be added, changed and deleted from the database without affecting existing programs.
5. It also includes data security features at database level, record level and even at field level to provide greater flexibility of restricted data access.

(b) Explain CSMA/CD access method used in LAN. How is it used for collision detection in LAN?

Refer to Page No.-114, Q.No.-3(a) 2nd Para onwards

(c) Discuss DES and RSA algorithms.

Refer to Page No.-112, Q.No.-1(f), June-2002 and Refer to Page No.-211, Dec-2007, Q.No.-2(b)

(d) List and explain the use of various "disk utilities" in Windows 95.

Refer to Page No.-35, Q.No.-1(c)

(e) Write a step by step procedure to create network connection by using dial-up network connector in Windows 95.

Refer to Page No.-59, Q.No.-1(i)

Q2. (a) Explain the purpose of following in MS-Word.

(i) Mirror Margin

Refer to Page No.-166, Q.No.-1(a)(ii), June-2006

(ii) Gutter Margin

Ans. The additional white space in the inside margins $\rightarrow$ to compensate for paper tucked away in the binding of a two sided book that would be unreadable. The gutter width which are specify in Margin tab of the Page Setup dialog box $\left(\text{File} \rightarrow \text{Page Setup}\right)$ reduces the text area.

We can simply increase the size of inside margins of our document to accommodate binding space by setting gutter margins.

(iii) Header

Ans. It is a place where we can put repetitive information in a document's top margin. Header is used to print something on each page, as title of document, your name, some graphic etc. stylized text, dates and automatic page numbering can all be included in headers.

We can add identical header on all the pages of document or we can change header for each page or each section of the document.

Steps to Add Header in our document are:

Menu Bar → View → Header and Footer

(iv) Footer

Ans. Footers are involved simultaneously with headers. Footer are the bottom places where we can write repetitive information in our document like page number, author of document etc.

Header and Footer editing is always done in Page Layout View. We can work right in header and footer area of our document after double clicking to unhide it. We can also apply any paragraph or character style to our header and footer using formatting toolbars and rules.

We can add Footer in the same way as header except that we are working in Footer window.

The Layout tab of the Page Setup dialog box helps in:

1. Creating Different Header and Footers for add and even pages.

2. Creating Different Header and Footer for the first page.

(v) Page Break

Refer to Page No.-184, Q.No.-4(a), Dec-2006

(b) List the salient features of fourth generation languages (4GL). Also, compare with the features of procedural languages.

Refer to Dec-2002, Page No.-97, Q.No.-1(e)

Q3. (a) What is the difference between subroutine and function? Give an example of each.

Refer to Page No.-79, Q.No.-1(e) = see Page No.-83

(b) What is meant by term *"multimedia"*? What are minimum hardware and software requirements for running Windows 95 multimedia?

Refer to Page No.-188, Dec-2006, Q.No.-5(b) and Refer to Dec-2007, Q.No-1(d), Page No.-208

Q4. (a) What are the different ways by which you can connect to the network?

Refer to Page No.-199, June-2007, Q.No.-4(b)

(b) Explain various services provided by ISDN.

Refer to Page No.-226, Q.No.-5(c)

Q5. Describe following Windows 95 Accessories in brief:

(i) Calender

Ans. Windows Calender is used to view the current month's calendar that shows the day and date and also the current day showing the timings to keep track of your appointments. We can easily view the day schedule or the selected month's calendar using calendar program at Accessories:

Steps to select calendar are:

Start → Programs → Accessories → Calender

(ii) Character Map

Ans. It works only with windows based programs. Character Map is used to insert a special character into a document.

Steps to select Character Map are:

Start → Programs → Accessories → Character Map

(iii) Clipboard viewer

Ans. Clipboard is the invisible holding area for copy and cut operations, but we can save for later use only in clipboard viewer.

If the current information of cut and copy commands are not saved in the clipboard, then it is lost for the next time copy or paste operation.

Clipboard is mainly used to transfer information between applications.

Steps to activate clipboard:

Start → Programs → Accessories → Clipboard Viewer

(iv) Card file

Ans. We can use card file to organize and manage information, such as names, addresses and phone numbers. The two ways in card file are:

1. Card View

2. List View

Card view displays our file as series of cards. List view displays the index line of every card in the file in alphabetic order.

Index Line is the bar at the top of each card file that contains the title of the card.

(v) MS-exposition

Ans. It is used to learn about Microsoft products, in categories such as Entertainment, Business and Kids.

Steps to select MS Exposition are:

Start → Programs → Accessories → MS Exposition

CS – 611: COMPUTER FUNDAMENTALS AND PC SOFTWARE
June, 2009

***Note:** Question number 1 is **compulsory**. Attempt any **three** questions from the rest.*

Q1. (a) What is the use of RAM and ROM in a computer? Also, differentiate between PROM, EPROM and EEPROM.

RAM and ROM-Refer to Page No.-43, 5th Point and Page No.-136, 137

PROM: Programmable Read Only Memory

There are two types of Read Only Memory (ROMs):

(1) Manufacturer programmed

(2) User programmed

A user programmed ROM is one in which the user can load and store "read only" programs and data. Such a ROM is known as Programmable Read Only Memory (PROM), because a user can program it. Once the user programs are stored in a PROM chip, they can usually be executed in a fraction of time. PROM is a non-volatile store i.e. the stored information remains there, even if power is switched off.

EPROM: Erasable Programmable Read Only Memory

It is possible to erase information stored in an EPROM chip and the chip can be reprogrammed to store new information.

EPROMs are useful in case of those applications where one may like to store a program in a ROM which would normally not change, but under some unforeseen conditions one may like to alter it.

EEPROM: Electronically Erasable Programmable Read Only Memory

The stored information of the EPROM is erased by using high voltage electric pulses. Such EPROM is known as EEPROM.

The programs or information can be easily altered in an EEPROM chip. Due to ease with stored programs can be altered. EEPROM is also known as Flash Memory.

(b) Describe the role of parity bit in asynchronous transmission and SYN character in synchronous transmission. Explain the answer by using a suitable example for each.

Ans. Role of Parity Bit in Asynchronous Transmission: In Asynchronous Transmission, the parity bit is used for error checking while transmitting the data. In asynchronous transmission, each character is transmitted separately, that is, one character at a time. Each character begins with a start bit, which tells the receiving device where the character coding begins and ends with a stop bit, which tells the receiving device where the character coding ends.

The next character is sent, with start and stops bits. The parity bit is used for checking errors while transmitting the data using even parity check or odd parity check method.

SYN character in synchronous transmission are used to synchronise the flow of data so that the receiving computer can read at the same speed at which the sending computer transmits. In synchronous transmission characters are transmitted as groups, with control characters (i.e. SYN character) in the beginning and at the end of the bit train.

(c) What are the steps involved in recording a macro in MS-WORD? How one can run a recorded macro?

Refer to Dec-2007, Page No.-212, Q.No.-3(a)

(d) What is the importance of Backup utility? Can a user take backup on any computer in its network? List the steps to install the Backup utility.

Ans. Importance of Backup Utility: We can take backup of our important files to floppy disks, compact disks or another computer on our network. When we have made a backup file, we can easily restore our original files which are damaged or lost.

Steps to start the Backup Utility:

1. Click Start and Select Programs.

2. Select Accessories from the Cascading menu and then click on System Tools.

3. Now click on Backup.

Steps to Install Backup Utility in our System Tools:

1. Start the Add/Remove Programs utility from the Control Panel window.

2. Click the Windows Setup tab and click the Disk Tools option in the window.

3. Then click OK to install the Backup Utility and follow the instructions on the screen.

(e) Write the steps involved in creating a presentation using powerpoint to perform the following tasks:

(i) To include a picture and text on the same slide

Ans. 1. Select New from File menu, to display the presentation dialog box.

2. Click the Blank Presentation and click OK.

3. Select Slide from Auto Layout dialog box and click on OK.

4. It will display the blank title slide to enter information.

5. Type the title and sub-title.

(ii) To include a table and text on the same slide

Ans. Tables are used to display text in a columnar form.

Steps to create a Table are:

1. Click on New Slide button on the status bar to display Auto Layout dialog box.

2. Select Table Layout from the Auto Layout list and then click on OK to display a blank Table presentation slide. From where you can add table.
3. Double click on Table Box to display Insert Table dialog box.
4. Type number of columns and number of rows in respective boxes of your requirement and click on OK to go in Word table form.
5. And lastly type your information in the cells.

(iii) Add the text as a hyperlink in an object

Ans. It is very easy to add a Hyperlink in Powerpoint.
Simply highlight the text we want to use as a Hyperlink and press Ctrl+K. The Insert-Hyperlink dialog box will appear, we can now enter the URL for webpage or another document address which we want to link, click the appropriate icon in the Link To Pane.
We can also link to a specific file by clicking the Browse button and choosing the file we want. Click OK when we have made the link.

Q2. (a) Differentiate between simplex, half-duplex and full-duplex mode of transmission. Also, give an example for each.

Simplex	Half-duplex	Full-duplex
1. In simplex transmission, the communication is unidirectional.	**1.** In half-duplex transmission, each station can both transmit and receive, but not at the same time.	**1.** In full-duplex transmission, both stations can transmit and receive simultaneously.
2. It transmission is like a one-way street.	**2.** It transmission is like a one-lane road with two-directional traffic.	**2.** It transmission is like a two-way street with traffic flowing in both direction at the same time.
3. Example : Keyboards and Monitors, the key-board can only introduce input; the monitor can only accept output.	**3.** Example : Walkie-talkies & CB radio.	**3.** Example : Data transmission over Telephone lines.

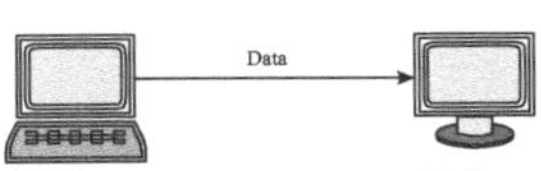

E.g keyboard, monitors are e.g. of simplex device

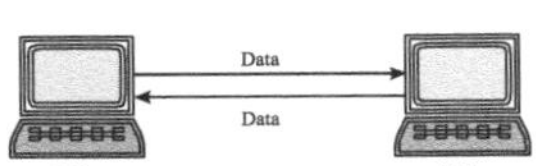

E.g Walkie takies is example of Half duplex

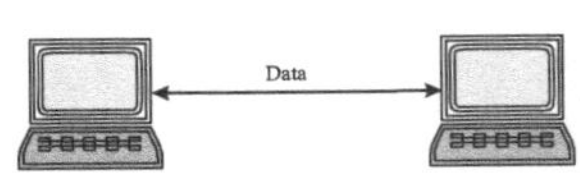

Telephone network is example of Full duplex.

(b) What is a scanner? Can we use scanner as an output device? Briefly describe any two source of data automation equipments:

(i) MICR
(ii) OMR
(iii) OBR

Scanner-Refer to Page No.-7

No, we can't use scanner as an output device because it is an input device.

MICR: Magnetic Ink Character Recognition is used by the banking industry for faster processing of large volume of cheques being handled in every day by this industry. The bank's identification code, account number and cheque number is preprinted by using characters from a special character set on all these cheques with a special ink, which contains magnetizable particles of iron oxide, before the cheques are given to the customer for use. These cheques are processed by using an MICR reader sorter.

Optical Mark Reader (OMR): It is capable of recognizing a pre-specified type of mark made by pencil or pen. For example, many students might have taken objective type tests, in which they had to mark their answers to questions on a special pre-printed test scoring sheet by darkening the small squares, circular or oval shaped box by a pencil, to indicate their correct choice out of various given options. These answer sheets are directly fed into a computer for grading with the use of an optical mark reader.

OBR: Is is a object bar reader.It scans a set of vertical bars of different width for used to read tags and merchandise in stores,medical records, library books.etc. these are available as hand held devices.

Q3. (a) What is RISC? Explain the important characteristics of RISC.

Refer to June-2002, Page No.-113, Q.No.-2(d)

(b) What is the purpose and benefit of disk-defragmentation? Do we have any tool to perform the task of disk defragmentation in windows, if yes then write the steps to perform the task.

Refer to Dec-2008, Q.No.-1(d)

Q4. (a) What are the main components of an operating system? How an operating system provides convenient and efficient utilization of the computer hardwares?

Ans. Operating System: An operating system is a large collection of software, which manages resources of the computer system, such as memory, processor, file system and input/output devices.

Operating system keeps track of the status of each resource and decides who will have a control over computer resources, for how long and when. The positioning of operating system in overall computer system is as follows:

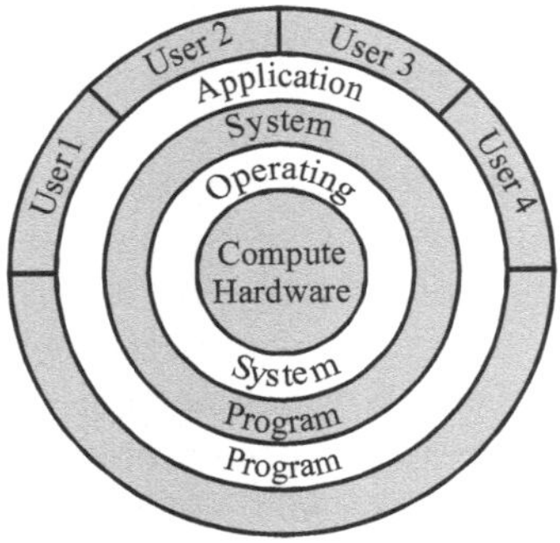

Fig : Component of Computer System

Operating system provides a number of services At the lowest level, there are system calls, which allow a running program to make a request from operating system directly. At a higher level, there is a command interpreter, which supports a mechanism for a user to issue a request without writing a program.

Main Components of Operating System are:

1. Computer Hardware
2. Kernel
3. Shell
4. Users

(b) What is meant by the term message encryption? Briefly describe, how RSA algorithm perform message encryption?

Ans. Message Encryption: It is a process of conversion of plain text message into cipher text message. It is also known as Enciphering or Encoding. Message Encryption is done by a key that is known as data string that controls the transformation of data. Encryption is normally done at sender's end of a network.

RSA Algorithm: Refer to Page No.-112, Q.No.-1(f)

Q5. (a) Assume you need to send a letter of "new year wishes" to all of your friends and relatives; which feature of MS-WORD you will use to avoid writing multiple letters? Write the steps for using this feature of MS-WORD.

Refer to June-2006, Page No.-177, Q.No.-5(b)

(b) What is a difference between WAN and LAN? What are the various devices which operates in WAN, explain their utility also?

Refer to June-2002, Page no.-110, Q.No.-1(d)

CS – 611: COMPUTER FUNDAMENTALS AND PC SOFTWARE

December, 2009

Note: Question number 1 is ***compulsory.*** *Attempt* ***any three*** *questions from the rest.*

Q1. (a) What are the differences between Primary and secondary memory? If the primary memory is overflowed then secondary memory can be used or not? Justify your answer with suitable arguments.

Ans. Primary memory is a large memory, which is fast but not as fast as internal processor memory. This memory is accessed directly by the processor. It is mainly based on integrated circuits. Each storage element of the memory is directly (randomly) accessible and can be examined and modified without affecting other cells and hence it is also called RAM. The memory unit stores all the information in memory cells also called memory locations, in binary digit. Each memory location has a unique address.

Secondary memory in fact is much larger in size than main memory but is slower than main memory. It normally stores system programs (programs which are used by system to perform various operational functions), other instructions, programs and data files. Secondary memory can also be used as an overflow memory in case the main memory capacity has been exceed. Secondary memories can not be accessed directly by a processor. First the information of these memories is transferred to the main memory and then the information can be accessed as the information of main memory.

If Primary memory is overflowed then secondary memory can also be used as a primary memory. Its acts as a buffer area of main memory and pages can be stored to and fro temporarily. After the work is done the memory buffer area is free but the space we allotted will remain with main memory. It uses a technique called paging.

(b) How an Array processors architecture is different from data flow architecture? Explain the term pipelining with the help of an example.

Ans. Array processors are parallel architectures, which deal with repetitive operations. These are an example of SIMD architecture, with applications varying from mathematical array operations and in structure in which data objects are known well in advance.

Data flow architecture is functionally distributed architectures, in which the operations are triggered with the arrival of data at these processors. They may be viewed as very general MIMD parallel architectures.

Most of these parallel processor computers follow an important concept called pipelining.
The basic idea behind pipeline design is quite natural. The key contribution of pipelining is that it provides a way to start a new task before an old has been completed. The concept can be better understood by taking an example of an industrial plant. To achieve pipelining, one must subdivide the input task into a sequence of subtask, each of which can be executed by a specialized hardware stage that operates concurrently with other stages in the hardware. Successive tasks are streamed into the pipe and get executed in an overlapped fashion at the subtask level. Hence the completion rate is not a function of total processing time, but rather of how soon a new process can be introduced.

(c) Explain the working of CSMA/CD LAN access method. Also, compare it with token passing method.

Ans. Refer to Q.No.-3(a), Page No.-114
Toke passing:- In token passing the control token is passed from one node to another according to a defined set of rules understood and adhered to by all nodes. A node may transmit a frame when it is in possession of the token and after it had transmitted the frame. It passes the token to the next device in a predetermined sequence.

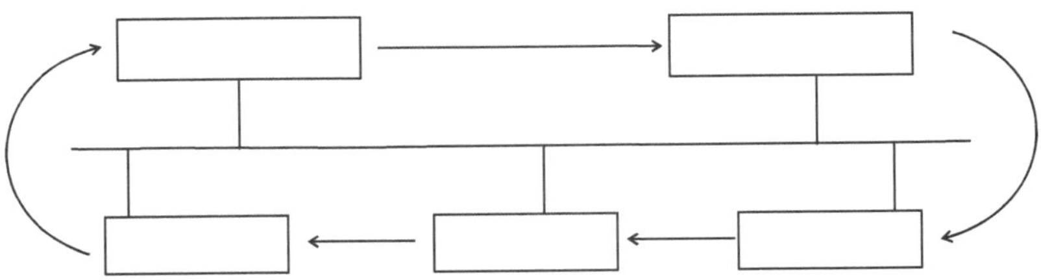

Token bus

In token passing, a logical ring of all nodes connected to the physical medium is first established and a single token is generated; the control token passes from one node to another traversing the logical ring. The token keeps on circulating the logical ring until it is received by a node waiting to send a information frame. After receipt of token to the next node in the logical ring. For token passing, the physical medium need not be a ring topology's it can be used to control access to a bus network also.

(d) How do viruses infect and spread in a computer system? Can viruses also damage the computer hardware Components? If yes, how? If No, why? Also, differentiate between BOOT infector and system infector viruses.

Ans. On booting, the system carries out the ROM instructions, the first being the power on self Test (POST), which is followed by the boot strap process of reading the boot record and loading of the disk operating system. In MS-Dos, it involves the loading of IBMDOS.COM, IBMBIO.COM and COMMOND.COM along with some optical files like CONFIG.SYS and AUTOEXEC.BAT. The booting process culminates into system prompt displayed on the VDU. The infection may begin as soon as a computer system boots from a contaminated disk or executes on infected program. Whatever viruses are presents gets activated, which immediately begin to spread throughout the system.

Yes viruses can damage the computer hardware components for ex:- virus can damage the boot sector or zero area of the disk and after the system startup can be directly loaded in the system and causes hardware parts to malfunction.

Now Refer to Page No.-190 (Boot Infectors)

(e) What are the various views available in Power Point? Briefly describe any 4 views. How do they help in preparing and maintaining a presentation?

Ans. PowerPoint has four main views. (i) Normal view, (ii) Slide Sorter view (iii) Note page view. (iv) Slide show view. Use the right view for the job when developing your presentation. What was known as the view menu in earlier version of PowerPoint is now the view tab in Microsoft office PowerPoint.

Normal view:- is the main editing view, where we write and design our presentation. This view has four working areas:-

(i) Outline tab:- This is the great place for writing our content to capture our ideas, plan how we want to present them, and moves slides and text around.

(ii) Slide tab:- This is a great place to view the slides in our presentation as thumbnails size images while we edit. The thumbnails make it easy for us to navigate through our presentation and to see the effect of any design changes.

(iii) Slides pane:- the slide pane display a large view of the current slide with the current slides shown in this view. We can add text and insert pictures, tables, smart art graphics etc.

(iv) Notes pane:- In the notes panes below the slide plane, we can type notes that apply to the current slide. Later we can print our notes and refer to them when we give our presentation.

Slide sorter view:- is view of our slides in the thumbnail form.

Notes page view:- We can types our notes in the notes pane, which is located just below the slide pane in normal view.

Slide show view:- Slide show view take full computer screen like an actual presentation. In this view, we see our presentation the way our audience will.

Q2. (a) What are Document Templates? List their uses. Explain the format of at least three commonly used document templates and write the steps to use them in your document.

Refer to June–2007, Q.No.-2(a), Page No.-194

(a) Define the term multimedia. Explain any four multimedia tools.

Ans. Refer to P-172, Q.No.-2(a) and now

Volume control:- If we have a sound card, we can use volume control to control the volume and speakers balance when we play audio files. To adjust the volume for multimedia devices, open the multimedia properties dialog box. In the play back or recording area, drag the volume slider.

Q3. (a) How many layers are there in OSI model? Name them, further explain the role and functions offered by each layer of OSI reference model.

Refer to June–2007, Q.No.-3(b), Page No.-196

(b) Write the steps to share a folder among different users on the network.

Ans. To share the folder with other people on the network follows the following step:

I. In my computer, click the folder we want to share.

II. On the file menu click properties

III. Click the sharing tab, and then click shared as, if the sharing tab is not visible, we need to enable file and print sharing services.

IV. Chose the option and fill out the options.

V. Click ok.

Fields in the share area are:

Share name:- the name will appear to other users when they browse the network.

Comment: to describe the object.

Read only:- other users can only read and cannot make changes.

Q4. (a) Explain the purpose of following in MS-WORD:

(i) Soft page Break

Refer to Dec–2006, Q.No.-4(a)(a), Page No.-184

(ii) Hard page Break

Refer to Dec–2006, Q.No.-4(a)(b), Page No.-184

(iii) Repagination

Ans. Repagination:- In order to display and print page breaks property, word must recalculate page endings after we have made changes. Normally, this is done automatically in the background whenever word can steal some otherwise unused computer time. This process is called automatic repagination. Since page endings affects certain other features word always repaginates when we

- Ask it to print
- Are in print preview or page layout view
- Complete a Table of contents or Index.

(iv) Tab stops

Ans. By default, the Tab sops are set at 05-inch intervals from the left margins, respectively. The insertion points can be moved to the next tab stop in the current paragraph by pressing TAB Key.

Use the ruler to set a tab stop at a particular position or to change the way text lines up at a tab stop.

To set Tab stops-

- Select the paragraph in which we want to set or change tab stops.
- To set or change the top alignment, click the Top Alignment button at the far left of the horizontal ruler until the tab alignment is the way we want it to be.

(v) Right Alignment

Ans. Right Alignment:- By default, the text in word is left aligned. These alignments can be changed. We can change the justification of text by using the justification buttons on the toolbar from left to right. Right alignment justifies the text to right margins. When we justify text the current paragraph or selected text is affected.

(b) Explain three features of Dot-matrix printing. Also, Write differences among inkjet and Dot-matrix Printing.

Ans. Dot matrix creates characters by striking pins against an ink ribbon-Each pin makes a dot, and combinations of dots form characters and illustrations. This is type of printer which uses a series of pins to create an image on paper. Dot matrix printers are the most economical way to print information. Because the printing involves mechanical pressure, these printers can create carbon copies and carbonless copies. These machine can be highly durable, but eventually wear out.

Difference between ink-jet and Dot-matrix printers:-

- **Price:-** dot matrix printers are relatively cheaper than ink-jet printers.

and now Refer to Dec–2002, Q.No.-5(a), Page No.-104

Q5. (a) Briefly describe the important reasons behind the loss on manipulation of the data, belonging to a user.

Ans. Some of the ways in which data loss or manipulation can occur are:

(i) Theft of PC and media:- A smart person with a false calling card can take away the PC for repairs and may never show his face again.

(ii) Damage due to breakage:- Floppies are easily breakable. Damage can also occur due to natural disaster.

(iii) Inadvartent corruption/loss:- This can happen due to inferior media or Erasure of files due to incorrect options by the operator.

(iv) Modification Erasure etc:- The person accessing data files may be authorized to read the data only, but he would like to alter, modify or erase the data by writing into that file.

(v) Computer viruses:- This is the latest threat to computer users.

(vi) Data tapping:- In large computer systems or on network, data has to travel between the processing units and terminals, or different processors, over communication lines. Any person trying to get access to data can intercept the traffic on the circuit by tapping into the cable at convenient points. This may even enable him to send spurious channel over the network and access the computer itself by emulating terminal responses.

(b) What is an assembler? Write any four differences between Complier and an interpreter.

Ans. An assembler is a translator, which takes it input in the form of an assembly language program and produces machine language code as its output.

Different between compiler and interpreter:-

(i) Scans the entire program first and then translates it into machine code. Where as a interpreter translates the program line by line.

(ii) Compiler converts the entire program to machine code. When all the syntax errors are removed execution take place. Where as in the case of the interpreter each time the program is executed, every line is checked for syntax error and then converted to equivalent machine node.

(iii) Compiler is slow for debugging (removal of mistakes from a program). Whereas Interpreter good for fast debugging.

(iv) Compiler execution time, is less whereas Interpreter time is more.

CS – 611: COMPUTER FUNDAMENTALS AND PC SOFTWARE
June, 2010

Note: *Question number **1** is **compulsory**. Attempt **any three** questions from the rest.*

Q1. (a) What do you mean by term Memory hierarchy? Differentiate between Primary and Secondary Memory with their exclusive characteristics.

Ans. Refer to Dec–2007, Q.No.-1(a), Page No.-203 and;
Refer to Dec–2009, Q.No.-1(a)

(b) Mention any four topologies available that are used in LAN, along with their application areas.

Refer to Dec–2006, Q.No.-3(a), Page No.-182

(c) Write a step by step procedure to do the following activities in WINDOWS:

(i) BACKUP

Ans. Refer to Q.No.-3(a), Page No.-49

(ii) To play sound files

Ans. Refer to Q.No.-(c)(iii), Page No.-156

(iii) Controlling Access to files

Ans. Controlling Access to files

We can control access to our folders by using password or by listing names of peoples we want to have access to these resources.

Following are the steps to control access to a folder files:

I. In my computer, click the shared folder we want to limit access to.

II. On file menu, click properties

III. Click sharing

IV. If we are using user-level access control, click Add to specify the people we want to be able to use ours resources.

V. If we are using share-level access control, type the password we want to use for the folder;

Refer to Page No.-156 (access file remaining)

(d) Explain the utility of the following features of MS-WORD:

(i) Mail merge

Ans. Refer to Q.No.-5(a)(i), Page No.-140

(ii) Macros

Ans. Refer to Q.No.-5(a)(ii), Page No.-140

Q2. (a) Define operating system? Explain its function in computer systems.

Refer to June–2009, Q.No.-4(a), Page No.-233

(b) How do you ensure physical security to the computer? Also mention about steps to be taken to ensure data does not get corrupted.

Refer to Dec–2005, Q.No.-2(b), Page No.-160

Q3. (a) Discuss any five salient features of Power point with examples.

Ans. PowerPoint is a powerful presentation graphics package. It allows the presenter to create his own high quality presentations. A powerpoint presentations is a collection of our slides, handouts, speaker notes, and our outline, all in one files. As we create slides, we are creating a presentation- we are designing how our presentation should look and giving it a format that carries through from beginning to end.

It gives us the flexibility of switching between different views during the creating of slides for a presentation.

• **Animation and sound:-** animation effects and sound effects, which make the presentation all the more effective. Animation effects are effects that can be provided to each part of a slide, so that the presentation becomes visually more appealing. For example, one can make the title of a slide zoom in from the left, then the first line of the slide appear swirling. A second line can be displayed in checkerboard style, while a third can be shown as a spiraling line.

• **Slides:-** are the individual "pages" of our presentation. Soon, you'll be creating slides with powerpoint. Slides can have titles, tool, graphs, drawn objects, shapes, clip art, drawn art and visual created with other applications and more.

• **Handouts:-** supports our presentation. We have the option of providing handouts for our audience. Handouts consist of smaller, printed versions of slides.

• **Speaker's Note:-** Can be created and printed. We will see a small image of the slide on each notes page, along with any notes we type on the notes page.

• **Outlines:-** As we are working on a presentation, we have the option of working with our presentation in outline view. In the outline, our titles and main text appear, but not our art or the text typed with the text tool

(b) Explain the utility of any two devices used for LAN.

Ans. The two devices used for LAN are (i) Network Interface unit (ii) Servers.

(i) Network Interface Unit:- Network interface unit connects each device in the LAN network to shared transmission device. It contains the rules or Logic to access the LAN. NIU is also used to implement LAN protocols and for device attachments. Its functions depend on the type of topology used in LAN. In macro computers, NIU may be installed as an add-on-card.

(ii) Servers:- one of the major benefits or implementation of LAN is sharing expensive resources such as storage device, printer etc. This is achieved through providing servers on the LAN. It is a dedicated computer, which controls one or more resources. This contain both hardware and software interface for LAN. Three major categories of servers used in LANs are :

(a) File server (b) Printer server (c) Modem server.

Networking file server is used to share storage space for files. Besides providing storage space for files in a LAN environment. It is used for taking periodical backup, and also to provide gateway to other servers within and between lans. Similarly printer server is used to handle printing works of all work station connected in the network.

In LAN environment also modern is required to get connected to other network or simply to use a telephone. A modem server is used to share few telephone lines and modems by all connected workstations in a network.

Q4. (a) How do you ensure secure message delivery in a system?

Ans. There are various ways to ensure secure message delivery in a system. One of the method for secure message is cryptography. It is defined as "the design and analysis of codes and ciphers. It used some unusual important methods of cryptography transformation of the text it was not secret writing 'one of the important method of information. The method consists of replacing the letters of alphabet in the original text by letters that are fixed number of places away. For example, 'A' could be replaced by 'D', 'B' by 'E' and so on. Thus the key for the cipher. Would be as follows:-

Plain:- ABCDEFGHIJKLMNOPQRSTUVWXYZ

Cipher:- DEFGHIJKLMNOPQRSTUVWXYZABC

Using this system, the secret message "ZHOFROPH WR WKH FRPSXWHU FRXUVH' would actually mean "welcome to the computer course".

There were of course other system developed around the similar time in history which included approaches such as

- Writing secret messages backwards
- Writing messages vertically rather than horizontally

Cryptography is the process of transforming plain text or original information into an unintelligible form (cipher text) so that it may be sent over unsafe

channels for communications. A data string (key) controls the transformation process. Anyone getting hold of the cipher text while it is on the unsafe channel would need to have the appropriate key, to be, able to get to the original information. The authorized receiver is assumed to have that key.
The stage of conversion of the plain text into a cryptogram is called Encrypting or enciphering or encoding. Reconverting the cryptogram back into the original form, when done by the authorized/person is called decrypting or deciphering or decoding.

(b) Write the characteristics of RISC architecture.
Refer to June–2002, Q.No.-2(d), Page No.-113

Q5. Write short notes on the following:
(a) Control Panel
Ans. The control panel is a collection of small applications used for changing settings in the computer systems, such as screen colors, fonts and other features. When we click on the option control Panel from the cascading menu of settings, a window is opened that contains the icon of the utilities for changing hardware configurations or customizing the window 95 graphical interface. The control panel will include options like Add New hardware icon, Add Remove programs to change the setting of programs, Display settings, Fonts, keyboard setting, Mouse setting, Network setting etc.

(b) Different Modes of Transmission
Refer to Dec–2003, Q.No.-1(d), Page No.-67

(c) System call
Ans. Refer to Page No.-14 (System Call)

(d) Any two source of data equipments
Ans. Most recent trends for data input are towards source data automation. The equipment used for source data automation capture data as a by- product of a business activity there by completely eliminating manual input of data. Some examples are:-
(i) Magnetic Ink Character Recognition (MICR) devices are generally used by the banking industry to read the account numbers on Cheques directly and does the necessary processing.
(ii) Optical Mark Recognition (OMR) devices are generally used by computer devices. OMR device is used by academic and testing institutions to graduate aptitude tests where candidate marks the correct alternatives on a

special sheet of paper. The OMR recognition device then directly read these answer sheet and information sent to a computer for processing.
(iii) Optical Bar code Recorder (OBR) scan a set of vertical bar of different widths for specific data and are used to read tags and merchandise in stores, medical records, library book etc. These are available as hand held device.

(e) System Programs

Ans. Apart from system calls, user may interact with operating system directly by means of operating system commands. E.g. if we want to list Sub-directories in MS-Dos, We invoke dir command in either case, the operating system acts as an interface between users and the hardware of a computer systems. The fundamental goal of computer system is to solve user problems. Towards this goal computer hardware is designed since the bare hardware alone is not very easy to use, programs are developed. These programs require certain common operations, such as controlling peripheral device. The command function of controlling and allocating resources are then brought together into one piece of software; the operating system.